REPORTAGE PRESS

ABOUT THE AUTHOR

David Charles Manners enjoyed an eclectic education in Epsom, Lichfield, Bath, Paris, Frankfurt, Stockholm and Kalimpong. He studied music and physical medicine, and now maintains an international reputation as a physical therapist and teacher of Shaiva Tantra Yoga, primarily to professional musicians. He is the co-founder of *Sarvashubhamkara*, a charity that provides medical care, education and human contact for socially excluded individuals and communities on the Indian subcontinent. For the past sixteen years, David has spent his life between the Sussex Downs and the Bengal Himalaya.

REPORTAGE PRESS

Published by Reportage Press
26 Richmond Way, London W12 8LY United Kingdom
Tel: 0044 (0)208 749 2731
Mob: 0044 (0)7971 461 935
E-mail: info@reportagepress.com
www.reportagepress.com

David Manners © 2009

British Library Cataloguing in Publication Data.

A catalogue record for this book is available from the British Library.

ISBN-13: 978-1-906702-06-9

Cover design and layout by Henrietta Molinaro.

Printed and bound in the UK

IN THE
SHADOW OF
CROWS

BY DAVID CHARLES MANNERS

REPORTAGE PRESS

Endorsements

'A journey into another world that tells a story which is at once accomplished, intriguing and moving.' – Gilda O'Neill, novelist and author of *My East End*

'I was so moved by this extraordinary story, and by the spiritual strength of the rejected people it describes. We have material wealth but are lost: they have nothing and are found.' – Dame Felicity Lott, CBE, Soprano

'The interwoven narratives that form the core of *In the Shadow of Crows* are about transformation and redemption, of working through places of darkness and loss, and of finding wisdom in the unlikeliest of places. This is storytelling that touches the heart, a much-needed reminder in this time of fragmentation that it is only through our connecting with each other that we can fully realise our humanity.' – Manjari Mehta, Doctor of Anthropology

*In memory of Marie-Paule Mourik –
inspirational tutor and extraordinary friend –
who taught and loved me fearlessly.*

At the moment of a man's death, all knowledge acquired, all wisdom learned through the living of life is liberated from the confines of his body. With the final, exhaled breath, it passes first to the gathered crows, who, for ten consecutive days, are respectfully fed by the family of the deceased. Only then do the grateful birds share his learning with earth and sky, stone and wind, fire and water.

It is thus that nothing and no one is lost. It is thus that the universe forever changes, learns and grows. Therefore choose well the knowledge you acquire in life. Seek out and nurture wisdom.

Kushal Magar, *jhankri* of the
Eastern Himalaya

Chapter One

I was not a nervous child.

Only the prospect of plunging stockinged feet into red Wellingtons caused anxiety to rise. My mother would insist I wore them if the barometer even hinted at the possibility of Change.

My single demand was that we delay our daily excursions for the ritual banging-of-the-boots on the kitchen step. I would drop in stones and give them a shake. I would poke in a long stick and wiggle furiously. I would peer into the musty darkness and give a short, sharp blow.

One could never be too cautious when dealing with scorpions.

My mother would patiently watch and wait, straightening the finger seams of wrist-gloves, tending to the powder on her nose.

It was all quite unnecessary, she would impress.

We lived in Surrey.

The legacy of my father's upbringing in the Punjab and along the North-West Frontier during the struggling death-throes of the dinosaur Raj touched every aspect of my life. I could ask the time in Urdu, even before I was able to read a clock in English. I could have told the *chowkidhar* to tiptoe, the *mali* to hurry with his hoe, or the *khansamah* to bring me eggs "rumble-tumble", had we had staff. I could have confidently talked about *mahouts* and *moonshees*, *bhisti mussaks* and *missy babas*, *ping-jams* and *burra sahibs* had anyone shown an interest.

I would roll my eyes and smack my youthful lips in longing for chapati doused in creamy ghee and palm-sugar jaggery, or for hot, crisp *jalabies* dripping with syrup, even though I had never tasted either. And had I come across a Salt March, I could have spotted

1

Gandhi in the crowd and knew to avoid National Congress supporters in their tidy, *khadi* homespun caps, even though India had been a republic for over twenty years.

My mother understood.

When I lifted the cloth during dinner to check for cobras around the table legs, she would smile. When I interrupted our walks in the park to scan the poplar trees for full-bladdered langurs, she would forgive me.

My little white legs may have been stuffed into red Wellingtons as I waddled across Epsom Common to feed ducks with stale Hovis, but my head was filled with monkeys and tiffin-tins. My heart was in Simla, Peshwar and Rawlpindi.

It started with a birthmark.

Bindra first noticed it as she took her morning bucket bath. She thought the pale patch on her slim, dark leg was dust. Perhaps the last of the *atta* flour from the *roti* breads she had made for her family the night before.

She rubbed it with her thumb. It did not smear. She rubbed it with the ball of cooked rice she used in place of unaffordable soap. The new, pallid birthmark did not change.

Bindra pushed the bamboo door of the wash house with her foot to let in more light. The sun had not yet broken over the mountains and the children were still sleeping. Her cockerel was unusually slow to herald the new day. This was inauspicious. Instead, the crows were arguing in the dawn.

"Kali Ma," she whispered, in honour of the Dark Goddess, "what news do your black-plumed messengers bring?"

There was a sudden explosion of life as every crow on the hillside simultaneously took flight. They filled the air with wing and claw, tearing apart the stillness, scratching out the sky.

"Kali Ma," Bindra whispered again. "Dark Mother, protect my children."

2

At that moment, the new day burst its brilliance across the eastern peaks that mark the border with Bhutan. Bindra looked back to the indelible mark on her left shin. She ran her palm across it. Smooth, though slightly raised.

There was another on her right leg. She pinched both marks. She pinched them hard, but they were numb.

A growing panic, of which she could make no sense, began to submerge her chest. Some distant memory, so deeply hidden that she had lost its name, was cleaving through her core.

Bindra threw her cotton *pharia* sari around her wet torso and stumbled out into the yard, suddenly, inexplicably unable to breathe. She turned her face towards the sun, seeking comfort in its emerging warmth.

Instead, her eyes were drawn to the crows. They were reeling in a vast mass above her hut. A whirling, ominous veil. Screeching squadrons were tearing away from the looming mass to plummet to the ground and rip into a ruptured pillow of bloodied feathers.

"Oh, Kali Ma!" Bindra cried aloud. "Not this!"

But even she could not say to what she referred. The dead and broken body of her cockerel, or the instinct of an unspeakable discovery of her own.

ψ

My maternal Grandmother was a witch.

Or so the villagers claimed. They said she cast spells to make them pregnant. She caused their hay bales to spontaneously ignite. She spoiled their butter.

Grandmother would have none of it. She did not cast spells, she would scoff in contempt of her ignorant neighbours. She cast "hoodoos".

Grandmother only augmented her reputation by keeping a malformed runt of a cat, called Cesspit. "Familiar" or not, never once did Cesspit catch a mouse or bird. His deformed nose had afforded him an interminable snore.

Grandmother also kept a big black crow, called Bird, who slept balanced on a tea-towel rack in the kitchen. He spent his mornings perched in the lowest branches of the walnut tree, from which his tiny eyes would follow her every movement through the windows of the centuries-old cottage. Bird was always watching, always plotting.

Bird would accompany Grandmother on afternoon errands, riding through the village on her bicycle handlebars, head down, wings outstretched, chuckling at the pedal-born breeze between his quills. Only if he spied a queue of prim, prinked ladies at the bus stop would he free his grip to molest their shopping and tangle their hair.

Back at home, Bird would terrorise the cat, tossing Cesspit's fishy biscuits from their saucer until Grandmother was forced to chase him from the scullery. In retribution for such chiding, Bird would pluck the inkwell from its stand to stamp devil's pitchforks in Parker blue across bureaus and blotters. He would nibble through the button-thread of every dress and blouse on the airer, until none retained the decency of fastenings. He would steal her keys and safety pins, the Morello cherries, sultanas and milk chocolates. He would hoard Muscovado beneath the doormat, and gobble custard so hot that he habitually spewed bright yellow splatters across curtains and visitors. And when at breakfast Grandmother's back was turned for but a second, sausages would vanish from the pan, rashers from the grill. It would take days for the meaty morsels to reappear, found stuffed behind the cushions of the sofa, poked behind the settle in the hall.

The day the grumpy next-door neighbour saw fit to shoot Bird dead for removing the pegs from his wife's washing-line, dropping every Lux-brightened garment to the ground, his barn went up in flames. We never knew about his butter.

When my father's managerial posting with a major multinational took my parents to a new life in Munich, I stayed on at school and Grandmother was assigned to be my guardian. Her joy at this new role was such that I could never once admit the cruel regime of classroom violence and playground bullying that I daily endured.

For liberating frogs from the biology lab to a life of waterweed, spawn and heron, I was punished with the cane across bare buttocks and a slow month of solitary calculus in an unheated stockroom. For suggesting in Divinity to the Very Reverend Master that the plagues of Egypt may have been little more than Hebrew hype, I had homework and head flushed down the toilet by the committee of the Junior Christian Fellowship. And when I was found by a prefect with a Windy Miller toothbrush and a secret store of Oxo stock cubes in my bedside locker, I was held down behind the refectory and forced to swallow dandelions until I was sick.

School ever remained both mystifying and friendless, an inexplicable game in which I felt I played no part. It could not have helped that, due to my noisy nightmares, I had been ejected from the dorms to be placed in the annexe, where I was expected to sleep amongst a dysfunctional set of sleepwalkers and bed-wetters, all of whom dedicated their night-time reading to Günter Grass, Kerouac or Kafka. The label earned of "outcast" may have further explained the regular defacement of my textbooks and the stealing of my tuck, the daily kicking of shins and toe-crushing stamps, the pulling down of trousers and Chinese burns.

My annual reprieve from term-time brutality was the Blyton-worthy summers spent with my grandmother in the depths of Sussex. There, she called me Johnny Sparrow, and taught me to treasure the poetry of a Bengali named Tagore. To find in the fields dropwort, trefoil and rampion. To squeeze sap from a bluebell for the mending of books. To nurture caterpillars gathered from lace-leafed cabbages, and tadpoles from the murk of Pigwood Pond.

We would climb abandoned windmills perched high upon the Downs. Lie amongst buttercup and cowpat to let yearlings lick our naked toes. String seagull skull necklaces on Clymping beach and pick bones from owl pellets to be glued into fantastical beasts. We would dance to scratchy Schubert on the gramophone, a tea towel in each hand "for self-expression". Run like the clappers and vault farm gates to rehearse our flight from gore-minded bulls. Picnic by the Arun on wild garlic and cheddar cheese, bloater paste and granary crusts.

"*I will be the waves and you will be a strange shore,*" she would recite from a favourite volume printed in Calcutta before the War. "*I shall roll on and on and on, and break upon your lap with laughter,*" as I dozed amongst daisy and speedwell, "*and no one in the world will know where we both are.*"

The highlight of each summer, however, was the hours of breathless wonder spent together in Potter's Museum of Curiosities. Shared shudders of delight at two-faced pigs in pickling jars and four-legged bantams stuffed with sawdust. Rabbits with tusks and mummified cats. Kittens at a tea party and toads on a seesaw. A hanged man's finger and a shrunken head, which Grandmother insisted looked like her cousin Fresden in a fit.

Grandmother was tender, funny and deliciously irreverent. She would spontaneously compose rude rhymes about the vicar: "*Through the lych with his twitch and perpetual itch, he grins through his hymns till he gives himself stitch . . .*". She would teach me new card games, called Klabberjass and Hosen Runter, then change the rules with every hand to ensure she won the promised humbug. She would hide a lump of Sunlight soap or a dead crane-fly from the windowsill in her scones, just to see how priggish parish callers would respond. She would find inventive ways to slip the word "pee" into polite conversation, then shake with barely contained laughter in her secret triumph.

I adored my Grandmother. She, in turn, made it clear that she adored me.

If further evidence of her affection were required, on my twelfth birthday she presented me with a bottle of biker's leather oil – and a stuffed crocodile on which to apply it.

Bindra's hands were full. She clasped a bag of sugar balls, an egg, three scarlet hibiscus flowers, a pack of red bangles, a clutch of incense sticks, a one-rupee coin and a small clay pot of vermilion *sidur*.

The walk towards the steep heights of Ringkingpong had moistened her brow and back. Since the pale patches on her legs had faded some months before, Bindra had noticed an inexplicable change in her gait. She laughed at herself, waddling like an old *hās* gander.

Bindra paused to look out towards the Kanchenjunga. The mountain soared above her, its peaks of snow and ice so bright in the afternoon sun that she had to squint, she had to smile. There was comfort in the unchanging presence of that constant guardian, even when heavy monsoon cloud and wet winter mist veiled it from all view.

Bindra did not feel the cold, stone floor of the temple courtyard beneath her bare feet as she stood before the shrine of Ganesha at its entrance. She placed the sugar balls and dappled egg at the feet of the plump-bellied, elephant-headed boy.

"Shri Ganapati, I need new strength," she whispered. "Change is coming. Release my fear and brighten my awareness." She bowed her head in *pranam*. "*Shokavinashakarakam namami vighneshvara padpankajam*," she quietly intoned. "Destroyer of Grief, I bow to the lotus feet of the supreme Remover of Obstacles. *Aung gang Ganapatye namah-aung*."

As Bindra mounted the marble steps of the temple, she kept her eyes to the ground. She knew that she was now standing before the life-sized *murti* image of Kali Ma.

A young *panda* priest padded up behind her, yawning. Without a word, he plucked the hibiscus flowers from her outstretched palms and placed them in a metal bowl. He hung her bangles on the rusty spikes of an iron trident. He struck a match to light the incense sticks and marked her forehead with a little *sidur* from her proffered pot. She bowed in gratitude and slipped her precious coin, the *dachinaa* fee, into the prominently positioned donations box.

Bindra began her slow *parikrama* circumambulation of the central shrine. She had become aware of a weakening in her grip in the previous months, and now held the bundle of smouldering incense sticks in both hands as tightly as she could. She wafted the pungent smoke before her as she walked, softly muttering, "*Aung*

7

kring kalikaye namah-aung," to invoke in herself the force of transformation embodied in the image of the Dark Goddess.

Back before the *garbagraham* inner sanctum, she laid her *majetro* shawl on the ground and sat upon it. Only now did Bindra feel ready to look into Her face.

Kali stood tall and beautiful, as black as the darkness that enables man to perceive the Light.

Bindra looked to the *mala* of severed heads, the necklace that represents man's egotistical belief that he is separate from the universe. Separate from his fellow man and from the divine that is all life. Separate from the Knowledge, Wisdom, Truth for which he seeks.

Bindra looked to the blood-red tongue of Unspoken Knowledge, its tip so far extended that it touched Her perfect chin.

Bindra closed her eyes.

"Jihvarasajña," she mouthed. "You who have the nectar of Wisdom on your Tongue, may I find in myself the Joy that underlies all life, through which I may weather the coming storm."

Bindra paused.

She listened as the breeze sounded not only the little *ghanti mala* bell chains above her head, but also the strings of wings of numerous, giant, shiny beetles.

"*Didi!*" the young priest suddenly shouted, "Elder sister! Your hands!"

Bindra started and cried out in alarm.

The bundle of incense sticks had burned down to its base and was flaming. The tips of her fingers were blackened and blistering.

Bindra had not felt a thing.

🔱

Grandmother filled my head from childhood with our family's history.

When I reached the age of fourteen, she judged that I was of sufficiently sober mind to receive a more intimate introduction to my ancestors and withdrew from its hiding place the Victorian family album. The heavy, leather-bound volume had been so long locked away in her tall, dark dresser, I had not even known that such a book existed.

As she leafed through each delicately decorated page, I stared in wonder at the faces of my forebears, of whom she had so often spoken. Through her spirited recountings of their exploits and their tragedies, these ascendants, so long asleep, had become the fairytale characters of my childhood imagination. They were more real to me than any Wicked Stepmother or Prince Charming, for her home was filled with evidence of their fading, sepia-tinted lives. Every piece of furniture and flatware, each walking-stick and brolly in the hall-stand, had once belonged to them. The miniature Goldilocks tea service, rocking horse, and musical box that played Strauss waltzes. The lace-trimmed petticoats, silk combinations and soft cotton camisoles in the chests of drawers. The Noah's Ark in the back bedroom, with its zoo of painted animals and grumpy Mrs Noah. The *Bruin Boys* annuals on my bedside table, with their tales of Wee Woolies, Dolliwogs and Tiger Tim.

And when we sat at breakfasts of ginger porridge, Marmite crumpet, shirred bantam egg and fresh mushroom from the meadow, she would protest our Dead-'n'-Gones had kept her wide awake with their rapping on the windows, twiddling of the doorknobs, winding of the chiming clocks and whispering in the dark.

Grandmother's troublesome ancestors had also lived in India. Unlike the sober administrators and moustachioed army majors of my father's family in the Punjab, hers had been hedonistic merchants, artists and planters in the "up-country" states of the distant North-East. So vivid was her unfolding of their lives that they would pervade the daydreams of my waking hours and nightly flood my sleep.

Grandmother raised me on the ransom paid by a kindly maharaja upon the kidnap of Uncle Hillebrand, a man so unpopular that at the news of his felonious removal the family had cheered. The impulsive suicide of Aunt Totty in a public pond at Tollygunge, after an unnecessary scene at breakfast when, at the bottom of the kedgeree, there was found a jammy spoon. The inadvertent flattening of cheery cousin Dill by a passing steamroller in the Simla Hills, and the scandal of his wicked wife, who had everyone convinced that she was both an archbishop's daughter and the Queen of Madagascar, until she died of plague contracted by the licking of a postage stamp.

Grandmother nurtured me with tales of cousin Inchiquin, who not only had a passion for pet porcupines, but lived on a train to ensure he passed his favourite Himalayan views twice a day. Aunt Chibi, who was hit on the head by a Bengali coconut and forever after made to wear around her neck a label with her name and address in a prominent script. Cousin Milas, who took to dressing in private as the Begum of Bhopal, then shot his wife dead over an unwanted Christmas present whilst on a pig-stick in Cooch Behar. Devout Buddhist Uncle Bertle, who had accompanied an expedition to Tibet, dared desecrate a hallowed mountain to attend a call of nature and caught cholera from its curse. And poor Captain Cundee, who fell from a balloon at the Durbar onto the gilded caparison of a state elephant, only to be denounced in the Club, during a protracted convalescence, for his ungentlemanly habit of not wearing cufflinks.

ψ

Bindra had tried to keep the sores on her fingers out of sight. She wanted to avoid all questions.

For many months she had applied poultices of ground turmeric root to reduce the swelling, crushed neem twigs to disinfect the blisters. And though some had now begun to ulcerate, had now begun to smell, she thought it miraculous that she had no pain. In fact, to her dismay, no pain at all.

When Bindra settled on the dusty ground at the edge of the *haat* market and laid out her produce on her shawl, she kept both hands out of sight, despite the fact that she had been careful to bind her fingers in strips of cloth. She sat in silence all morning, watching what seemed to her to be the entire world walk by.

Smiling Lepchas, with their kindly manners and playful faces. Broad-shouldered Bhutanese, swathed in cloth beneath which she always sensed some fearsome weapon lurked. Woolly-hatted Bengalis on a cheap holiday from the Plains, who seemed to shout in anger at everyone with whom they spoke. Pot-bellied Marwaris, little liked for their buying up of the place and their pulling down of the old town in preference for concrete blocks at extortionate rents. Stocky-legged Tibetans, twirling *mani* prayer wheels and fingering *japamala* prayer beads, even as they bartered with characteristic ruthlessness. And then her own Nepalis, as cheeky and as chatty as children, talking over everyone else at the tops of their voices.

Few took any notice of Bindra. Few even knew she was there.

This was the season for wild avocados and oranges, and the stalls were filled with mounds of both the dark, bitter and the plump, sweet fruits. Compared to the abundance of the bazaar itself, the few offerings on her shawl were meagre. The dry, stony ground she called her vegetable patch struggled without a direct source of water. The little it managed to produce was stunted and deformed. Bindra and her children did not mind. There was usually enough. But still she needed money to buy rice, mustard oil and the freshly ground *atta* flour for *roti* breads.

Bindra waited until late afternoon, but nobody had stopped to even cast a curious eye across her wares. She conceded defeat and pulled herself onto her knees. She stretched her aching back before bending to gather up the few red carrots and withered radishes. The wilted cauliflower and mustard leaves for *gundruk*. The foraged moss and sticks she thought she might have sold for kindling. As she wrapped them back into their cloth, an unkempt boy left a group of skinny children scavenging in the rubbish piles to confidently approach her.

"*Didi*," he whined, "big sister, anything to give me? Anything in there you don't want to take home?"

He smelled unwashed, his jumper little more than an erratic, green spider's web across his small, dark bones.

Bindra smiled. "I don't have much you'd like, *bhai*," she apologised, slipping her hand into the bundle. "But you can take these, little brother."

The boy stood still. His grubby face had fallen silent.

"They don't look much, but they're sweet and have a good crunch," she promised, rubbing two thin, dark carrots on the sleeve of her tatty cardigan before thrusting them towards him.

The boy stepped backwards. He was staring, not at her offering, but at the loosely bandaged hands and swollen earlobes.

He looked hard into her eyes.

"*Kori!*" he whispered. "Leper!"

Bindra suddenly could no longer stand. She slumped sideways and hit the ground. She could not breathe.

Her vegetables rolled out across the floor.

But the children did not snatch them.

They all just ran away.

Chapter Two

I had three heroes as a child.

Ricky from *Champion the Wonder Horse*, who lived with his cowboy uncle in a dusty land, got into endless scrapes with local rogues, yet always managed to be saved by an indefatigable team of feral stallion and wily dog.

Rabindranath Tagore from Calcutta, who never had his own television theme tune, but had written poems that showed me the world was brim full of beauty, if only I would take the time to notice.

And Uncle Oscar.

Uncle Oscar had been a pioneering tea planter in the storyland-sounding Assam and Bengal, a fact for which we all felt inexplicably grateful. I was told he had never drunk tea on the few occasions that he had come back to visit, which had made everybody laugh. He had said English brews were made from floor sweepings, over which everybody had laughed still more.

I laughed too, every time this family anecdote was recounted, even though I did not understand the comparison. I had never tasted tea. My parents would not touch it. They only drank dandelion roots, roasted barley and ground acorns.

Of the lives of my many relations, as related by my Grandmother, it was undoubtedly Uncle Oscar who most captured my juvenile imagination. It was not just his reckless derring-do of first sailing to India with nothing but a frock-coat, a pair of home-made pyjamas, a copy of *The Pilgrim's Progress*, and a loaded rifle. It was not just his courage in navigating the full length of the Brahmaputra, from the great Ganges Delta into Upper Assam, when still a fresh-faced youth, to commence, as he put it, "the uncertainties of a jungle life." It was not just the prestige of surviving the great Darjeeling earthquake of 1898, which he had barely allowed to disrupt his tennis match at the Amusement Club. Nor was it just his heroic status amongst the locals, earned by his introduction of hygienic milk to protect them against TB, cinchona trees to produce quinine for malaria, his hunting down man-eating tigers and rogue elephants, and for generally saving the day.

No.

It was because, Grandmother hinted, Uncle Oscar had taken a native princess to wife in those deep, dark jungles.

It was because, she whispered, I had secret cousins hidden in those distant hills.

ψ

"Silly boy!" Bindra scoffed as she walked home from the market that evening. "Such foolish words."

Yet still she trembled.

Bindra lived some miles beyond the lights of the busy town and its jeep-filled lanes, below the step-cut paddy fields and farms. When the floods had swept her husband and some seventy other passengers in the crowded Kakariguri bus off the road and to their deaths in the surging Teesta River two monsoons before, she had been unable to meet the rent on their little house.

They had never found her husband's body. The fact that the *jhankri* mountain shaman had been unable to carry out the proper death rites still haunted her. Unfinished business. Not good for the dead or the living. Ill-boding.

The farmer had promptly thrown her out of their home with her four fatherless children. To prevent their return, he had immediately moved in a *phing*-maker. Employee of the Dalai Lama's wealthy brother, the new tenant could at least guarantee the monthly dues through the profitable production of glass noodles, despite the paucity of his wages.

Bindra had begged and sobbed, but her superstitious landlord had not wanted a young widow on his land. Inauspicious.

"Leave this place!" he had spat. "And take your miserable fate and your feathered demons with you, Dhumavati!"

Bindra had recoiled. He had called her by the name of the large-nosed goddess, who rides a chariot drawn by crows. A widowed goddess whose name is normally only ever spoken as a curse.

ψ

Grandmother and I were sitting by the fire.

We had just finished one of our Naughty Teas of "noisy toast" topped with marmalade on chunky cheese. Beetroot soldiers with horseradish pickle so strong it made our noses run. Pilchards in a pepper sauce, with all the bones "to make our hair grow curly". And then the seedy cake we had baked together in the afternoon, with such a dousing of condensed milk and lemon curd that the very thought of it made our hearts hurry.

Grandmother now sat sunk into a sagging, ancestral armchair, surrounded by a clutch of crocheted cushions. Cheek resting on the back of graceful fingers. Tiggy-Winkle legs draped with new knitting.

I was perched on some great-aunt's harlequin leather pouffe that had long leaked its horsehair innards onto the scorch-spotted hearth rug. I listened to the grandfather clock counting out another generation in the hall, as Grandmother hummed one of her nondescript tunes in time with the ticks and Cesspit added a wheeze of syncopated snores. I stared into flames guttering in the grate, and breathed in the ever-present reassurance of coal smoke, well-Vimmed sink, mint humbugs and lavender wool-wash that pervaded her cottage.

"Johnny Sparrow," Grandmother murmured, reaching out to stroke the arc of my ear. I looked up, smiling in intuitive expectation. "Fetch me the key in your Grandfather's shaving mug," she instructed with a twinkle, the soft white waves of hair around her face revealing in the embers' glow a memory of the rich auburn they had once been.

I had never met my Grandfather, and yet I knew and loved his face that smiled with tenderness from behind framed glass on piano and wall. I often gazed into his kind, unblinking eyes, his silent, ready smile, and thought he looked a lot like me. He may have died too soon, the year before my birth, yet I knew where to find his gloves and braces, his goat-head inkwell and farmyard gaiters, his unused cut-throat razorblades still in their printed paper wrappings, his penknives, collar studs, draughts board – and his china shaving mug.

"Now open the dresser drawer, darling," she instructed. "And bring me the rosewood box."

I rattled the poker in the grate with no real purpose as she rummaged through old letters written on lilac paper, funerary ribbon, ration cards and a pressed posy of desiccated violets.

"Ah, here he is!" she beamed, studying her find with unguarded affection.

She handed me an old photograph taken in Burma. The young man looking back had a sensual mouth and intelligent, gentle eyes.

"Handsome, isn't he?" I observed with interest.

"Oh, Theo was beautiful!" Grandmother agreed, her face and hands suddenly busy with memories. "So elegant. So witty. A voice like sweet, soft fudge before it sets. We girls all fell in love in a moment and would just sit looking at him, quite unembarrassed by our stares. You see, Theo was like a prince from a storybook, brought to life before us!" she enthused.

Gazing into the finely formed features, now faded by time and Sussex damp, I knew that I too would have been sufficiently captivated for some surreptitious staring of my own.

"Uncle Oscar only let him come to London between the wars, because he was ... well, more European than the others," she revealed. "Very important in those days, I'm sorry to say. My father did not approve, of course. All the same, we girls once secretly saved our pocket money just to buy our lovely Theo a box of chocolates. Very bold back then, when we were forbidden to skip in the street, or swing on a gate, just in case we showed the hem of our long knickers!"

I wanted to know what had become of this entrancing new relation.

"Dead," she sighed, melting back into the faded chintz. "Long dead. Left rubber in Rangoon for confectionery in Putney – but didn't survive the *Luftwaffe*."

I was intrigued. "Then who was he, Grandma?"

She leaned close to me and laid a papery palm on my shoulder.

"Why, Johnny Sparrow, Theo was the eldest of Oscar's secret sons!"

The stars were bright that night, bright enough for Bindra to pick her way down the hillside path. She struggled to cling to the low tree branches as she climbed from boulder to boulder, a bundle of unsold vegetables and kindling twigs tied across her back.

"No rice again," she sighed to herself. "Just more carrots. More woody radishes. More chewy *gundruk*." At least there were now only two mouths waiting to be fed.

The previous summer, she had given her eldest daughter as a maid. Only eleven years old, she was now working as a house-servant to a wealthy poultry farmer, down in Kakariguri. It gave Bindra peace of mind to know that her beloved Jayashri was no longer hungry and had hot milk tea to drink every day.

Her second, Jamini, had been taken away by a Christian "orphanage". In exchange, the owners had paid Bindra enough to buy a *bakhri* goat and daal lentils to feed the remaining children for a full three months. The Christians had promised to teach Jamini to read and write, on the strict condition that she changed her name to Mary, wore a wooden cross around her neck, and slept with an American Bible beneath her pillow. It had seemed a small price for an education and the daily doling out of a millet gruel that had earned the school its local name of "St Porridge".

And yet, Bindra knew that if she allowed herself to stop and think too long, she would unleash a weeping cry for the loss of her daughters that would never cease. Every day she doubted that she had made the right choice for her girls. So every night she reminded herself of their shared hunger, huddled together for sleep in the bamboo hut they had built for themselves on the abandoned burial ground, the only land for which nobody demanded payment.

There had been a time, and not so long ago, when there had been no hunger in their home, with food enough for all six members of the family. Food enough, until the day Kailash had not come home. He had been a good husband and father, a good friend. Now waiting for her tonight were just the two boys, Jyothi and Jiwan. Light and Life. So long as they kept hunting out wild *iskus* and tapioca roots in the forest, they could manage. So long as they still came home with a pocket of spilled grain collected from the roadside, she could keep them together a little longer.

It was as she approached the *shaktiko roukh*, the dedicated Shakti Tree, its broad trunk bound with offerings of coloured thread, that Bindra slipped and fell on the stones.

"Twice in an evening, you clumsy thing!" she groaned. "Come on now, you're better than this."

Bindra sat to rub her shins and elbows with wrists and forearms. "No harm done," she assured herself.

It was dark beneath the spreading branches. Bindra found her way to the painted image of Durga that lay embraced amongst the tangle of roots, daubed with dung paste. She sought the remains of any *sidur* at the feet of the tiger-riding goddess and marked her own forehead with a smear of the scarlet pigment, to remind herself that she was as much an expression of the universal forces represented by Durga as the bark of the distant dogs, the moon above, the breath in her lungs.

"Jaya Ma," she voiced into the darkness. "Give me victory."

Bindra took a carrot from her bundle and winced at the deficiency of her gift as she placed it amongst the roots.

"*Aung hring dhung Durga devyai namah-aung*," she repeated, even as her voice wavered and the hands clasped at her heart trembled. She had determined to invoke the strength and wisdom in herself to overcome what she knew to be her gathering enemies, Fear and Despair.

As she approached the shack, Bindra could see through the wide gaps between the bamboo slats that her two boys already had a low fire burning on the mud floor. With a single call, they came running to relieve her of her bundle.

"What did you sell, *Ama*? And what did you buy?" they both asked with excitement.

"Nothing and . . . nothing!" she smiled with disappointment. "But fetch the *tasala* and I shall make us a feast!"

The boys cheered just to brighten her and ran to lift the blackened pan from its hook on the wall.

As Jiwan turned, his face drew tight with horror.

"*E Ama!*" he gasped, his finger pointing to the little toe on her right foot. Whilst they had seen it gradually curling under during the past months, the toe was now twisted, torn and bleeding.

Bindra looked down and cried aloud at the sight of tattered flesh and splintered bone.

She had not even noticed.

I met Priya at a party.

My eyes were first drawn to the Siouxsie Sioux backcomb as it bobbed through a crowded, monochrome kitchen. I had heard her name for weeks as two acquaintances had independently confided that they intended her for themselves. I leant with calculated disinterest against the black Formica breakfast bar to watch Tom and Toby take their turns with practised chat and artful nonchalance. I sipped at something sickly in a plastic cup, looking on in envy at their boldness and in pity at the impotence of their stumbling seductions.

It was as her glazed gaze drifted from their competitive attentions that Priya discovered the intensity of my interest amidst the throng. I felt my face flush furiously, but could not look away. I had never seen such beauty without vanity. It quickened my heart. It silenced my self-consciousness. She glanced at the floor to veil her own blush, then back at me to reveal with her dark, kohl-stained eyes that we had shared a secret intimacy.

I made my way towards her through what had suddenly become an empty, silent room. I could hear nothing but a pounding in my ears. I could see nothing but a shy and tender smile I knew that I would kiss.

At midnight, we wandered away from the house to talk without interruption and to escape the fierce disdain of friends who would never find it possible to forgive me.

Priya was intelligent, but shy. Self-possessed, yet vulnerable. She made me laugh. She made me laugh a lot.

We walked back holding hands and sucking on humbugs from my pocket, indifferent to the threat of a chill, hair-flattening drizzle.

"Can I phone you?" I asked, above the clamour of twenty-five at breakfast, above yet more Stranglers and The Jam.

"I'll have to ask my father," she replied.

It was not the response I had anticipated.

She put a hand to her mouth and giggled at my silence.

"It's just that he's never let me see a boy before," she confessed. "And I don't know if he'll approve of a white one!"

ψ

Bindra had been walking since before dawn.

As she had pushed through the towering *dhatura* she had repeated the name of Shiva, to whom these plants with their hanging, trumpet flowers were dedicated. She had walked so far that lush jungle had become scented pine and dark oak. Where there had been bamboo thickets, scarlet poinsettia and rhododendron, there was now maple, birch and knee-high cardamom, their soft leaves brushing against her legs and sweetening the air of the *bindra ban* deep forest, after which she had been named. And as she walked, Bindra sang softly to warn the *Punyajana*, the Good People who live in trees and plants, that she was passing through their world.

Bindra gradually climbed the steep path to the cave temples. She gave a handful of *bhui-kaaphal* wild strawberries to the docile *sadhu*, who had watched her difficult, rolling approach. The wandering ascetic looked her in the eyes, then narrowed his own, as though with misgiving.

"Funny old man," she giggled to herself. "He surely recognises me. I've met him in these hills for years!" She turned to sound the bell above the gateway, to wake the deity within. She did not see him toss the sweet, red fruit to the floor.

Bindra crouched down and eased herself into a crevice in the rock face. Before her stood the row of *lingams*. She touched her head, mouth, heart and pubis in *pranam*, reverently saluting the divinity in all life, of which she recognised herself as but one expression. From an old medicine bottle in her bundle, she poured a little goat's milk over each of the stone-cut symbols of universal union. She laid an offering of large, white *dhatura* flowers and then *belpatra* leaves from the woodapple tree that she had collected on her slow ascent. Both were favourites of Mahadeva, as the androgynous Paramshiva was better known in the Hills.

"*Aung namah Shivaya*," she softly sang to the Lord of Yoga, Lord of the Mountains. "Shri Sakha, my Supreme Friend, your *lingam* reveals the stability of the cosmos. May I recognise that same stability within myself," she began. "May I understand better that there is no separation, no difference between you, the universe, and clumsy little me."

"*E!*" a gruff voice shouted from behind her.

She turned with a start. Silhouetted against the sky beyond the entrance of the temple crag stood a *Bahun* priest. She had heard that a Brahmin had been recently posted to the cave temples. His job, it was said, was to wean the villagers away from their ancient, unorthodox, mountain traditions.

"Come out here, where I can see you!"

She waddled on her haunches, until she reached the entrance and could stand again. Even in the sunlight, Bindra struggled to draw herself upright. The bindings on her feet, which protected her increasingly clawed toes, had caused her to limp the entire length of the morning's arduous trek. This, in turn, was causing a new and unrelenting pain in her lower back.

"Where have you come from?" he asked, with his heavy Hindi accent.

There was a mystifying aggression in his voice. She felt no inclination to converse with this hostile stranger, so waved vaguely towards the mountain road along which she had walked.

"What's wrong with your hands and feet?" he almost snarled.

She looked down at herself. "It's nothing," she joked. "Just silly accidents."

She noticed the *sadhu* standing to one side, watching.

The Brahmin stared at her dirty cloth bindings and made a loud clacking sound with his tongue.

"Leave here," he said, his face suddenly expressionless.

"What did you say?" she asked in disbelief.

"You heard me, leave here!"

He had raised his voice to her. The men in these hills did not raise their voices to women. Women were shown respect. Women were honoured for the divine qualities they embodied. Men bent to touch the feet of their *cheli-beti* sisters and daughters. Men undertook day-long fasts if they raised their voices to women.

The Brahmin turned to pick up a long, metal *trishul* from a pile that lay against the rock face. To Bindra's utter dismay, he abruptly, forcefully jabbed her with the ritual trident.

"Leave here!" he bellowed, thrusting at her again, so hard that he caught her between her ribs.

She looked into his eyes with bewilderment.

All she could see was his fear.

For three years I loved Priya.

Together we cooked curries, made our own clothes, and hiked the Stiperstones and Clees. We spent rainy afternoons in matinees and galleries, our evenings outside theatres and concert halls in hope of cheap returns. We took Philosophy and Art at college, music lessons, language classes, and night trains to Bavaria. We sailed the Baltic with a Finn, then spent a spring in an Amsterdam squat, living on old Edam and peeing in a sink, until a pot-headed neighbour fell through our roof and brought in the weather.

Back home, we would seek out ruins to explore by starlight, twist our ankles and dent our shins. And when the weather warmed, we would cycle after country graveyards with picnics in a basket, to dream of our shared future and fall asleep in each other's arms on time-worn tombs.

For three years, Priya loved me.

"*I seem to have loved you in numberless forms, numberless times,*" she would recite from Tagore, as though to prove it, "*In life after life, in age after age forever.*"

For three years, I did not live a day without Priya. I did not sleep a night without whispering her name.

And yet, my father's mother was not happy.

"Listen dear, she's a nice enough girl, but we don't want her sort in our family."

Her sort?

"Are you referring to the colour of her skin?" I asked, struggling to remain respectful, "because, as Priya likes to point out, I go darker than she does in the sun!"

This was evidently no argument, but I persisted.

"In fact, she jokes that I must have more Indian blood in my veins than she has in hers!"

My humour was not shared.

"You have not been listening," she replied, with calculated restraint. "So listen now and listen well: No. No. Never!"

☡

Bindra had scurried down the hillside, back to the road. She was panting and perspiring.

When the Brahmin had said she did not deserve to step onto consecrated soil, that her *karma* denied her the right, she had pulled herself tall and had felt the fire of Kali in her bones.

"Your talk of *karma* is not our way in these hills," she had protested. "*Karma* is your *Vedanta*, used to justify unkindness, dishonourable thoughts and acts towards others. And this because you judge them to have 'sinned' in a previous life, according to your own, man-made laws!"

"*Aap apne aap ko kya sumujhtey ho?*" the Brahmin had hissed, suddenly reverting to his native Hindi. "Who do you think you are? Preaching to me your *jungli* superstitions!"

He had reluctantly returned to Nepali and continued with tight teeth.

"I am a *Brahmana*! Whilst what are you? A woman! A mere phase of illusion! Don't you know that your sex is the root of all worldly attachments?" He had barely been able to catch his furious breath to repeat, "I am a *Brahmana*! Keeper of the *Vedas* and the *Manusmriti*! I am the *mahanta*, the owner of this temple! And what are you? Nothing but an illiterate, black-faced female, whom God has seen fit to suffer the foulest of His curses! For your audacity to one of His chosen, twice-born sons, divine justice will return you to your next miserable life as a mange-ridden pye-bitch!"

Bindra had listened with astonishment.

"*Dajoo*, elder brother, your attachment to the divisions of caste is not ours," she had asserted. "All such hierarchies only undermine the many to afford an imagined superiority to the few. They are a falsehood, leading humankind ever deeper into the delusion of division and separation, and yet further from the underlying truth."

Her voice had stayed steady.

"And how can you claim ownership of something that cannot belong to anyone?" she had challenged. "This cave temple has been here, open to all, without restriction, since the beginning of time!"

His face had flushed florid.

"But you and I have no argument," she had softened, with a conciliatory smile. "Our ways may be different, yet still you and I are one! All life is Mahadeva! All life is Kali Ma! You are Shiva! I am Shiva!"

The *sadhu* had looked on, motionless and silent.

"And brother," Bindra had continued, roused with new courage by the naming of the Dark Goddess, "do not be deceived that that *janai* sacred thread across your shoulder makes you any more pure, any more worthy of respect than the penniless crone who span it. It is only a length of greasy old twine!" she had chuckled, playfully. "No more or less holy than the soil at our feet or the hair on my *jungli*, uneducated, 'black' head . . ."

It was then that the Brahmin had spat at her.

☥

Grandmother was delighted.

"She's perfect! You're both perfect!" she exclaimed at the news. "And both your names mean 'Beloved'! All I could have ever hoped for you, my darling boy!" she burst, with enough excitement for the both of us. When I revealed that the gold jewellery had already been entrusted to the post by Priya's family in Gujarat, she visibly trembled with tingles.

"Do let me buy the silk for the bridesmaids' saris!" Grandmother insisted. "Just imagine, the ultimate Anglo-Indian wedding! Let's have kedgeree with your favourite eggs 'rumble-tumble' at the breakfast! *Bel puri* and cucumber soup, *gajar halwa* and warm plum cake with cardamom custard at the lunch!"

I threw my arms around her. "Thank-you-so-much-Grand-ma," I tapped out on her soft cheek in Morse Code kisses.

"You-are-wel-come-John-ny-Spar-row," she pecked in reply.

☥

Bindra broke into a lumbering trot, despite the bruising of her ribs, until she reached Lapu *basti*, the village of Lapu. She made her way directly to the narrow path that would lead her to the *jhankri*.

At the sight of the smiling man, sitting on the steps of his simple wooden temple, Bindra burst out with an explosive sob.

"Come, *bahini*," Kushal Magar beckoned. "Sit with me. Drink hot *masala chiya*."

She eased herself down beside him and sipped at the brew of tea leaves spiced with black cardamom, peppercorns, cloves and ginger root. It was sweet, milky and deeply comforting.

"I remember when you made this journey once before, sister," the *jhankri* smiled, "when the monsoon took your husband. So what brings you back today?"

"I need your help, *dajoo*," Bindra stated, with newly restored composure. "There is something wrong, elder brother. There is something very wrong with me."

He looked her kindly in the eyes.

"Fear diminishes understanding," he offered. "It reduces man's inclination towards compassion. Fear only gives rise to conflict, both within and without. So do not be afraid, *bahini*. You are Durga. You are Shiva. You are Kali Ma."

Bindra laughed and wiped away more tears. "I used almost those very words this morning to someone else who was afraid. It is a lesson indeed to have them returned to me."

The *jhankri* left her sitting on the temple steps. She looked out to the relucent peaks of the Kanchenjunga, whilst he prepared himself. He donned his *jama pagri* white tunic, then the headdress stitched with feathers and precious *kauri* shells, symbols of the Goddess, the active force of the universe. He began to intone the mind-focusing syllables of *mantras* as he opened the red doors of the little shrine.

Kushal Magar took up his *mura*, the sanctified drum that would take him into trance, enabling him to perceive beyond the boundaries of mere intellect, beyond the debilitating confines of petty ego.

He unwrapped the *thurmi* from its cloth binding and raised the ceremonial dagger with both palms. He repeated resonating syllables and clasped the rock-crystal handle between firm fingers to draw a circle on the dry ground with its iron tip.

"*Aung satom bhi dhumba damdim . . .*"

This was now the ritual space, the focus for all his will and power, for all the knowledge bequeathed to him by innumerable preceding generations.

Kushal Magar sat cross-legged, facing the *than* altar. He burned handfuls of mountain herbs in metal bowls. He lit cones of heady *dhup* incense in scorched clay cups. And all the while he muttered an endless stream of anciently configured "seeds" of sound, *bijas* with the vibratory power to effect a change in consciousness.

To Bindra, the air seemed to thin, the air seemed to shine, as the *jhankri* closed his eyes and started to tremble.

His journey beyond all limitations had begun.

$$\psi$$

She was found by children on a muddy track we often cycled together.

She had been crushed against a tree.

The driver was never discovered. The accident never explained.

Beautiful, bright, funny, loving Priya – she who had become the reason for my every waking hour, my every breath – had died alone.

None of us had had the least idea. I thought I might have felt it.

It was my mother who had to tell me. Ringing from a distant telephone. Line crackling. Voice strained.

Two days later, Grandmother slipped away into her lawless reaches for one last time.

She never again awoke from sleep.

$$\psi$$

Kushal Magar's drum lay silent. He blinked vaguely towards the mountains.

"*Bahini*," he whispered. "I have passed through *Akash*, the world of the gods. Through *Dharti* and *Patal*, the worlds of man, of water and crystal upon which all else sits. But, there is nothing I can do. You are bearing the one affliction I have no power to heal. Forgive me."

Bindra dared not take another breath.

The *jhankri* moved decisively. He threw a length of scarlet cotton over her head and gave the instruction that she was to listen with her heart.

He drew her close, lifted one corner of the cloth and whispered an urgent but precise stream of sounds directly into her right ear. *"Aung tato purushaya bitnay madevarcha . . ."* he began.

Three times he repeated the same torrent of syllables, blew smoke from newly ignited plants into her face, anointed her forehead with dark oil.

Kushal Magar turned to her other side. He lifted the opposite corner of the cloth and repeated the long mantra three times into her left ear.

"Aung tato purushaya bitnay madevarcha . . ."

Again, three times the aromatic smoke. Three times the benevolent anointing.

Bindra remained slumped and silent.

"Younger sister, take these," he said, thrusting into her bound hands a small cloth bag. "In here are balls of cremation ash mixed with buffalo *ghiu*. When you believe you have no more choices, repeat the mantra and throw one ball for every *bija*, every seed of sound, into fire," he instructed her with urgency. "Forgive me. I have nothing more . . ."

Bindra rocked her head from side to side in resignation and understanding. She listlessly handed him a small bunch of carrots, held together with a cord that had been tied to her waist. But Kushal Magar shook his head.

"You have far greater need. Now hurry, sister. Hurry home. The storm has come."

Chapter Three

It was still night when I was shaken awake.

"Time to get moving, mate," a voice was saying. "This is no place to kip, believe me."

I was shaken again.

"You've got to have somewhere better to sleep than this, surely?" the voice insisted.

I stared up at a policeman.

"Sorry," I mumbled, wiping sticky lips.

"You know you stink, don't you?" he added.

"Sorry," I repeated. My mouth tasted poisonous.

"Do you know you're on a roundabout?"

"Sorry," was again all I could manage.

"Well, how about moving your 'oh-so-sorry' backside and getting yourself off home?" he suggested.

"Thank you," I muttered apologetically.

I did not look back after I crossed the road. I knew he was still watching. I pretended to know where I was going, yet had no idea in which town I was that night.

The dying bulb of a public lavatory flickered up ahead. I glanced behind to be sure he had not followed.

I took a newspaper from a rubbish bin, then locked myself in a cubicle. I laid the paper on the floor, curled up around the pan and struggled back into a difficult sleep.

The sky was darkening as Bindra reached the top of the path that led to the abandoned burial ground. Her mouth was parched. Her knees, hips and back painful.

As she broke through the tree line and the dimly lit valley opened up before her, she stopped. She looked beyond the Shakti Tree to where her home stood. She had lost her bearings.

Again she looked at the tree, and then beyond.

There was smoke in her nostrils. There were embers in the gloom.

Bindra's heart violently twisted in bloodless dread. Her knees suddenly buckled beneath her. And as she fell, she vomited.

"Jyothi, Jiwan! *Mero choraharu!*" she screamed, as she began to scramble down the stony hillside. "My boys! My boys!"

Bindra rolled and slipped, lacerating her clothes, her skin, until she fell against the tree's solidity.

"*Ama!*" a hoarse voice gasped. "Mother!"

Bindra's sons burst towards her from the darkness of the hollow.

"They're still here!" both boys cried, as she gathered them into her arms. "*Ama*, they're still here! They're waiting!"

ॐ

I looked without recognition at the reflection in the window of the off-licence.

Gaunt features blinked back.

I had no sense at all of who it might be.

I was knocking at the door, when the "Open" sign was slipped into place and the bolt unlocked.

"Alright, alright!" the plump-calfed woman barked.

I had the bottle in my hand and the two pound notes on the counter, even before she was back behind the till.

"Have a nice day!" she sneered, as I skulked out and made towards the park.

I pushed deep into the bushes, away from any paths, any dog walkers, any police. I unscrewed the cap and gulped down foul, burning bitterness until all was gone.

I laid my head on soft, damp ground.

I breathed the sweetness of dark soil deep into my lungs.

And then, again, the blissful, empty darkness.

ψ

Bindra peered down the smoke-swept hillside for a moment.

"Who has done this?" she asked the frightened faces pressed against her legs.

"*Ama*, they're still here. Stay safe by Durga's tree," Jyothi pleaded.

"But this is wrong. This is nobody's land. We owe nothing. No one comes here."

Kali Ma surged back into her bones and Bindra stood tall again.

"Stay here," she whispered. "Pray to Mahishasura-mardini, She who is the Slayer of the Buffalo Demon. Pray for victory, my strong sons!"

Bindra touched the two dark heads as she left the sanctuary of the Shakti Tree, placing on them a blessing before she stepped towards the dying bonfire that had once been their home.

ψ

I was naked beneath the blanket. Naked and cold.

"What're you on then, eh?" some man was saying to me, clenching tight his grey face as he examined my eyes.

I stared back, frightened.

"Know where you are?"

I shook my head.

"You're in a police station, mate. In a lock-up."

Again I shook my head.

"Oh yes you are!" he replied with a bored laugh, pushing my chest with such force that I fell back onto cold concrete. "What do you expect, walking around in the altogether? Not nice is it, for the rest of us? However pretty your mother thinks you are."

"My mother?" I asked in confusion. "You know my mother?"

"Night night, pretty boy," he chuckled.

And the lights went out.

I lay still and silent.

I lay still and silent for a long time.

And then:

"Enough. No more. It ends here."

Bindra approached the smouldering pile of bamboo.

She stopped and stared in disbelief at the complete destruction of all she had struggled to provide for her children. Forcing back a pressing wail, her bewildered gaze rested on the scorched-scalp dome of her *tasala*. The sight of her old cooking pan emerging from the embers, like the dark skullcaps she unearthed amongst her vegetables, gave her momentary comfort. Her boys would still have hot *tarkari* before sleep.

A spectre of bright sparks suddenly scattered into darkness, drawing Bindra's eyes to narrow on a twisted chair. She owned no furniture. She looked again.

"*Mero bakhri!*" she choked in rage and confusion. "My goat! Why kill my goat?" She put her hands to her face and began to cry. That sweet-natured she-goat was a friend to the children. She gave good milk. She even slept with them when the cold was too hard to bear.

"Who did this?" Bindra screamed into the enclosing shadows. "Show yourselves, *kaapharharu*! You cowards! Who would do this to my children? And me, a widow! With nothing! Who has hurt none of you!"

A murmur made her turn.

A group of men and women were standing some yards from her, their faces flickering in the dying fire.

For a moment, she thought they were *bhutharu*, spirits of the dead bones beneath her feet that she found caught amongst her carrots.

But she knew these people. They farmed the land around her. They were her neighbours. She had laboured hard in their fields during harvests of buckwheat and kodo, pearl millet and mustard. She had planted their paddy until her feet had swollen and split in exchange for a measure of daal. She had fried them gifts of sweet, rice-flour *phinni* during *Dasai*, during *Durga Puja*. She had brought them tasty, baked *iskus* when the forest vines hung heavy with yellow squash gourds.

"You?" she faltered. "Why would you do this?"

There was no shame in their eyes. Only a look she had seen earlier today, in the cave temple.

"You are afraid!" she gasped in realisation. "Why? What have I done? What have any of us done to you?"

They blinked back in motionless silence.

A man cautiously stepped forward.

"Woman, you are cursed. And now you curse us. My children are sick because of you."

A young woman joined in. "My belly is full of worms, *bokshi*!"

"It is you, Witch, who has fouled our water and soured our milk!"

"Our cows are dry!" cried another.

"I am no *bokshi*!" Bindra laughed in astonishment. "What are you saying? You know me! You are my neighbours!"

"We do not know you, Leper Witch!" an elderly man shouted.

Bindra looked back, up to the Shakti Tree. She did not want her sons to hear such wicked words. Such cruel names. Such lies.

A sharp stone struck her shoulder, causing Bindra to stagger backwards in shock and pain.

"Leper!" shrieked a woman. "What sins are yours that you'd punish even us for your crimes?"

Bindra looked up to the tree, to her boys. She turned to stumble back into the darkness, to hold her sons again. Her Light and Life.

A sudden, rushing movement and Bindra's clothes were clinging wet against her skin.

The brutal reek of kerosene.

She turned her face towards the flickering group of spectral *bhutharu*, standing silent, staring with their hollow eyes.

And then a gleaming flame, spinning, spinning in the dark.

The thud of a burning stick against her back.

Bindra was on fire.

Chapter Four

As the plane began its descent onto the myriad Diwalian lights of the city in the early hours of the morning, I quietly wept. I had finally arrived in a land and amongst a people so loved by my rosily reminiscing father and enigmatic Uncle Oscar that I felt as though my entire life had prepared me for this moment. I had, at last, come home.

The Indian crew was busy securing tray tables and luggage lockers, even though the passengers were few and scattered through the cabin. I put out my hand to touch the empty seat beside me. Priya and I had imagined making this journey together.

"Such adventures to be had!" Grandmother had cheered, when I had first intimated our intentions. "Be sure to sit with a *sadhu*, eat a warm mango straight from the tree, hug an 'untouchable' – and bring me a stone from Uncle Oscar's grave!"

It still made no sense to me that I was travelling alone. It made no sense that I was about to step onto Indian soil, breathe Indian air, without Priya's slim, dark hand to gently trace the contours of my own.

"*I shall become a delicate draught of air and caress you,*" she had once written in a letter, purposely quoting Tagore for me, "*and I shall be rippling in the water when you bathe, and kiss you and kiss you again.*"

I returned my face to the window. The lights below me blurred as the transparent reflection that returned its stare began to distort and shake. I was vaguely aware of a man sobbing.

A soft, dark hand alighted on my shoulder. I turned, to look into the eyes of a sari-draped stewardess.

"Are you alright, sir?" her lipstick smiled with concern. "May I offer you a boiled sweetie?"

Outside the main entrance of Bombay airport, a man flashed me a tatty grin of broken enamel and inflamed gums.

"Where are you intending to be going, sir?" he asked.

I replied that I was bound for the city's Central Station.

His thick, black eyebrows rose and fell with acrobatic pretensions. His dry lips puckered into a well-practised sphincter of concern and sympathy.

"No good, sir. Central Station blown up yesterday! All rubble and not one train!" he cried out, his arms flailing wildly in all directions to illustrate the calamity. "One hundred and forty-two dear foreigners coldly-bloodly murdered! Not safe for not one young man. You, sir, must be coming with me!" he ordered and began tugging on my rucksack.

I was disinclined to follow him into the pre-dawn darkness. For all his apparent interest in my well-being and safety, I did not trust the man. I thanked him for his advice and politely explained that I now wished to return to the taxi queue from which he had somehow managed to lead me.

His pleas to follow him became vociferous. The tugging intensified. It was all becoming rather unpleasant.

How he managed to shuffle me backwards, around the corner of the building, out of sight of the airport officials who were ferrying newly arrived passengers into the comparative safety of yellow Ambassadors, I could not say. But in a moment, he laid hard into my chest with one great shove of his unctuous head. I staggered backwards helplessly, at the mercy of my backpack, when my impending topple was providentially interrupted by an object unseen behind me. It crunched audibly, and let out a Marathi expletive, much muffled by the tight packing of my travel wardrobe.

I swung around, inadvertently knocking to the ground my tourist-guide-cum-assailant, and was astonished to discover that he had prepared an open car door, towards which he had been stealthily directing me. He also had a henchman, who was now winded and sliding down the vehicle to the floor, gasping for breath.

I swiftly kicked away a slender knife that had apparently fallen from the crushed hand of the newly incapacitated felon, whereupon, for some absurd, British-bred reason, I calmly apologised to them both, before strolling back to the official taxi rank to hail a cab.

🔱

Bindra had lain amongst the discarded wadding and cockroaches in the hospital corridor all night.

The medical staff were little interested in the motionless bundle watched over by two silent children. With neither money nor relations to settle the "unofficial debts" she would inevitably incur, Bindra owned nothing that might convince any nurse to dirty their hands on her damaged body. There were too many other would-be-patients blocking the doorways, crowding the corridors, offering bribes for a bed, to bother with a quiet one. Besides, they knew that if they waited long enough, the penniless widow was likely to die of infection or shock.

The hospital had been founded by the British a century before, in the days when all natives had been forbidden within the boundary gates. Only those who had removed the waste, or emptied the bedpans and lavatory boxes had been permitted entry. Now, the hospital was a government institution and open to all. Now, the waste was simply tossed straight down the hillside. The sewage simply ran into the river.

Bindra had no memory of climbing the steep hill to the hospital grounds. She only recalled a confused and terrible night of searing light, deep darkness and extraordinary pain.

Jyothi touched his mother's brow.

"I have water," he whispered in her ear. "Jiwan-*bhai* has bananas. I'm sorry, *Ama*, he had to take them from someone's garden."

Bindra blinked slowly.

Again, he softly touched her brow.

"Shall I sing for you, *Ama*?" he whispered.

She made no reply.

Jyothi rested his cheek against hers and softly began, "*Resam phiriri, resam phiriri udera jauki darama bhanjyang, resam phiriri . . .*" – "Little bee who likes to fly, little bee who likes to fly, go and rest at the top of the hill, little bee who likes to fly . . ."

A nurse in a second-hand uniform stopped and turned. "*E bhai,*" she called, "a little louder, so I can hear too!"

Jyothi stopped singing. He drew Jiwan to him and the two boys sat close together, as though in defence of their mother.

The young woman approached. "You have a sweet voice, *bhai*, and your song reminds me of my village." She peered over their dusty mops of hair, at the bundle of rags they seemed determined to keep hidden. "Who's this?" she asked gently. "Your *ama*?"

Jyothi barely tipped his head to one side in nervous affirmation.

"May I see her?"

The nurse squatted to lift the thin blanket that covered Bindra. "What's happened here, *didi*?" she asked, her mouth a taut grimace, tongue held between her teeth. She turned to the frightened boys. "Stay here with your mother. I'll come straight back," and she hurried away.

Jyothi and Jiwan did not move. They watched the woman trot up the corridor, enthralled that they could still hear her shoes, long after she had disappeared from sight.

ψ

The taxi journey to Bombay's Central Station was not an obvious place for schoolboy Dante to come flooding back. Still I muttered, "*Lo! Dis; and lo!*" beneath my breath.

My dreams of noble natives draped in embroidered silk, my visions of mongoose and tiger, raja and palanquin, had not prepared me for such scenes of pitiful deprivation. Mile upon mile of tightly packed hovels constructed from bamboo and grass. Extensive villages of intertwined bark and cardboard bound into wigwams. Vast camps of rag tents, stitched together and stretched across spindly frames, swart and sticky, as though pitched. Shadowed and silhouetted in the low morning sun, the squalid shacks of Dharavi, Asia's largest slum, took on the appearance of famine-withered cattle. A diseased herd grovelling amongst hills of pestilential excreta, heavy bovine heads bent, bony shoulder blades hunched and jutting.

My taxi spluttered to a wheezy halt.

"Is this it?" I asked the head of dark, oiled hair in front of me. I turned from side to side, in search of any building that might suggest a railway terminus. In every direction lay the same post-apocalyptic landscape. Nothing but goats, dogs, cows, rats and crows picking their way through infernal filth with hoof and claw.

"No, sir!" the driver laughed. "Breakfast *chai*!"

He left the door open and wandered towards a stall piled high with red clay cups.

I squirmed uncomfortably in my gummy seat. Beyond the dusty windows, as early morning sun and heat and stench continued to rise from amongst the stifled dens around me, innumerable generations of sons, fathers and grandfathers stretched their chicken-instep limbs. They pulled away tatty loin cloths to expose heavy, dark appendages, then crouched naked on the roadside to release new stygian brooks from straining, emaciated bodies.

The air was physically thick, soup-like to my nose and throat. I fought to hold my breath and swallowed hard to quell the forceful contractions of my stomach. I battled to contain my need for reaction, to repulse the inconceivable vision now coursing, unchecked, into my incredulous eyes and nostrils.

Suddenly, he was back.

"Good *chai*, sir!" my driver said with a broad grin. He was bearing a cup of murky, ash-strewn brew, which he pushed towards my lips. I declined. "No, please sir. My gift. Welcome to India!"

I performed my very best sipping act, without once letting my neurotic mouth approach the greasy liquid. My pretence evidently pleased him. Not until he turned away was I able to toss it out of the side window.

Where slum ended and cosmopolitan city started was not easy to determine. My Virgil at the wheel sped us well away from the main roads, in preference for wretched, labyrinthine lanes. It did not help my fragile belly that, whilst he was careful to avoid the long-eared cows, which wandered untethered at their pleasure, he made no attempt to swerve for dogs or children in our path.

We stopped again. Time to relieve his tea against a boundary wall. The efficiency of his kidneys was certainly impressive.

I looked out across the road to another desolate inner-city wasteland that seemed to be home to many thousands. As the sun's blast drove billowing storms of flies from evaporating cesspools and into shade, I observed its inhabitants step from sordid hovels dressed in laundered shirts and pristine saris, their hair immaculately groomed. I watched entranced as they began to mend and stitch, mould and saw, to massage, play, laugh and sing.

And in that moment, sitting alone and bewildered in a filthy Bombay back street, I recognised in these vibrant smiles something of the magic of India in which, since childhood, I had believed. In this exuberant humanity in the most inhumane of realms, I had already discovered the enchantment beyond fairy tales in search of which I had come.

ψ

"You can't be here!" the matron spat. "Who let her in?" she glared accusingly at the Nepali nurse. "Get her out immediately!"

An orderly was summoned, but as he bent to lift Bindra he caught sight of one bare foot. He stood bolt upright.

"No, madam!" he stated defiantly. "Do not ask me to touch her!"

The young nurse gave him a harsh stare. He had used a linguistic form of "her" that is normally applied only to animals. The man glanced once in apprehension at the matron, then bounded straight up the stairs.

Enraged, the matron turned to the nurse, dropping her voice to a vicious hiss. "I don't care how, you hear me, but just get rid of her before word spreads!"

The nurse bent down. "*Didi*," she asked softly, "can you walk?"

Bindra did not know.

"*Didi*, we cannot treat you here. You should not have come. You must apply to the medical officer for your district. There will be trouble. You must go with your sons. Please, sister, can you try?"

Bindra turned her eyes to Jyothi and Jiwan.

The sight of a woman on her hands and knees, draped in a blanket, crawling from the hospital, provoked stares and laughter. The nurse stayed close until they reached the gate. She crouched down and pressed a few crumpled rupee notes into Jyothi's hand.

"*Bhai*, take your *ama* straight to the Tibetans, near *Mangal Dham mandir*, you know, Guru Shri's Krishna temple," she hurriedly instructed. "Do you understand? Take your *ama* to Doctor Lobsang Dhondup."

⚕

Five long hours on a slow train, stuck to grime-coated bench seats.

Five long hours of eyes and mouth gritty with the thick dust and black flies that squalled through the windows. My illusions of the glamour of Indian train travel had been fast shattered.

It was all so unlike the descriptions of passage across the Subcontinent by rail as promised in my guidebook. I flicked again through its finger-stained pages.

I was tempted to read aloud the paragraph which stated with conviction that "*the Indian railway coach is arranged to give all the comfort possible to the hot-weather traveller.*"

Where, then, was the "*dressing room at the end of the compartment providing a cool comforting wash whenever desired*"? What had happened to the "*stained glass in all the windows to modify the glare*"? And what of the "*disk-shaped curtain of scented grass that can be revolved by means of a small handle and which at each revolution dips into a concealed basin of water, whereupon the air delightfully refreshes the interior of the coach*"?

I glanced resentfully at my fellow passengers at the printed assurance that "*one is almost sure to have the coach to himself, so he may lounge as lazily as he pleases on the long, leather-cushioned seats, which, with the addition of pillow and rug, make excellent*

41

beds at night." As for the guarantee that one "*can obtain delicious tea and toast, or, by telegraphing ahead, a very good and substantial meal,*" I openly scoffed.

But then my Grandfather's guidebook had been printed in London. In 1916.

I squirmed on the hard seat and wandered in and out of an awkward half-sleep – until I inhaled a plump currant of a blow-fly. I woke in convulsions to find the compartment for six persons now snugly accommodating a perspiring and attentive audience of seventeen.

The train had strained and ground its heavy way northwards, through the fertile plains of Gujarat, to the little market town of Valsad. I had in my pocket the name of Priya's grandfather, the name of his village and the nearest railway station, at which I had now alighted.

I squinted in the scorching noonday brilliance and stared at the sea of faces that swelled before me. Westerners were rarely, if ever, seen in these parts. They blinked in hushed amazement at the sight of a doughy-faced stranger, cheeks scarlet after hours of near asphyxiation amongst the scrum of bodies piled into the train. They blinked as I stood wilting, dwarfed by the excessively-pocketed luggage rising high above my shoulders, bottle of warm water in one hand, address on a greasy scrap of paper clutched optimistically in the other.

I, in turn, blinked back at them. Tired and dazed. Nervously expectant.

With a simultaneous roar, the crowd burst into raucous laughter, clutching each other as they squealed and hooted. I had clearly under-estimated the comedic potential of my travel wardrobe. All dubiety was dispelled and in one great surge, they ran at me.

"Halloo!" they cried through their communal hysteria. "How a'you fine?" and "Wilcum kind chup!" they hooted with unrestrained enthusiasm.

Now at close quarters, they scrutinised my clothes and studied the address scrawled on my paper. A highly animated discussion ensued, whereupon they triumphantly led me to one of the awaiting rickshaws, where innumerable friendly hands helped me with the rucksack, guided me onto the seat, secured my luggage and vigorously patted me on the back.

The chuckling mob crowded around, whilst some amongst them lifted their arms and bent their elbows, indicating to me that they wanted to see my biceps. I obliged, whereupon delighted cheers shook the banyan trees. Thin hands extended to stroke my skin and squeeze my thews, whilst wide eyes peered down my shirt front and up my shorts. Never had I thought myself physically broad or particularly tall, but amongst these slender Gujaratis, I was veritably strapping.

The only exchange of words between myself and the locals, which did not involve an awful lot of clumsy hand-waving and uninformed guesses as to an approximate interpretation, was with a young lad who pushed up beside me and asked, "A British sir?"

I affirmed that I most certainly was.

"Lovely marvellous!" he grinned, brown eyes sparkling. "My uncle, he living in Leicester! My next-year wife in Parsons Green!"

Before further familial details could be gleaned, the motorised rickshaw spluttered into action and, like a wild boar unleashed, immediately plunged at full speed towards the profusion of potholes that passed as a road. With hearty reiterations of "How a'you fine?" and "Wilcum kind chup!" now adopted as a farewell by the waving crowd, I quickly left the bustle of Valsad far behind, with its jolly population which had found me such a wag.

We sped through a flat, lush landscape of crops ripening and steaming in the sun, passing ox-drawn, hay-high carts rumbling along on timber discs, as I clung tightly to the hood-struts to prevent myself from being flung out into the road. We caused alarm amongst young men strolling hand-in-hand. We frightened women compressed beneath water-filled urns and crop-packed baskets. I tried throwing myself from side to side in the futile belief that it might in some way assist the driver to avoid the craters and dustbowls in our path. The broken branches and the herds of goats. The nonchalant water buffalo and the whoops-was-that-a-chicken?

"Dalba?" my driver asked herdsmen drinking from a wooden bowl at a well. They shrugged and shook their cloth-bound heads.

"Dalba?" he asked a line of *Advasi* Tribals who had evidently come from the remote *mofussil* regions of the interior to work the harvest. They rimpled sun-scorched brows and stared at me, transfixed.

I had begun to believe that I had taken down the name incorrectly, when a near-naked holy man repeated, "Dalba," and rocked his head from side to side in recognition. He bowed to me and pointed with a heavily knuckled finger across the fields.

If he did indeed know Dalba, then it was somewhere amongst the dark mango groves. A tiny village hidden deep within the leafy haunts of serpents and wild monkeys.

Chapter Five

Bindra could not determine how long she had slept. Hours, days or weeks? The air of the little room in which she lay was heavy with the scent of plant oils.

"*Kasto cha, bahini?*" a broad-faced Tibetan woman smiled, asking how she was in perfect Nepali.

"Better," Bindra replied, surprising herself.

"*Timilai pira cha, bahini?*" the woman gently asked. "Do you have pain, younger sister?"

"Little," Bindra replied, again in surprise at the change she felt in her body. "My boys!" she suddenly gasped.

"Listen," the woman grinned, emphatically cocking her head towards the open door.

Bindra could hear Jyothi and Jiwan's voices flooding into the room on the bright sunshine, with the pungency of fermented lentil *phing* noodles drying outside on bamboo poles. The boys were playing a boisterous game of cricket.

"We said they could stay in the house and keep my Dawa and Pemba company," the woman explained, rolling a string of coconut and carnelian *dzi* prayer-beads between thick, stained fingers. "But every night, they sleep here on the floor, to be near you. You have good sons, *bahini*." She opened a large bottle, from which she removed two pungent balls. "Now's time for more medicine," she smiled, and popped them into Bindra's mouth. They were chewy, gritty and slightly sweet.

"*Mithai cha?*" she chuckled. "Taste good?" The Tibetan woman raised a broad hand to her dark-skinned face to conceal her amusement. "Last week, *bahini*, you were still spitting them out!"

45

Bindra moistened her mouth and rasped, "I thought you were feeding me *gobar* goat dung!"

As Detchen Dhondup's broad shoulders began to rock with boomy chortles, Bindra's smile returned.

ψ

I wiped my face with a sodden handkerchief and squinted through the brilliance. Five kohl-eyed girls at Dalba's single stone well released the bucket-rope. They left their water-pots and scurried on flat feet for the darkness of doorways.

I stepped out of the rickshaw into the midst of a handful of cow-dung houses, bleaching, splitting and crumbling in the summer's blaze. Not until my eyes adjusted to the glare could I discern silent figures clustered together in the shade, scrutinising me with a contradiction of delight and alarm.

"*Salaam-alaikum,*" I offered towards my umbral Hindu audience in uncertain and starkly inappropriate Muslim greeting. "*Mehta ka ghar kaha hai?*" I attempted, asking in self-conscious, "kitchen" Urdu where I might find the Mehtas' house.

There was no response.

"Mehta?" I persisted, convinced that the clipped, Anglicised pronunciation I had inevitably inherited from my Raj-born fore-bears had rendered my limited vocabulary unintelligible. "*Mehta ka ghar?*"

A sudden clamour of Gujarati made me start.

Two grinning boys were escorting an elderly, near-toothless woman draped in mazarine silk. All three were talking at once, waving their arms at each other and at me as they approached. I put my hands together to greet them, at which the boys hid behind the woman, giggling.

"*Salaam-ji,*" I bowed. "Mrs Mehta-*ji?*"

Priya's grandmother nodded her head from side to side and began to chatter at me in excited Gujarati.

"*Kiy aap angrezi boltay hain?*" I fumbled, in the hope she might speak at least some words in English. She shook her head. She scolded the boys who were staring at me with wide eyes from amongst the drapes of her sari, and shooed them off to fetch a bilingual relative.

I rapidly dredged through the vague remains of courteous childhood phrases and found, "*Aap se milkar khushi huye.*" Accordingly, I declared that I was pleased to meet her.

Mrs Mehta rocked her head in incomprehension and sucked her remaining teeth through an unconvincing smile.

I decided it prudent to remain silent, leaving Mrs Mehta and me to stand blinking. Politely. At one another.

To my great relief, the boys soon returned, escorting a cheerful young man who introduced himself as Mukund. His English was admirable. My arrival, he explained with embarrassment, was entirely unexpected. The letter sent had not arrived. The embarrassment, I insisted, was all mine.

Back in England, where affluence abounds, an unexpected stranger could be most unwelcome. The arrival of an unplanned guest could inflict havoc upon schedules and diaries. Hands might be thrown up and excuses voiced of unprepared larders and low-stocked fridges, imperative Scout activities and Church meetings, insufficient bed linen and no clean towels.

But here – where the people lived from hand to mouth, fighting against the seasons to feed their families when one bad crop could bring starvation – they offered me their all.

I was led away from the low mud houses, across a rough dirt yard, to a building that stood beneath the welcome shade of tamarind and neem trees. Fronted by a finely carved, wooden verandah, this was by far the grandest house in the village. I was invited into the central hall and directed to an old, wicker-seated chair. The room was dark, lit only by shafts of spiralling dust that broke through the fine filigree of closed shutters. The house was ancient and, although much decayed, retained an exquisite beauty in its intricately carved doors and cupboards, its chequer-board floors of green slate and pale cream alabaster.

Brusque orders were given.

In moments, the tepid water from the bottle I had been carrying was offered to me in a metal beaker, on a tray engraved with dancing deities. The clatter of pans, the hiss of oil and the ambrosia of cooking spices drifted from an unseen kitchen. Through open double doors I could see a broad wooden bed being stripped and hurriedly remade.

Sad eyes lingered on me for a moment. Whispers were exchanged.

I wondered whether they were saying that if I had arrived with Priya, they would have been scattering the sheets with flowers.

I pressed hard against the sudden, waxing weight in my chest, as a steady stream of women, young men and children, some thirty in all, were presented to me. They bowed shyly, smiled and departed as quickly as they came. I gave up trying to remember their names, and hoped they did not notice the quaver in my pleasantries. In every pair of dark, bright eyes I had seen only hers.

Mukund stayed by my side. He politely clarified that *Namaste* was the appropriate greeting in Hindu company and laughed out loud at my earlier blunder.

"Please no need for apologising, Mr David," he assured me. "No offences being felt. We are rather most tickled to be hearing our Muslim brothers' salutation in our village for the first time in history," he grinned, squeezing my shoulder as though to indicate a new affection.

Mukund explained that he was visiting from Bombay, on study leave from college. He told me that the men of the house, Priya's Uncle Piyush and her grandfather, were out giving offerings at the temple of Hanuman, the Monkey God, far across the fields, but that they would return before dark. He enquired after the health of English cricket and the Queen, Winston Churchill and Mrs Thatcher. He asked if his three cousins, who were standing against the wall and whispering, could feel my arms.

"What do you eat, Mister David, to make you grow?" he translated for them.

The second time in one day that I felt big and butch.

"How am I?" Bindra asked.

"Doing well, *bahini*," Detchen smiled reassuringly. "Doctor Dhondup's very pleased. You are healing. Your thick woollens stopped the burns from going too deep. The shawl you were wearing protected much of your head and face. Gu-Lang, our Protectress of Mothers and Children, was with you that night."

"Thank you," Bindra tried to say, but her voice broke. "I have nothing," she choked, "nothing to pay for all you've done here."

The Tibetan placed a hand on Bindra's arm. "*Bahini*," she gently said, "those who can, pay for those who can't. You owe us not one *rupiya*, younger sister. We can treat your burns and ease your pain, but you need still more."

Bindra seemed to know the words she was about to hear and held her breath.

"You have a great sickness," the woman began softly, "that even the wisdom and knowledge of our *Bönpo* cannot cure. For this, my husband-doctor says you need *paraiharuko dabai*," she explained. "Foreigners' medicine. You must leave the Hills and go down to Kakariguri. Ask for the Gad Sap Hat Ashram, where free medicine is given. They will want you to pray to their dead god that hangs on the wall and bleeds. But do it, *bahini*. Do it for the *paraiharuko dabai*."

Gad Sap Hat Ashram. The Tune-Snake-Hand Ashram.

Bindra repeated the peculiar name to herself and weakly rocked her head from side to side on the hard, flat pillow to show she had understood.

The woman drew closer.

"But, *bahini*," she almost whispered, "you know you cannot come back to this place, even when your sickness is cured. They will never let you return. Your children will not be allowed in the school. Your money will not be accepted at the *haat* bazaar. You must find a new life. Away from here. Where nobody knows."

Bindra turned her head towards the doorway. She knew these words were true. She closed her eyes tightly and held her breath again, as the streams of tears across her face sparkled brightly in the sunshine.

☫

"Hot or cold, Mister David?"

Nothing in the world had I wished for more than Mukund's kind offer of a bath. He and the muscle-squeezers had led me to a small stone room leading off the busy kitchen.

I blinked at the single tap protruding from the wall. "Oh, cold, please!" I said, wondering how I could possibly have a choice with only one oxidised pipe. I looked around, unsure what I was expected to do. The boys pressed into the doorway, grinning in anticipation.

"Do you wish a seat, Mister David?"

I declined the offer. The potential addition of furniture in such a confined space only seemed to further confuse the situation.

I wondered whether an audience when visitors bathed was customary, as I tentatively began to undo my shirt. It was the sign for which they would seem to have been waiting and all joined in my undressing with unreserved delight. One of the boys promptly whisked off my dust-impregnated clothes to the *dhobi* washerman, whom I had noticed beating brightly coloured bundles against broad, smooth stones at the back of the house. Farewell buttons, I thought.

Now naked, I declined their repeated requests for limb-feels or an exploratory finger in the navel, however politely translated by Mukund. Instead, I gently ushered them out, enabling me to shut the door and squat in private. With a deeply instilled fear of contracting amoebic dysentery, I kept my lips tightly closed as I poured the cool water from the tap over my head with a wooden bowl.

Even above the splash of water, I could hear the boys whispering and giggling outside. Even with sandal soap in my eyes, I could see them peeking through the gaps around the door.

☫

Bindra held her sons close as they pressed themselves into the crowd that forced itself onto the Kakariguri bus. She was wrapped in a full shawl, given to her by the Tibetan doctor's kindly wife. Detchen Dhondup had also ensured that the telltale signs on her feet were covered with woollen socks and protected by loose flip-flops.

Around her middle, wrapped in a long cloth, Bindra carried a bundle of food and medicine. Amongst the crisp rice-flour *phinni*, the crunchy sesame *til mithai*, the soft yak's cheese *churpi* and the spicy potato *aloo dum*, she had tucked the little bag of ash balls given to her all those weeks ago by the *jhankri* at Lapu *basti*. Jyothi had two small blankets tied across both shoulders and carried the heavy canister of water. Jiwan had a strap bound around his forehead, from which a string bag of *suntalaa* oranges hung down his back.

Bindra found movement painful. Her back and shoulders remained unforgivingly tight. Still, she pushed her way to a seat on the bus, perched on its edge and drew the boys close. All were silent and kept their eyes away from their fellow passengers. She had not told the full truth to her boys. And yet they sensed they all bore an unspoken secret, for which others would willingly punish them without warning.

As crowded town and busy shops quickly became lush forest and plunging valleys, Bindra looked up the hillside towards the white pinnacle of the Kali temple.

"Kali Ma," she whispered, "protect my sons and daughters. Remove my fear. And brighten my understanding."

🔱

Refreshed from my bucket bath and satisfyingly fragrant once more, I stepped back into the kitchen.

To my irrepressible surprise, the aunts, cousins and loosely-relateds had returned. They were standing, quietly awaiting the completion of my ablutions and, though I was skimpily towel-clad and struggling to retain my modesty, they led me directly to the table.

Spread before me was a great feast of *khichdi* rice, *kadhi* buttermilk, *papads*, *achars*, fresh *kachambar*, crispy *farsans* and curd. I assumed we were all to eat together, but they impressed that this gastronomic prodigality was for me alone. The gathered kin were merely onlookers, a position which, by their delighted smiles and enthusiastic nods at my every mouthful, they seemed to find most satisfying.

I ate heartily. The merest suggestion of an empty space on my plate, and a host of female hands lifted spoons and bowls to pile high new, spicy servings, despite my protestations. When I could eat no more, they presented me with a harvest festival of village-grown bananas, chicoos, guavas and mangoes.

Mukund impressed that they were very touched by my willingness to adopt their custom of only eating with my right hand. I did not tell him that my left had been fully occupied holding down my towel, his rorty young cousins having spent the entire meal peering steadfastly under the table.

Fed and dressed, appreciative audience departed and scallywag cousins dismissed, I lay on the bed that Priya and I had been meant to share.

I fought to drive away the pervasive thoughts that threatened to stifle both mind and breath by trying to remember the many new names of the unreservedly smiling, gentle faces I had met since my arrival. The honest warmth of these strangers was conferring on me a comfort that, until now, I had not allowed myself to know. Whilst I had rejected any possibility of the least expression of sympathy back in England, here my careful restraint was yielding to the unqualified kindness of Priya's relations, the tenderness of a family that had so nearly been my own.

I distracted myself by considering the fact that the Mehtas were probably more affluent than the others in the village due to the benefits of their emigrant son. Where others were dependent upon the communal well, their house had a tap. Where others had beaten-dung floors and walls infested with sore-inflicting, vampiric pests, their rooms were stone-tiled and plastered in pale yellows, pinks, blues and greens. In these pigments the humidity had painted figures, faces and fantastical beasts, which seemed to breathe, move and converse in the torrid air.

My room span with the tickling twitter of sparrows that nested on cupboards and shelves, and sat in restless lines on the top of the mirror. The sultry skies beyond my windows throbbed with the percussive calls of insects. The warbling song of girls pulling water at the well. The pounding of soapy cloth as my dirties had their seams and gussets sorely tested on the *dhobi*'s wash-stone.

And yet, as my mind began to slide and my eyes were overwhelmed by the weight of their lids, all I could hear was the excited chatter of the boy cousins on the verandah, relating I-dared-not-think-whats to their curious friends.

ψ

The bus spluttered to a temporary halt at Teesta Bazaar, affording its passengers a chance to purchase a cup of hot *chiya* tea and an array of local fruit, nuts and vegetables. Bindra had no intention of losing her seat, but Jyothi and Jiwan needed to relieve themselves.

"Don't let go of your brother's hand," she instructed Jyothi as the two boys climbed down the metal steps onto the roadside. "And keep away from the wheels!" she called, but they had gone.

Bindra looked out to the low huts that balanced precariously on bamboo stilts along the steep hillsides. Below their unstable balconies, she could see the raging torrent of the deep green Teesta.

She thought of Kailash. Her sweet, simple Kailash. She thought of him sitting in the bus as it slipped off the monsoon-shattered road and plummeted into the swollen river. She thought of him trapped in his seat and the water flooding in.

Bindra leapt to her crumpled feet and struggled to the open door.

"Jyothi! Jiwan!" she called, her heart gripped tight with terror. She climbed down into the crowd and called again, "My sons! My sons!"

Bindra pushed through the meandering throng, towards the row of shops that stood above the river's edge. A little hand suddenly took hold of her elbow. She dropped to her knees and tightly held both her bewildered boys to her chest. "Just for a moment . . ." she gasped. "Just for a moment I thought . . ."

"I know you," a poorly dressed Marwari interrupted her admission. Bindra looked up. The man had had an accusation in his statement. "You're the widow from the old burial ground," he affirmed, his pox-marked nose and forehead starkly revealing their shadowed craters in the low morning sun.

Bindra stood up with difficulty. It was essential that she was not known, that no one recognised her. Holding fast to her sons, she turned and, without a word, hurried back towards the bus.

"Keep away!" the man shouted to startled onlookers, as he followed close behind them. "Keep well away!"

Bindra reached the steps and pushed the boys ahead of her into the sanctuary of the vehicle, urging them to slip between their fellow passengers who were already returning to their seats.

"*E bhai!*" the Marwari bellowed at the conductor, who was nonchalantly leaning against the front wheel, sharing a Shikari cigarette with the driver. "You have a leper on your bus! I know this cursed woman. She's a leper and a witch!"

Bindra swung around to face her denouncer, her eyes wide beneath the shawl, her mouth too dry to speak. Passengers were now leaning out of the windows. A crowd was gathering in the road. All were staring at Bindra, at her bandaged hands and frightened children.

"Is this true?" the conductor asked, approaching apprehensively.

"I am no witch!" Bindra cried. "Let Kali Ma be my witness!" The very pronouncing of the name of the Dark Goddess began to dispel her timidity.

"But are you *kori*?" he pressed.

Before Bindra could respond, a foot kicked her from behind. She tumbled off the bottom step and hit the floor. The crowd cried out. Her shawl had slipped off her head to reveal a large patch of ugly, hairless scalp and swollen ears.

"*Ama!*" Jiwan cried out from within the bus.

Bindra clambered to her feet. The crowd shuffled back yet further. She brushed off her clothes and called to her sons. Jyothi and Jiwan leapt down the bus steps and ran to stand beside her.

"Do not fear us!" she said aloud, fighting with herself to calm the trembling that now threatened to defeat her limbs. "We are not different from you! It is only man's limited understanding that sees division where there is none. Your pain and suffering is ours. Our pain and suffering is yours. We are each but one expression of the same Truth. May Kali Ma brighten all our understanding!"

The crowd was unresponsive.

They parted to allow Bindra and the two boys, who now clung to her, to shuffle away. Not until the little family was out of the village and some distance from its rickety bridge and busy market did Bindra speak.

"My good, strong sons, the foreigners' medicine I need is perhaps five or six days' walk away, if we stay to the road," she breathlessly explained. She could hear the Kakariguri bus growling its way towards them and turned awkwardly to glance behind her. "But we may have to walk in the forest . . . away from the wheels."

"Don't worry, *Ama!*" grinned Jyothi. "I shall sing to the *Punyajana* and they will watch our path."

And, thus, as Bindra quickly led her sons off the tarmac of the old trunk road and into dark, dense jungle, the Good People in the trees were serenaded by a solitary voice confidently singing, "*Resam phiriri . . .*"

ॐ

I awoke to find an elderly man sitting on the bed beside me. He looked into my eyes and smiled.

"Mister David, you are most welcome."

Priya's grandfather was a striking figure, tall and elegant in the pure white *dhoti* cloth that wrapped around his waist and drew up between his legs. With his thick, white hair and dark, omniscient eyes, he looked to me like Rabindranath Tagore, the illuminating narrator to my life, the bright lantern that, since childhood, had chased my shadows.

I was momentarily transfixed by Mr Mehta's sun-creviced forehead with its generous daub of deep-orange ochre from his *puja* to the Monkey God. I then remembered myself, placed my hands at my heart and thanked him for the generosity of the welcome I had received, even though I had not been expected.

"You are the first Westerner this village has ever seen," he smiled broadly, in flawless English. "You have now become part of our people's history. They will still talk of you in fifty years' time!" His face became serious. "And your welcome is such because, for all we know, you may even be God come to visit us."

Before I could respond to such a startling suggestion, his eyes welled with tears and he wrapped his arms around me. Mr Mehta held me to him with tender, quiet strength. It was as though he sensed the burning blur of previous months had been dominated by such a profound sense of loss that I had become entirely accustomed to an enduring, ill-lit hollowness. I had existed in a void, deprived of any depth of feeling or constancy of thought, from which I had been unable to find the least escape. My only means to maintain control had been to isolate myself, to become anonymous, denying all contact with friends and family.

The facts had been irrefutable: Priya and Grandmother were gone.

No awkward condolences, no pity in self-consciously averted eyes would restore them to me.

However, to be held now by this stranger whom Priya had loved enabled me to soften in his supporting arms. To rest upon his shoulder. To cling to him and weep.

I only pulled away to wipe my face when Priya's Uncle Piyush entered the room. He was strong, handsome and confident, yet waited with respect until I had regained composure.

"*Our guest from the dark of the infinite,*" he quoted, with a broad and honest smile, "*the guest of light!*"

"My Grandmother and Priya were the only other people in my life able to recite Tagore!" I stumbled in recognition, astonished to hear their names together on my tongue.

As I continued to sniff my nose and dry my eyes, Uncle Piyush joined us on the bed and held my hand. The unexpected company of Tagore in our first meeting provided a safe foundation on which to cultivate an association. We compared our favourite poems, preferred passages from his prose, and found ourselves engaging like old friends.

Mr Mehta sat by, watching us attentively. He then announced, "I shall no longer be calling you 'Mister David'. You are my own son, we are your family, and this is your home."

I suddenly remembered my purpose and turned to my rucksack. I dug deep for two carefully wrapped boxes and hesitantly handed them to Priya's grandfather.

"The wedding gold," I murmured. "I have come to return the wedding gold."

He slowly placed the boxes on his lap and stared hard at the unopened lids.

Again, he took me in his arms.

Again, we wept.

☗

By dusk, Bindra, Jyothi and Jiwan had travelled little distance. They had been unable to climb the steep, forested mountainside, unable to clamber across the deep, rocky gullies cut by monsoon streams. Bindra had felt she had no choice but to return them to the "black-top" road, despite her trepidation.

Jiwan had tired quickly, but his exhausted mother had found herself unable to carry him. The new skin across her back and shoulders was still too fragile, too sensitive to bear any weight. As the light had fallen and the traffic had dwindled, she had led the boys back to the ease of tarmac.

By nightfall, they had reached a promontory, high above the river, designated a "viewing point" by the West Bengal Tourist Board. Where once there had been virgin jungle, now the State offered a pot-holed car park, a pair of dilapidated concrete benches and a roofless shelter for the recreational pleasure of holidaying visitors. The two boys wrinkled their noses as they entered the place. It stank of stale urine.

They were not the first that evening to settle at the "viewing point". Two tall, lean *roti-wallahs* had already lit a low fire and were laying out their bedding. Such itinerant pastrymen were a common sight on these hill roads. They came from the distant Plains to walk between mountain villages with large, metal trunks balanced on their heads. These black cases were filled with such tasty and rare delights that the appearance of the *boxies* in any hill community remained a source of great excitement as the enduring chill of a long winter slowly began to thaw.

Bindra drew the shawl close around her face and tucked her bandaged hands up inside, well out of sight. The men stared hard as they approached.

"*Namooshkar,*" they offered in mumbled Bengali greeting.

"*Namaste dajooharu,*" Bindra replied brightly in her own tongue. She indicated towards their small fire with a lift of her eyes. In answer, they both briefly nodded for them to share the warmth.

Whilst she encouraged the boys to run ahead, Bindra moved closer with caution. Bengali *roti-wallahs* were well-known for their coarse manner and assertive appetites, and these men were eyeing her with more curiosity than she felt comfortable.

She crouched down at a distance, taking care to keep her back to the two strangers. The men watched intently as she discreetly unwrapped her food parcel and passed one piece of soft *churpi* to each of her sleepy boys. The fragile *phinni* had been reduced to nothing more than flakes and crumbs, but the boys scooped them from the cloth and licked them off their fingers. Bindra held back Detchen Dhondup's potato *aloo dum* and sweet sesame *til mithai*, in the hope that she could make it last until they reached Kakariguri. After that, she had not yet dared to think.

It was still the custom in these hills to share provisions, however poor. Bindra asked Jyothi to offer a piece of *churpi* to their camp mates. Both men declined. They had never been able to develop a taste for the pungency of fermented yak's cheese, so prized amongst these hill people in their jungle-clad mountains. One of the men returned the hospitality by unlocking his metal trunk and handing Jyothi three pastry *shingara* stuffed with spicy vegetables.

Bindra smiled in gratitude as her boys tucked hungrily into the crisp crusts. The *roti-wallah* offered a bloody grin in return, his mouth and teeth scarlet with well-chewed betel nut, but Bindra quickly turned away.

She had never felt comfortable with Plains-men.

ॐ

Dawn had barely dissipated the bug-drummed darkness, yet the village was already wide awake and working. I breathed in the sweetness of warm cow dung steaming in the yard, the comfort of spices tempering brightly in the kitchen. I stretched my toes and rolled onto my back to listen to the harmony of voices, tools and animals, the concord of a whole new world beyond the windows.

Suddenly, an anxious cry. Mr Mehta.

I leapt from the bed, wrapped around my waist a *lungi* cloth, and ran out onto the verandah.

Priya's grandfather was bending over the buckled body of a perspiring stranger. The man's head was bleeding badly.

"What's happened?" I asked, as Mrs Mehta hurried to join us. Her hands were already heavy with clean cotton and a bowl of steaming water.

"This fellow is a *Dalit*, from the edge of our village," Mr Mehta said, gently laying a hot, wet compress across the man's wounds. "You understand the term *Dalit*?" he asked.

I shook my head.

"*Dalit* means 'broken', 'shattered', 'oppressed'," he explained. "This fellow is an *Achut*, an Untouchable – even though Untouchability has officially been illegal in India since the days of the Mahatma!" he added with manifest frustration.

I crouched down to meet the eyes of the ostracised man, whose sort my Grandmother had told me to embrace.

"His name is Pankaj – 'mud-born'," Mr Mehta said in introduction, quickly adding in response to my look of surprise, "like a lotus, not a worm! He and his wife are permitted no land. Instead, they must deal only with dead livestock and the removal of the other villagers' faeces from the fields with their bare hands. Can you imagine such a scavenging *bhangi* life?"

I could not.

"Gandhi-*ji* referred to such people as *Harijans*," he continued, "Children of God, just to make his point. But you think caste-minded people really understood then, or begin to understand today? Do you think they would ever allow this man to enter their homes, or even to take water from the same well?"

Pankaj looked up at me and smiled shyly, even as he winced at another application of scalding cotton. I laid my hands on his shoulders in an attempt at comfort. He looked too hurt to hug. In response, Pankaj placed his pale palms together and drew them to his heart, even as tears trickled down his bruised cheeks to darken the dust.

"Has he had an accident?" I pressed, as Mrs Mehta returned with more clean cotton and a honey-pot. She removed the wooden lid and handed the small clay container to me.

"Son, this is no accident," Mr Mehta replied, shaking his head and tutting in despair. He dipped in the proffered spoon, then let the viscous, antiseptic syrup drip onto torn flesh. "Neither is this uncommon, nor infrequent. I am sorry to say there are some, even in our own community, who have not yet learned the inherent value of all life. Some who do not yet see that all is one . . ."

A sudden shout interrupted his explanation. Its vehemence caused Pankaj to flinch and retract his undernourished, scab-dappled legs. I had not noticed the gathering of agitated villagers that kept its well-judged distance.

A gaunt, tense man stepped towards us. He seemed angry.

Mr Mehta responded with a pacifying smile and uplifted palm. He refused to be dissuaded from his attentive ministrations, revealing the same quiet strength of character and conviction that had once been Priya's.

A second, quarrelsome voice was raised, sustained by the swell of a communal grumble.

Mr Mehta turned to face the bared hostility of his neighbours.

I could not understand a word of his Gujarati, yet was transfixed as he addressed the crowd with calm authority. What I took to be his defence of the damaged man, who now cowered at our feet, was such that all dissent was immediately silenced. Every one of the villagers dropped their eyes as though in shame, then silently shuffled back to homes and duties.

Mrs Mehta returned to the kitchen to pile a *thali* plate with hot *khichdi* rice and daal for their unexpected guest, whilst Mr Mehta indicated to me for more honey.

"In the old days," he confided under his breath, as he continued in his care, "my whole family would have now been outcast."

A restored and reassured Pankaj was soon sent off home in the protective company of Uncle Piyush, whilst Priya's grandfather carefully cleaned his hands and I quickly bathed in preparation for morning *puja*.

"The villagers obviously respect you," I said to Mr Mehta as we walked across the fields towards a little white-washed temple. "Priya told me that you were once a schoolmaster."

"Indeed," he confirmed, "some miles from this very village. But that was long, long ago, when I was a young dreamer of a fellow."

"So, you must have been teaching under the Raj," I asserted.

Mr Mehta slowed to a halt and took hold of my arm, as though preparing to steady himself.

"Son, when the Quit India agitation was escalating in '43," he began with sudden solemnity, "news reached my schoolhouse that British troops were on their way to suppress the demand for *Purna Swaraj*, for totally independent rule, in our district."

I remembered hearing that my grandfather had regularly knocked *Gandhi topi* hats off the heads of Congress supporters in the street, with a swipe of his regimental swagger-stick. I now cringed at my own juvenile naivety that had been amused at the Chaplinesque slapstick of such a story, without a thought for the remarkable self-determination of a subjugated people that underlay it. I now found myself wondering at the colonial fantasy that I had been fed and so easily, if not mindlessly, accepted.

"The moment the warning came, I ordered the children straight home," Mr Mehta continued, an undisguised strain now tightening his voice. "But word had arrived too late. My pupils met the soldiers on the road. In the impulsive bravery of their youth – enthused,

I have no doubt, by the popularity of Non-Cooperation – some of my older boys defiantly mocked the Tommies. In response, the British soldiers emptied their guns into the children's legs. I heard the volleys from the schoolhouse – *tat-tat-tat-tat*! I ran to them, ran just as fast as I was able. But all too late. When I saw what had been done to my students, my innocent boys and girls, I fell flat to the ground . . ."

Even as Mr Mehta said the words, he clasped his chest and belly. I held him fast to keep him upright, as, almost half a century on, he sobbed into an empty, sun-baked field the raw lucidity of his memories.

ॐ

Fire-warmed and well-fed, the two boys soon fell asleep.

Bindra, however, forced herself to remain awake. She could feel the *boxies* staring at her back, but could understand nothing of the muttered exchanges they shared.

"*Ei-je!*" one of them whispered towards her.

Bindra pulled her shawl close and looked over her shoulder. He had gruffly called her attention. Both men grinned in unison and raised their dense eyebrows. One was rubbing affectionately at a gathering in the *dhoti* cloth around his loins. Bindra's heart began to pound. She turned back to her boys and pretended to busy herself with their blankets.

"*Ei-je!*"

This time, the whisper bore yet greater intent, whilst his companion could barely contain his giggles. Bindra had determined not to turn around again.

Suddenly, an extended finger prodded her back with forthright purpose. She winced with pain and pulled away.

"No, brothers, I am hurt!" she cried, exposing the fear she was fighting to contain. "I am hurt beneath my clothing. You are not to touch me. Please, for the sake of my fatherless boys . . ."

The men burst out laughing. "*Nepali oto bhalo bolte pari na!*" one mocked in Bengali. "Can't speak Nepali that well, love!"

Bindra could not be sure what they had said. To make herself clearly understood, she lifted her shawl, deliberately uncovering a broad swathe of burnt, bare scalp. The men gasped and drew back.

"Now leave us be!" she growled, revealing a bandaged hand as she pointed for dramatic threat into the impenetrable shadows. "Kali Ma is watching!" she added for effect.

Both men had lost their juvenile banter. They were puzzled by the unsightly signs of damage this woman had unveiled. They were now unsure with whom they shared the comfort of their fire.

The two *boxies* had long made their living amongst these hill people at the end of the cold season, but still they were unsettled by the tales of *bhut* ghosts and *bokshi* witches, *hikman* chanting women and *mata* seers. They feared the headless *mukatta* that bore eyes in their shoulders and stepped from the trees to bring nausea. The tattered *tangare*, who had died as men in the snows and now latched on to the living to sap them of life. The stories of *bijuwa* who spoke with the voices of the dead, and *madre* who crouched in the shadows at dusk to wreak confusion. But most of all, they feared the *bojudeuta* who, it was claimed, inflicted insanity, infected food and ate the hearts of children.

The disquieted Bengalis settled down to sleep. They eyed the woman and her sons one last time with uncomfortable suspicion, then cuddled up together, blankets drawn over their faces to keep in the warmth and keep out the mountain magic.

The night vibrated with insect life and the clamour of testy monkeys in the dark. Bindra looked up towards Shiva in his form of the moon god, riding his chariot of glazed water through the darkness.

"Soma-shambhu-paddhati," she whispered, in search of comfort, "look over my fatherless boys and my lost girls as I sleep. Sweeten their dreams."

Bindra drew up her knees and rested her head on her forearms. There was no position that did not cause new pain.

When next she opened her eyes, it was light. The fire was long out.

The moon and the pastrymen had gone.

63

ψ

Before the evening meal, Uncle Piyush and I walked through the sugar cane to his mango orchards. They appeared fiercely aflame in the sinking sun.

"Priya loved this place," he smiled, his arm sweeping wide as though to encompass all fields, trees, cows and crows as far as the distant, darkening horizon. "*Gloom in the forest and glamour in the sky*," he wistfully murmured, as his hands alighted on my shoulders.

I nodded, but found no words to offer in reply. However hard I looked, I would not find her.

"So, now you must take care," Uncle Piyush hissed into my ear. "There are snakes here!"

As we stepped beneath the dense canopy of thick leaves, I could not initially see a thing and wondered just how he meant me to "take care" of venomous fangs gleefully primed and waiting in the shadow.

"*Pitaji* says that man has disturbed the balance in the world, because snakes, monkeys and birds all behave differently from when his father was alive," he explained in whisper. "You see, the snakes are cruel today, they attack for no reason."

Comfort indeed.

Once our eyes had become accustomed to the darkness, Uncle Piyush tenderly fingered the heavy fruit that hung around us. Having judged one ripe for plucking, he carefully rotated it from its hold and handed it to me.

"Mangoes are always best eaten fresh from the tree," he advised with an encouraging grin.

"Right again, Grandma!" I smiled to myself, as eager fingernails revealed the fragrant flesh beneath smooth skin, and keen teeth plunged deep into succulent, golden glory.

Far ahead, beneath the sunless ceiling where wild peacocks courted, the solitary tongue of an oil-fed wick flickered weakly. We had come to check on the Rajasthani *chowkidhar*, hired to guard the fruit from thieves. Despite our underfoot twig-crunchings and constant chat, the watchman did not wake from his slumber until Uncle Piyush had shaken him roughly by the shoulders. He was dismissed the following day.

Back at the village, the women were already extinguishing the lamps. Husbands were returning to waiting wives, whilst young men mounted the flat roofs of family homes to lie together on communal beds. I had been invited by cousins Mukund, Harsad, Amul and Tapan to share their sleep, so climbed the stairs to join them on a mattress of dry rushes, spread out to modify the temperature of the house below.

Beneath the lambent gaze of Orion and a lucent moon, we talked late into a night heady with the scent of liberally oiled hair, salty skin and fervent, fertile earth. The boys asked after their cousins, Priya's brothers, in England, of the crops they grew, the cows they kept, the women they loved. They discussed test matches and spin bowlers, hooks and yorkers, glides and googlies. They guided me through gods and goddesses of a teeming, joyful pantheon that encompassed all that is, or was, or could be. They told me tales of relentless wars and irrepressible passions, defeated demons and unconquered kings. They described the affectionate intimacies shared in India between closest friends, and, with the names of Lord Krishna and Prince Aravan on their lips as though in benison, tenderly entwined their limbs in mine.

The week had passed too quickly and I now regretted that my time in the village was to be brief. I had so feared meeting Priya's family, in selfish anticipation of the crippling pain it might expose, that I had purchased in advance a train ticket to leave the following morning. I was about to commence my journey northwards, in search of whatever remained of a distant childhood that had so inspired my own. I had determined that, from amongst the ruins of an empire, I would find some remnant of my father, an echo of a man who had remained so inaccessible in my life and yet so influential in his distance.

However, for that one night, all remorse at my imminent departure was short-lived. The gentle touch of responsive hands and the cool air, so deliciously balming after the searing onslaught of the day, soon seduced me into a depth of sleep I had not known for many months, as heat-lightning illuminated the tops of the mango trees and gave the monkeys nightmares.

$$\psi$$

The mountain was foggy that morning. A dispiriting drizzle was fast dampening Bindra's shawl.

Before continuing their journey towards the Plains, she gave the boys a little of the *aloo dum* from its greaseproof paper. They both ate the *shingara* she had saved from the pastrymen, with a sprinkle of extra salt from its newspaper twist. And they all shared one orange.

Back home, it was *haat* market day and the road was already busy with buses and jeeps as both shoppers and merchants wound their way up to the old hill station. Bindra kept to the dark tree line as often as she could for protection from both the weather and cruel eyes.

Jyothi cried out in triumph when he spotted an *iskus* vine heavy with fruit. Together, they gathered the squash gourds and bound them in Bindra's cloth. Although they hung heavily around her waist, the promise of baked *iskus* for dinner had already lightened the load.

The drizzle was fast becoming rain, so Bindra called for the boys to find shelter until it passed. She laughed as Jyothi and Jiwan ran ahead, kicking up their legs and whooping in the wet.

When Bindra reached the broad-leafed tree selected as the driest spot to wait out the weather, Jyothi was sitting alone.

"Where's your brother?" Bindra asked.

Jyothi stared back, his face expressionless.

Bindra swung around and called out, "Jiwan! Where are you hiding?"

She looked back at Jyothi. His silence had begun to frighten her.

"Son, where's your brother?" she asked again with greater urgency.

Something was very wrong. She recalled the talk of tigers in these lower slopes, when she was a girl. Her heart began to deafen her ears.

She stumbled towards Jyothi and cried, "Where's your brother?"

Jyothi looked up at her and shook his head.

"Tell me!" she ordered.

"Jiwan-*bhai* was behind me, running, *Ama*. But when I reached the tree, he wasn't there any more."

Bindra turned to retrace their path, calling for her little boy at every step.

The forest was silent.

The pain of panic in her chest was catching every breath. She turned back to Jyothi, who had not moved from the shelter of the tree.

"You heard nothing? Saw nothing? Your brother did not call out?"

"*Ama*, I saw a man ..." Jyothi muttered in fear, his cheeks beginning to run with tears.

Bindra's eyes darted wildly as she scanned the undergrowth. No man could move in silence across these *thumki* hillsides. No man could move without leaving his trail.

"Where was he?" she hissed in whisper, certain they were now being spied upon.

Jyothi pointed towards a towering peepal tree, the sacred fig of Shiva, symbol of the liberated mind. Some said that to tell a lie beneath its shade brought upon the culprit the very affliction his mother now bore, yet Jyothi had only ever known her to speak the truth.

Soft rain rustled the tree's vulva-shaped leaves, symbols of the Goddess, as Bindra forged into the undergrowth towards the pale, peeling trunk. At its base stood an old stone *lingam*, emblem of universal union. The upright stone was garlanded with an offering of fresh flowers, and yet she could see no footprint, no broken foliage. She touched the base of the tree, touched her heart, then waded back to Jyothi.

"How did he look, this man?" she asked, in heightening alarm.

Jyothi shook his head.

"Son, tell me!" she cried out.

"He was like a child. Small, like a child. A red child," he blurted.

"Red?" Bindra gasped. "Was he naked? Stained with *sidur*?"

Jyothi rocked his head from side to side in anxious affirmation.

"Wearing many *malas* around his neck? Around his arms? A drum in his hand?"

Jyothi had not stopped nodding.

Bindra put her bandaged hands to her mouth, as though to muffle the words she feared to say out loud.

"*Ban jhankri*!" she cried. "Jiwan has been taken by the *ban jhankri*!"

Chapter Six

First impressions of Gujarat's principal city of Ahmedabad convinced me to remain no longer than the time it took to travel between the train station and the bus depot.

Seven hours in a sweltering second-class carriage, with a projectile-vomiting infant beside me, and two itching strangers sitting on my backpack due to the lack of room, had left my nerves frayed and my patience worn. This city may have beckoned tourists to its splendid Indo-Saracenic architecture and the Mahatma's celebrated ashram, but the blinding dust, lung-solidifying pollution and relentless roar of the traffic drove me to seek an escape just as quickly as I could.

Unlike the cheery rickshaw-*wallahs* at Valsad, those waiting outside Ahmedabad station were aggressive and bad-tempered. They fought each other for my custom. They pulled at my dampening clothes from every direction. I defiantly ignored them all and marched straight for a young man, so thin that his eyes bulged from his face, so gaunt that his arteries pulsated visibly beneath translucent skin. He smiled weakly at me and glanced nervously towards his competitors who were now jeering as they wrestled with each other to be the first to reach us.

"Long Distance Bus Station *chalo*!" I shouted above the hullabaloo.

He shook his head in incomprehension.

As his native Gujarati was beyond me, I tried, "Drive me to the Long Distance Bus Station, please!" in my most pedantic RP.

Still no joy. I had thought that "Bus Station" was widely understood.

The other drivers were already upon us and had begun to pull at my backpack. As I struggled into his rickshaw, they punched my emaciated peddler with their fists. I hastily scoured my limited memory of childhood Urdu for some appropriate term for him to get going, while fighting with his rivals to retain my luggage.

"*So jao!*" I shouted at my driver.

I cringed. I had just ordered him to go to bed. Under such duress, my minimal childhood vocabulary had become completely muddled. I berated myself for never once having thought to learn a word of Gujarati from Priya, or her parents. I had never imagined that I would have had a reason to make this journey alone.

The crowd was now maddening itself into an incomprehensible frenzy. It seemed I was about to be dragged from the rickshaw, and the skinny man gripping the handlebars brutally concussed. Despite my dismay at the forceful fingers now trying to wrench the shoes off my feet, I was distracted by the physical state of my malnourished driver. As bare toes kicked hard into his spindle shins and stark knuckles slammed against xylophone ribs, he turned around to me with tears in his eyes and lips drawn thin. It looked to me as though he was about to expire.

"Go!" I yelled at him. "Drive! Pedal!"

This was ridiculous. I was being attacked and robbed on a busy station forecourt. My driver was having his bones broken by bullying competitors because he did not understand a word I said, yet still he patiently awaited my direction.

Utterly desperate, I shouted, "*Bawasir!*", a word with which I had vague recollections of my father's father once filling me with alarm. To my amazement, it did the trick. My rickshaw driver immediately began pedalling at top speed and fast pulled away from our abusers.

Not until the raging mob was far behind did I look down to find my clothes and skin covered with a Pollock-like paroxysm of dirty fingerprints in sweaty smears. I slumped against my rucksack in exhaustion, and puzzled at the dynamic response I had finally achieved. A fact made all the more inexplicable as the word I had inadvertently yelled was "haemorrhoids".

🔱

Bindra clung to Jyothi as they made slow progress through the dense undergrowth of mountain jungle. She called Jiwan's name at every difficult step, certain that the *ban jhankri* could not have taken him far. He was somewhere in the shadows of these misty trees. He was somewhere on this hillside.

The *ban jhankri* was a figure of mountain folklore, whose continuing appearance and interaction with the local population enabled the diminutive forest shaman to move with ease between myth and man. Many tales were told of children who vanished whilst walking in the forest, or working in the fields. Their disappearance was always so swift, so gentle, that even those by whose side they stood did not feel their departure.

It was said that the *ban jhankri* stepped out of the tree line and beckoned to those innocents he chose. It was only they who could see him. Some denied their capacity for the path he offered and ran straight home. Others willingly followed him into the jungle, where they were initiated into the limitless potential of the Words of Power.

Bindra had met a man when she was a child, who had been taken by a female *ban jhankri*. The *ban jhankrini*, as such mystical women were called, generally lacked the discretion of their male counterparts, and she had charged down the hillside, pendulous breasts slung over her shoulders, to simply snatch him as he had foraged amongst the trees. He had been returned two years later, barely recognisable to his own family. Bindra thought of him now and found herself sobbing into the damp quiet of the trees.

"*Ama*, look!" Jyothi suddenly tugged at her arm. "*Ama*, there are soldiers!"

Bindra peered down the hill to a large army truck drawn up against the roadside. A row of uniformed men was gathering along the cliff edge to urinate into the river below.

Bindra had forgotten her fear. She had forgotten the damage to her body that others found so threatening.

"*Dajooharu!*" she shouted as she stumbled, slid and fell towards the serpentine length of grey road below them. "Brothers, help us!"

The abrupt appearance of Bindra and Jyothi as they tumbled out of the undergrowth and hit the wet tarmac caused some of the young men to start. Bindra instantly became self-conscious again and prudently drew the shawl over her head, around her face and hands, as Jyothi helped her to stand upright. They both stared at the soldiers, at their mottled-green uniforms, their heavy, shiny boots and unwieldy wooden rifles. They had often seen the enormous army trucks grinding up towards the Tibetan border posts, but these Bengalis, Biharis, Rajasthanis and Punjabis, with their incomprehensible speech and inexpressive faces, were normally avoided by the local population.

"Kali Ma," Bindra whispered under her breath, and stepped forwards. "Brothers, my son is missing. My son is gone. In the trees . . ."

They stared back at her in incomprehension.

"Brothers, my son is gone . . ." she repeated. "I beg you to help me."

More men buttoned up their flies and joined their comrades on the road. A Bihari with a large belly that refused to be reined in even by his broad, regulation leather belt, laughed out loud. He crudely, flatulently encouraged the others to return to the vehicle.

"Please, brothers!" Bindra pleaded. "My son!"

The tumble to the road had loosened the long length of cloth bound around Bindra's hips. In a moment, its knot unravelled, releasing her meagre provisions to the ground. The scavenged *iskus* rolled straight toward the row of obsessively polished toes. Jyothi ran to grab the precious yellow gourds, but a tall, slender Sikh stepped forwards and caught the vegetables in his large hands. He walked across the road to help Bindra scoop up the few remaining items, then chased off three mangy rhesus monkeys that were showing a little too much interest in her greasy paper parcels.

"*Dhanyabad dajoo*," she said in thanks, her gaze exploring his finely coiled, green *pagri* turban and the impressive length of his well-shaped nose. "It's my son, my little boy. He's lost in the trees!"

The bearded Punjabi stood up and sought out Bindra's eyes. He did not speak Nepali. She looked straight back with an unfaltering gaze. This uncommonly tall man, with his noble, foreign features, was going to help her. She had decided.

The soldier turned and in English called, "Hey, Kabir! Nathu! Come out here a moment!"

Two dark, broad-cheeked faces peered through the canvas cover of the truck. Gurkhas.

"Brothers! Brothers!" Bindra called in excitement, her heart brightening in relief at the sight of Nepali-speaking kinsmen.

She quickly recounted Jyothi's sighting of the *ban jhankri* and Jiwan's disappearance. The two men listened intently, then turned back to their comrades. Bindra strained to hear, but could not understand the foreign tongue shared by the soldiers, into which her account was now translated.

"*Mero chora!*" she just kept repeating. "My son! My son!"

"Sister," one of the Gurkhas smiled, "we'll help you look, but we don't have long. We're expected up at Deolo camp."

And into the forest the soldiers swarmed.

ψ

The main road along which my scrawny Gujarati rickshaw-*wallah* and I trundled was melting and sticky in the noonday sun. The fablon-covered bench on which I perched, balanced atop rusty bicycle wheels, gave me little confidence. We swerved wildly between lorries, buses, motorbikes, ox-carts, pony-traps and count-less fellow rickshaws, my heat-plumped fingers whitening as I dug them deep into slippery upholstery.

Every jolt and slue drove us further into dark, obscuring fumes that billowed in aggressive threat from innumerable engines run on low-grade petrol cut with oil. I choked through my grimace, briefly clutching a handkerchief to nose and mouth until I had to concede defeat and, with near-feral gesticulation, direct my dishevelled driver to turn off down a narrow backstreet. He drew to a halt and turned to stare at me with vacant eyes. It occurred to me that in

our panicked departure from the train station, I had not yet
determined whether he had understood my desired destination. I
took the opportunity of comparative quiet to try again.

"Bus Station. Long Distance Bus Station."

My pronunciation was now that of a baritone Joyce Grenfell. Still
it did not appear to register with him. I had but one option and
winced in anticipation.

"Long Distance Bus Station, please," I said in an embarrassing
imitation of Peter Sellers' Doctor Ahmed.

"*Thik che*! *Thik che*!" he responded in delighted Gujarati,
releasing his grip on the handlebars to shake my hands in triumph.

"*Boom ditty boom ditty boom*," I sighed in relief.

I decided to celebrate our advance in communication by
dismounting to approach a *dhaba* food-stall, where I bought two
cold bottles of an over-sweetened fizzy drink called Limca. My
driver's delighted grin stretched his gaunt skin to its limit. Looking
into his face, I had the distinct feeling that this was a man whose
life would not be long. It was difficult to tell, but I guessed he could
have been no older than about twenty-five. Frustrated and angry
with my own helplessness, my impotence to make the slightest bit
of difference to his life, in a pathetic attempt at a philanthropic
gesture I returned to the stall and bought him a selection of savoury
pastries and fruit. Harsad, as his name proved to be, seemed
astonished, whilst I, with a pang of ancestral colonial guilt, fretted
as to whether I was, in fact, being condescending.

With new confidence and strength, Harsad pedalled on through
a squalid quarter of pollution-corroded tenements. As we rattled
over bricks, cracked pipes and spasmodic sections of crumbling
tarmac, we approached a young husband and wife struggling to
pull five small children and all their belongings on a heavy cart.
The wagon was also piled with cardboard boxes, scrap paper and
a mound of broken stones. Amongst this refuse, presumably
collected for reselling, lay a shrivelled old woman with watery eyes
who was partially covered in pieces of sacking and rag. She was
feverish and breathing heavily. Although the couple leaned into the
yoke with all their weight, they failed to move the wooden wheels.

I was still stupefied into pathetic inaction when, as we turned a tight corner, a violent buzzing filled the air and the sky turned black. We had disturbed a frantic swarm of innumerable flies. My driver had to swerve to avoid not only the reeking corpses of what appeared to have once been two dogs lying in our way – so bloated that their stiff limbs no longer touched the ground – but also the pack of hairless mongrels that now tugged with cannibal dementia at bulbous bellies and paws.

At the crowded depot, I purchased a ticket for the "luxury bus" to the city of Udaipur, which lay over the state border in Rajasthan. Harsad saw me right to the door. I put an arm around his fleshless shoulders to express my thanks for his courteous and efficient service. He weakly shook my hand goodbye, with a grin so triumphant that it seemed to threaten to tear his fragile face.

As he walked away on spindly limbs, proudly clutching the meagre bag of food I had purchased from the street stall, my head began to swim with the sights, sounds and smells encountered since boarding Harsad's rickshaw at the train station.

Distress, disease and death. Cruelty and corpses.

This was not the India of my father's stories and Grandmother's tales. Not the India I had tasted in Priya's burning kisses. This was not the India of my childhood imaginings, my lifelong dreams.

I was suddenly submerged in a confusion of memory.

I cried out and ran towards Harsad and his rickshaw, but he had gone. I had no idea what I might have done if I had found him.

I sat on my rucksack in the billowing dust, confused and disorientated.

I needed a moment. To catch my breath.

🔱

As the army lorry's grumbling roar faded, Bindra slumped to the sodden earth.

"I'm sorry, *Ama*!" Jyothi choked. "It's my fault. I wouldn't go with the little red man. So Jiwan went instead." He dropped to the ground beside his mother and covered his face in shame.

The soldiers had been kind to them. They had searched hard. They had shouted Jiwan's name loudly. None had called her *bokshi*. None had tried to hurt her. The Gurkhas had pressed a little money into Jyothi's right hand as they left. The Punjabi with the warrior eyes had given them *mewa* papaya that he had found growing in the forest. They had all been kind.

"It's not your fault, *mero ramro, shashi keto*," Bindra assured Jyothi, "my good, brave boy." She cuddled him to her breast and sought for words to comfort both of them. "We must believe that Jiwan is not gone. The *ban jhankri* are not bad men. They bring their chosen ones back, in time. We must just stay here and wait – until Jiwan is returned."

"But *Ama*, the doctor said I must take care of you. The doctor said I must see you get good medicine from the Ancestors at the Tune-Snake-Hand Ashram," Jyothi insisted.

"They'll have to wait," she replied with tired resignation. "Just as we must wait for your brother to come back."

"But *Ama*," he persisted, "where shall we live? We have no house here. No *bakhri* goat for milk. No *kukhurii* hen for eggs. No *haat* market for rice and daal!"

Bindra did not reply for a moment. She looked far into the trees.

"Then we shall sing sweetly for the *Punyajana*," she announced quietly. "This is their world and we shall show them respect. We shall apologise for the disruption we have already caused to their peace, and offer our best songs in our finest voices."

She smiled at Jyothi and wiped his dirty, tear-streaked face with the frayed hem of her shawl.

"There is nothing to fear, my darling son," she promised. "The Good People of the forest will watch over us."

The "luxury bus" was filthy.

The seats had lost much of their upholstery and rusty springs poked directly out of the exposed horsehair, which crawled with mites. I sat in the stationary vehicle at Ahmedabad for almost two hours of unexplained delays in paint-blistering heat. Not only was I sticking to the tacky seat and, though desperate for air, forced to breathe shallowly due to the abominable stench of the open cesspools outside the bus, but I had also begun to scratch.

I had convinced myself that our deferred departure had enabled some unseen miscreant to steal my backpack from the roof-rack above. My minimal funds would never accommodate a new wardrobe and I now mentally prepared to live in the same shorts and shirt for the coming weeks. In addition, I was trapped behind cracked windows, which would not open, and was drinking my bottled water too fast. I quickly realised that I would have to limit my intake if my diminishing supply was to last the journey.

My fellow travellers were all local and a sullen set, so unlike the hearty rurals of Valsad and Dalba. I tried to initiate conversation, but felt that I was regarded with suspicion and my attempts remained entirely without success. I did however discover that I had been charged over twice the price for my ticket than any other passenger.

Before I could muster the will to return to the ticket office and cause a scene, the engine burst into splutters. The new promise of escape from the insanity of the bus station and of a sewage-free breeze through the windows kept me in my seat.

However, as brakes squealed and gear-box grated, a dysfunctional cassette player also struggled into life. For the entire six hours of the journey, we were continuously blasted with a single tape of Bollywood favourites at double speed, while the speakers distorted and the screws worked loose.

And yet nobody seemed to mind.

Except the lone, sweaty, angry, itchy foreigner.

ψ

Bindra and Jyothi had sung their gratitude to the *Punyajana* before tearing into the perfumed orange flesh of the papayas.

"You see how good they are to us, the Good People?" Bindra affirmed, her mouth full of delicious sweetness. "The *Punyajana* are worthy of their name!"

"*Ama*," mumbled Jyothi, his face pressed deep into the skin, his teeth and lips still busy seeking out the remaining fruit, "why can't I see the *Punyajana*?"

Bindra cleaned her lips with her tongue and edged closer to him on the pile of large, waxy leaves Jyothi had gathered as a waterproof carpet on which to sit.

"The *Punyajana* are all around us in the forest," she explained, as comfort for herself as much as for her son. Jyothi loved his mother's stories and snuggled in, without once faltering in his busy exploration of the now bare papaya rind. "We see them in all the goodness that they offer us. In the trees that give us shelter, tools and honey. In the plants we use to heal and clean. In the *kapur* camphor that fragrances our *puja* fires. And in the *gurubuwa* flowers that give our hill *jhankris* and mountain *yogis* their secret knowledge."

"Does the *ban jhankri* have secret knowledge too?" Jyothi asked, lowering the limp skin to stare hard into the trees.

"The *ban jhankri* perhaps most of all," Bindra confirmed, following her son's anxious gaze. "And do you know the name of the King of the *Punyajana*?" she quickly continued to distract him from his quiet fear.

Jyothi shook his head.

"Why, it's Kubera, the best friend of Lord Shiva! He's a good king, who has a big happy belly and a big happy face!"

Jyothi smiled at the thought.

"And, do you know, he holds a mongoose in one hand that coughs up jewels of every colour, to remind us of the unfailing abundance of life? And a sour *kaagati* fruit in the other, to remind us that we have nothing to fear in death?"

Jyothi's dark eyes had opened wide.

"Now," she continued, "Lord Kubera keeps only eight teeth in his head, to teach us the eight qualities that afford us peace of mind and serenity of heart, qualities that we would all do well to strive for in our lives: tolerance and self-discipline, generosity and patience, contemplation and honesty, dedicated intention and knowledge."

"Does he live on our Kanchenjunga?" Jyothi asked, excitedly.

"Oh, very near by, in a beautiful city called Alkapuri, where all the riches of this wonderful earth are stored. It is Kubera who shares them out, to make sure we all have what we need."

Jyothi's forehead furrowed. "Do we have what we need, *Ama*?"

"Just look at us, here!" she burst in delighted reply. "We have our sturdy trees for shelter and our bed of soft leaves. We have a changing sky in our eyes and a chorus of birdsong in our ears. We have shawls to wrap around us in the cold, dry twigs to burn and fruit to eat. We even have a clean *kulo* brook that trickles by to ease our thirst. We have good memories of good people. We have stories to share. And we have each other. See how rich we are!"

Jyothi was still deep in thought. "But *Ama*, we don't have Jiwan."

Bindra did not reply, but looked back into the trees. The loss of her daughters had inflicted such grief and a torment of guilt that there had been many days and sleepless nights she had not believed she would bear. It was only the resolute repetition to herself that she had made the right choice for her girls, and the unwavering conviction that she would be able to reunite them, that had enabled her to endure their absence. To also lose a son now threatened to unleash a carefully contained despair. If only she could talk to the kindly *jhankri* of Lapu *basti*, he would know what she should do.

Bindra put out her hand to touch the little cloth bag of balls of cremation ash mixed with buffalo *ghiu* that Kushal Magar had given her.

"*Ama*, what if we were to do *puja* to Lord Kubera, and ask him to give us back my brother?" Jyothi suggested with great consideration. "He can ask the *Punyajana* to tell him where the *ban jhankri* has taken Jiwan-*bhai*."

"You are a gift to me," Bindra said softly, stroking his face with a bandaged hand. "And so very much your father's son," her smile warm in her remembering.

She sat upright to ready herself.

"Now, normally we would make Kubera *puja* on *Dhan Teras*, two days ahead of *Kaag Tihar*. You remember, the day we decorate the house with *saipattri-mala* marigold garlands? The day we feed

79

the crows before we eat our own meal, so that whenever we see their black plumage or hear their *kaag-kaag* caws we remember to look for the wisdom that every moment of every day brings?"

Jyothi grinned at the memory of the five-day-long festival of *Tihar*, and the deep-fried, rice flour *sel roti* fox-bread and *mulako achar* radish pickle his mother used to make to share with their neighbours.

Bindra's head was also filled with blissful memories of home, husband and four noisy, happy children lighting rows of little *diyoharu* oil lamps and singing in unison. Just the thought of the laughter and the galaxy of twinkling diamonds in the darkness cheered her heart.

Together, Bindra and Jyothi chose a long stone by the brook to stand on end. This would be the *lingam*, phallic representation of Shiva. Bindra reminded Jyothi that Kubera sported his own vertical *tesro khutta* "third leg" to show the underlying stability and limitless abundance of life, even in unexpected change and apparent poverty.

Around the *lingam*'s base, Bindra had Jyothi draw an eight-petalled lotus to represent Kubera's eight teeth of Wisdom, to prompt them to purify their intentions and their purpose. As he marked the lines in the ground with a stick, she impressed upon her eager son that the riches Kubera represented were never the wealth of personal gain.

"Such wealth," she insisted, "is not true treasure."

Together, they gave in offering three young leaves from a banana tree that was growing at the roadside. To this they added scarlet petals from a spreading *lallipatti* poinsettia tree. They had no honey, normally poured over the stone *lingam* in Kubera *puja*, so Bindra directed Jyothi to squeeze sweet juice from the remains of her papaya fruit.

"This symbolises the wealth of earthly delights," she explained. "When explored with bright awareness, no such pleasures need be an obstacle to wisdom."

Bindra and Jyothi knelt down together, facing eastwards, the direction of Kali Ma as Bringer of Knowledge. Bindra showed her eager son how to take water from the curled leaf of a tree and sprinkle it first on himself and then over the stone *lingam*. She took the *desalai* striking-matches from her cloth. Together they lit little twists of torn cotton as replacements for lamps, and a ball of pungent moss as incense.

Bindra then taught her son the words of the Kubera mantra, the Words of Power that would enable them to be open to the overflowing abundance of life from every source, even from within themselves.

"*Aung yakshyaya Kuberaya vaishravanaaya*," she began, "*dhanadhanyadi padayeh . . .*"

Jyothi followed, repeating each phrase after his mother.

"Never forget," she taught him, "Lord Kubera is not outside, but inside. This is the wisdom of the *Thuture Veda*, the Spoken Knowledge of our mountain tradition. We are calling on all that Kubera represents in ourselves. This is to help us learn to receive in order to give. And then, in turn, to give without thought of reward. This is the order of nature, the balance in the universe. This is wisdom."

Jyothi's tightly knotted brow indicated a pressing question.

"So, will Jiwan-*bhai* come back now?"

Bindra looked up to stare into the gathering darkness of the trees.

"Let's sing for the *Punyajana*," she said.

Chapter Seven

As the "luxury bus" crossed the state border, the landscape changed dramatically. Lush, cultivated plains withered into stony valleys incised by vast, empty riverbeds washing in dust. Gujarati villages clustered beneath palms evaporated in the desiccating heat, to be replaced by broad-roofed farmhouses squatting in solitude on arid hills.

I had entered Rajasthan, the Land of Kings.

Stones that were once great palaces and forts loomed from craggy heights, silhouettes of fallen majesty against cerulean skies. The Rajput warrior-lords who had once filled their marble-floored halls with courtly life and love, cruel vengeance and filial assassination, now surveyed their legacy through the eyes of red-necked vultures from tumbled battlements and toppled towers.

Far below, in the parched fields, sweating children slaved to break rocks into chippings, to mould head-high heaps of steaming dung and straw into blocks. Women, humped beneath stone-piled hods and sun-dried brick, laboured in half-sleeved bodices and billowing skirts of bright jasper, topaz, amethyst and cinnabar. Bare feet splayed beneath heavy anklets of silver and ivory. Necks and ears, noses and foreheads glittered with finely spun silver and thick cut glass.

The rugged route, across which the bald tyres of the bus lurched, bore the hefty hooves of arrogant, filthy camels. With jutting, tartar-clad teeth and long-lashed, indifferent eyes, they dragged leviathan tumbrels through deep dustbowls and drifting sand. Amongst their loads slumped sun-scorched men sporting soup-strainer moustaches and single hoop-earrings, narrow waists bound in pleated *dhotis*, heads wound in wide *pagri* turbans of riotously coloured cloth.

Far ahead, I caught sight of Brahminy kites and crested eagles gliding above white palaces, bleached temples and shining lakes. Through the haze of dust on the window, a dazzling, heat-inflicted mirage sparkled and reflected in the setting sun: the royal city of Udaipur.

The bus dropped me outside a solid gateway studded with iron spikes, once protection against the battering, armour-clad elephants of ancient enemies. I was genuinely surprised to find my dust-caked rucksack still intact on the roof-rack, with its promise of a change into clean clothes before dinner. It was thus with a renewed buoyancy that I hailed a rickshaw to take me deep within the confines of the city walls.

I had previously read that Udaipur promised a choice of many fine hostelries in which to stay, few of which I could afford on my budget. I had selected a cheap, though romantic-sounding establishment that had once been a minor summer palace. My rickshaw-*wallah*, however, exerted defiant independence by taking me to a hotel that was not the one requested. When I objected, he pretended not to understand. While I remonstrated with him, a crafty porter removed my rucksack from the seat. As I chased my vanished luggage into the wrong hotel, the driver received his commission at the front desk and disappeared. I was furious at the deception, but in my parched fatigue conceded that the dilapidated building with its neglected garden courtyard did possess a certain charm.

However, when the extortionate tariff was revealed by a churlish clerk, I exploded. I insisted that I was not some wealthy foreigner – of which my unkempt, smelly state was certain evidence – and could not afford the rates, whereupon an uncommunicative teenager was summoned to lead me through a maze of stairways, corridors and balconies to a small back room. The disappointing accommodation offered its own toilet, meaning an acrid-smelling hole in the floor with grimly splattered foot rests. A shower, meaning a heavily oxidised, dripping tap and dirty plastic bowl. A window onto the garden, meaning a sealed, opaque mesh that would not open. And even a rusty electric fan that flashed sparks and died as soon as the dour youth turned it on. None of this, however, deterred him from demanding a tip in "good dollars" for his courtesy.

Priya would have pinched my bottom and hooted out loud, to rouse me from my stupor. She would have grasped my hand and pulled me back out into the darkness, to shake me into action. But standing here alone in this oppressive heat, I was too exhausted and thirsty to think of trawling the city in search of better lodgings. My skin and clothes were black with dust and grime. My head was splitting.

Thus, despite the questionable methods of procuring custom, I resigned and, for this night only, grumpily took the room.

ψ

Bindra added more wood to the struggling fire and drew closer to Jyothi. Just to watch his little chest rise and fall as he slept gave her unspeakable joy.

The air was cold in her nose, the leaves beneath her damp. She loosened her shawl and tucked one end of it around the curled shoulders beside her.

Her eyes suddenly darted back amongst the trees.

Far across the hillside, a solitary drum had begun to pound the confluent rhythms of the three worlds, of *tintirilok*. The rhythm of the seasons. The cycle of time.

The *ban jhankri*?

Bindra turned from side to side, but the density of the forest confused the direction of the sound. The drums of the mountain shamans were common in these hills at night, as were the howls of the jackals they provoked. However familiar the wail of these wild dogs in the darkness was to Bindra, it still sounded like a murdering of infants.

"*Aung namah Shivaya . . .*" she sang softly to comfort herself, for jackals were considered to be companions of Shiva, principal deity of the mountain *jhankri*. "Svashva, Master of Dogs," Bindra whispered, "father and friend of the *jhankri* – and of me – may I learn to restore balance where there is instability. Compassion where there is anger. Harmony where there is inequality."

She touched her right hand to her forehead, mouth, heart, navel and pubis.

"May I, like you, be Asutosh, 'One who Quickly Calms'. Shankar, 'One who is unceasingly Benevolent'. Akrura, 'One who is unfailingly Kind'. *Aung namah Shivaya* . . ." She touched her heart once more.

Bindra cuddled down beside Jyothi and placed one arm, protectively, around her sleeping son. The drums and jackals seemed farther away now. Softer, kinder, gentler to her ears and heart.

She took one last look out into the blackness of the trees before braving sleep.

"Where are you, Jiwan?" she murmured. "We are waiting."

ॐ

Night had fallen when I left the hotel to explore the busy quarter. Even in the dark, there was no relief from heat or noise.

The narrow streets of Udaipur were jammed with hawkers and drivers. They hassled me at every step, tugging at my arms and clothes, pushing souvenir flutes, Mughal pornography and hotel advertisements in my face, attempting to physically force me into rickshaws and restaurants.

I walked into the first Westerners I had set eyes upon since alighting at Bombay airport. They were mostly young, red-faced Germans, the last stragglers of the tourist season. None was willing to respond to my gauche smiles or attempts to engage in conversation, even in their own tongue. A little despondent, having hoped for an exchange of words with someone in this city who did not just want my money, I approached the dark, stone elephant-flanked gates of a temple. The possibility of studying the lamp-lit images enshrined within its quiet precincts seemed a suitable distraction from the lack of financially independent friendship offered in the bustling streets.

At my appearance, the deformed and diseased who lined the entrance sprang into animation. They beat their metal bowls on the ground. They waved stumps of vanished limbs. They exposed running sores and infected wounds. I apologised to them all, above the clamour, above the persistent cries of "*Sah'b! Sah'b!*" For fear of pickpockets, I had left the hotel without my money. I had nothing with me but half a bottle of warm water.

I turned away and fought to quell the revulsion that was tightening my belly. I had to fight, because any aversion to the land of Priya's birth or its people felt like a rejection of the woman who had said we would name our daughter Lali, our son Milind – Darling Girl and Honey Bee. A rejection of the woman who had agreed to grow old and die in my arms. The beautiful, light-filled woman who had loved me far beyond my merit.

Suddenly, my knees lost all strength, forcing me to steady myself against a wall. I thought I must be reacting to the unrelenting heat and decided to make my way back to the hotel. The naked light bulbs dangling in shop doorways, the flickering oil lamps in niches and windows, the spluttering candles in jars that hung by string from lintels, began to blur into unfocused streaks of glaring luminescence. The clamorous bobbery of the streets smeared violently around my head, until the rebounding echoes made me stagger and sway like an intemperate, heavily laden station porter.

I struggled to mount the main stairs when I reached the hotel. No one came to the front desk, despite my determined pealing of the hand bell. I stumbled through the courtyard until I could no longer stand, then crawled up the flights of stone steps and along the balconies to my room. The violent speed at which the fever was defeating me was alarming.

No sooner had I reached my door than all the lights went out as the entire city plunged into the darkness of a power cut. I remembered having seen a stub of candle on the dresser upon my initial arrival, so explored its grubby surface until fingers fumbled to both waxy stumps and box of matches in my first aid kit, and drove the shadows into madness.

With a wet flannel flopped on perspiring head and a dose of general antibiotic forced down into queasy belly, I was finally able to totter into bed. My sleep, however, was fitful, troubled and tearful as the searing temperature played pitiless tricks upon a heat-demented mind.

It seemed that I was sitting in an orchard with Priya, sharing a picnic of *puri bhaji* and fresh peach chutney. Grandmother was softly singing, "Johnny Sparrow, Johnny Sparrow," as she laid mustard poultices along my spine. Mice were whispering secrets in my sheets. Spiders were whistling sea shanties from their corners. Cockroaches traversed my contorting face, a legion of furtive feelers fearlessly surveying the depths of mouth and nostrils.

By morning, my bed was sodden.

My disgust at finding mice droppings in my sheets was soon surpassed when I looked at my flushed and haggard features in the broken bathroom mirror. Stuck to my hair was a half-squashed cockroach with legs outstretched, as if suspended in an ultimate, energetic star-jump.

In revulsion, I leapt to turn on the taps. There was no water.

In anger, I kicked the corroded pipes. They did not even gurgle.

I sought a solitary comfort in the pristine whiteness of my toothpaste and scrubbed my teeth with vigour, determined that at least one part of my body would feel clean. I rinsed with a careful measure of depleted drinking water, then chewed at the brush's nylon bristles as though their residual mintiness might assuage my misery.

If only it could have been Priya's *puris*, or Grandmother's Dijon-drenched muslin that had been true.

Bindra woke to the sound of men in the forest. She opened her eyes and stared into the dawn. She quickly slid her hand around Jyothi's waist and drew him close.

The voices were approaching. She listened intently. Nepalis, who spoke her own dialect.

Bindra sat bolt upright.

The two figures in the trees stopped still.

She could make out the formal dress of white *suruwal* trousers worn tight on muscular legs, and the black *dhaka topi* caps on their heads. The white *daura* tunics drawn around their stocky torsos by a *patuka* sash, collars tied close to symbolise the serpent of liberating knowledge that enwraps Lord Shiva's blue-stained throat. She could see that one wore *rudraksha mala* strings and a cloth bag stitched with *kauri* shells across his chest.

The two men peered towards her.

"*Jhankri-jyu*! Kushal Magar *dajoo*!" she cried. "Last night I dreamed that you were coming to me! And here you are, brought with the sunlight!"

The kindly *jhankri* stared in astonishment. "*Bahini*? How can you be here, in this forest?"

"But *dajoo*, brother, how can you be here, so far from Lapu *basti*?" she gasped.

Neither seemed to need to answer the other's question.

"I knew you would come!" Jyothi smiled. He had been awoken by the exchange and clapped his hands as the *jhankri* and his companion approached, their strong shoulders laden with provisions. "We did Lord Kubera's *puja* one week ago, didn't we *Ama*? And his *Punyajana* brought you to us!"

Bindra explained that she and her sons were travelling to Kakariguri on the Plains, in search of foreigners' medicine to heal her. The *jhankri* was pleased. He said it was good and right. He in turn explained that he was travelling with his brother Darpan to an ancestral village on the Darjeeling road, to undertake the annual *baje-boju puja* for his mother's forebears.

"But, *jhankri-dajoo*," Jyothi interrupted with marked intent, "you are here to tell the *ban jhankri* it's time to give my brother back!"

Kushal Magar looked at Bindra. She rocked her head from side to side in anxious affirmation.

"*Bhai*," he said softly to Jyothi, "the *ban jhankri* are great masters. Not like me. I can ask for you, little brother. But I cannot promise that the *ban jhankri* of this forest will listen."

Jyothi stood up and boldly approached the two visitors, dragging his thin blanket behind him. "Yesterday I dug *iskusko jara* and *tarulko jara*. I shall light a fire, *Ama* will bake the squash root and tapioca, then you can ask the *ban jhankri* to bring my brother back!"

Kushal Magar laughed. "Then, *bhai*, you light the fire so your *ama* can cook, and my brother and I shall prepare for *puja*!"

Jyothi did not say a word, but ran towards the trees to gather fresh kindling, his whole face alight with new smiles.

ॐ

The air was still and stifling as I ventured out into the blinding daylight. I could feel the calenture coursing through my body with new cruelty, tearing at my mind with malicious intent.

As familiar rickshaw-*wallahs*, touts and erotic-miniature sellers ran towards me, the heat and filth, the aggressive demands for money and attempts at pickpocketing were suddenly no longer tolerable.

I had to get out of Udaipur. Now.

For two and a half hours, I queued in the train station, dragging my rucksack across the concourse floor. I filled in forms and queued again. I was sent from window to window, only to be told that there were no seats.

There were no seats on any trains.

There were no seats on any trains for the next five days.

I was convinced of some conspiracy between the hotel owners and the booking-office staff, so went in search of the senior station master. The man looked strained, as though permanently sucking in his belly in order to fit into someone else's military-style uniform. Barrel-chested and brusque, he barely deigned to rest even a glance on my perspiring figure before curtly ordering me to write him a formal letter, "for politely requesting a seat".

But where was I to find writing paper, pen and envelope? He ignored my impertinent question. Instead he made a loud, viscous snort, and spat a gelatinous projectile towards my toes.

Through the back door of a station office, I caught sight of a tubby little man dawdling beside an impossibly cluttered desk. He burst into life as I knocked on the doorframe, announcing with flamboyant pride that he was "Station-secretary-sixteen-years'-service-Sir!" With unabashed coquetry, he flashed his close-set eyes and well-formed teeth, and declared me "a-most-handsome-young-welcome-guest-in-my-country-Sir!" He was giggling and wiggling with such heightening ebullience that I had to look away with unease.

He did, however, agree to donate a piece of scrap paper and a pencil, on the condition that I promised to post him a generous selection of books from England.

"Only-big-lovely-colour-picture-volumes-and-expensive-to-buy-Sir!"

In that moment, all residual patience evaporated. Incensed with the absurdity of the situation, made fragile by my fever, and desperate to escape this suffocating office with its sticky-sweet, diabetic odour, I dishonestly agreed. Brightly coloured and costly beyond imagination the tomes would most certainly be.

In gratitude, he offered to spend a night with me in my hotel, if a seat on the train was not forthcoming. I politely declined, but thanked him for his inordinate, giggly, wiggly hospitality.

I immediately delivered a hasty letter to the office of the senior station master, and was instructed to return in five hours. Only then might a decision as to whether or not I would be allowed on the train be decided.

Five hours. I had to wait five hours.

I lingered outside the crowded "Men Only" waiting room, until I caught sight of the secretary through the doorway. He was still wiggling in his chair, flashing his teeth, waving at me with a little too much enthusiasm.

I nodded politely, turned my back, then promptly plunged into the riot of the station forecourt.

"*Aung Baneshkandaya nama . . .*"

Kushal Magar withdrew long chains of *ghanti* bells from his cloth bag, which he draped around his neck and across his chest. He tied a length of white cloth around his waist to represent the consciousness of semen: Shiva. He tied a length of red cloth around his waist to represent the energy of menses: Shakti. He knotted the sashes tightly on his left side, a reminder that he, like all existence, embodied both these principal forces in the cosmos.

Kushal Magar bound his head in a white scarf, over which he donned a headdress stitched with feathers and small *kauri* shells. The short pipe made from a human arm-bone was sounded. Kushal Magar unwrapped the *thurmi* dagger from its cloth binding and drew a circle on the forest floor. He marked the eight directions with the white, paper-thin *totala* seeds sacred to the *ban jhankri*.

"*Aung satom bhi dhumba damdim vajradhumbha . . .*"

He dipped the ceremonial dagger into the smoking ash of the dried *gurubuwa* teaching plants he had ignited in the *dhupauro* bowl. *Ganja* cannabis, *titepati* mugwort, *hasana* night jasmine. He dropped an intuitively measured portion of psychotropic *saal* resin onto the glowing embers of the new fire.

Finally, he offered two drops of his own blood to the flames, by the pricking of his navel with the consecrated *dumsi* porcupine quill, as evidence of his self-surrender.

Kushal Magar sat cross-legged in the centre of the circle. He offered his *mura* drum to the rising smoke, as his brother struck the brass discs of the *mujura* cymbals to sound the supreme union of the universe.

Kushal Magar placed on his tongue a small piece of cooked *gurboko jara* cobra lily root and closed his eyes.

The spiral journey of the *jhankri* had begun.

Outside Udaipur railway station, I bartered a price with a rickshaw-*wallah*. He agreed to cycle around the more pleasant and less crowded areas of the old city, whilst I sat huddled up and shivering beneath the rickshaw canopy.

Bounded by wooded hills and bathing *ghats*, we stopped at Lake Pichola, the "Sapphire Udaipur", in which stood two gleaming island palaces. As my driver wandered off to urinate and spit scarlet *paan* into the shallows, I sat in the sweet-scented, dappled shade of gaunt acacias to watch ducks dabble, swallows swoop and ioras flare emerald and amber like silk shot with gold.

A lithe young man rose from the lake before me, glistening in the sunlight. As he stood to wipe the water from his eyes and smoothed back his black hair, I smiled at the thought of my wan, von Aschenbach face blinking out from my motorised bathchair at this dark-skinned Tadzio. The boy looked up and cocked his head. He grinned with knowing, waved, then dived back into the blue.

Across the lake rose the towering walls, balconies, cupolas and hanging gardens of the largest palace complex in all of Rajasthan. Even in my fever, the temptation was too great.

It was thus to the carved-marble arches of its northern entrance, where Maharajas were once customarily weighed and their weight in gold or silver distributed to the populace, that I next instructed my driver to take me.

ψ

Kushal Magar slumped forwards.

The writhing and drumming had stopped.

The forest was quiet.

Jyothi looked to his mother. Her eyes were closed.

Kushal Magar stirred.

"*Jhanar*," he murmured. "The waterfall. The *ban jhankri* will return him at the waterfall."

ψ

I fought my way through the vociferous mobs of unofficial guides excited at the sight of an end-of-season visitor, and entered the relative cool of cloistered courtyards, mirrored hallways, pierced-marble corridors, and painted walls depicting extravagant courtly life and creative love.

I had vividly imagined Udaipur's City Palace as a child, for it had been from its royal menagerie that Kipling's *Jungle Book* Bagheera had escaped to forest freedom. Even as childhood had become adolescence, Kipling's panther had continued to stalk my dreams, and I now found myself astonished to be standing in a very real building that still maintained the appearance of my having stepped into a storybook.

I flopped faintly by an arid fountain, beneath the fragrant racemes of a graceful tree. I was shivering feverishly again. I had been unable to eat a thing since leaving Dalba, three days before, but now acknowledged that I needed to build my strength. I decided to search out plain rice and bland vegetables – "boiley-food", as my father's mother used to call such convalescent fare – only to find that I was struggling to stand.

I was the only customer at the rabble of plastic garden furniture beneath a sun-scorched marquee that passed as the palace restaurant. When my order arrived, I could distinctly smell urine. I concluded that I had become so accustomed to the all-pervading, frowzy stench that it was now permanently lodged in my nostrils.

I dabbed the perspiration cascading down my temples, neck and throat with a fist of pink paper napkins, before prodding at the limp vegetables. I had to try.

I thrust a single forkful of wet rice and unseasoned potato into my mouth, but could not swallow.

The taste of food on my tongue, taken from a bowl that I had been able to buy with such nonchalance, stirred visions of starvation, crippled limbs and reasty corpses. The vivid summary of images fused with a fearful guilt, revulsion and despair that now overwhelmed both heart and mind.

I slumped forwards in the chair to rest my burning head in moist, hot hands. I was on fire, giddy with resurgent fever, nauseous with shame and self-loathing for the naivety and indulgence of my life.

I did not want to remember why I had come to this place, to Udaipur, to India, to poverty, suffering and squalor. I did not want to admit that however far I travelled from a shattered tree in a quiet lane, the memories from which I ran would still be true. The broken ribs and bloodied lungs. The slow and lonely death.

I pushed the vegetables aside and spat the contents of my mouth into disintegrating napkins, as I struggled to contain compulsive retching.

ॐ

The climb was hard and long, and took two days.

Kushal and Darpan Magar led the way, but Bindra panted hard and often had to stop. Little Jiwan's legs could never have carried him this far.

As the watery rumble of the fall finally grew near, Bindra paused at a Shakti Tree. She bowed her head in *pranam*, both to catch her breath and show her respect to the tiger-riding Mother, whom she too embodied. Jyothi ran to her side bearing scarlet petals from a *lallipatti*, which he placed in reverent offering at the weather-worn feet of the Goddess held firm in its roots. It was Durga who represented the strength within that had sustained them in their sojourn amongst the trees. It was Durga who represented the strength that would enable Bindra to bear the challenges that she knew were yet to come.

And then, "*Bahini!*"

Kushal Magar and his brother were standing by the edge of a forest pool, into which bright waters pounded.

Bindra could not contain the cry that tore from her throat.

Seated on a rocky platform in the centre of the churning waters was a naked child. She stumbled forwards and fell to her knees, gasping. Jyothi danced around her in excitement, waving frantically to his brother.

"*Ama*, it's Jiwan-*bhai!*" he cried. "The *ban jhankri* has given him back to us! *Ama! Ama!*"

"*Dhanyabad*! Thank you!" was all Bindra could mutter, as she watched Darpan Magar quickly strip down to bare skin and swim towards the motionless Jiwan.

Chapter Eight

My obsequious letter to the station master at Udaipur had worked. I had been approved for a berth on the night train.

A buck-toothed teenager followed me from the platform to my compartment, where he proudly introduced himself as "Injan Wailrayz buk sellah, *sah'b*." He had made his poor clothes so presentable and had oiled his hair into the finest colonial-schoolboy parting-and-fringe that I felt obliged to purchase one of his prudently plastic-bag-wrapped, paperback books. With only a cloth sack around his narrow neck in which to carry his wares, the literary selection on offer was both limited and uninspiring. Neither the *Krishna Calorie Counter*, nor the Jackie Collins best-seller, discreetly bound in a disguise of brown paper, appealed.

I chose instead Agatha Christie's *By The Pricking Of My Thumbs*. However, the story would turn out to be much more of a convoluted mystery than the novelist had ever intended. Whilst the spelling in my Indian-published copy was creatively eccentric, the cheap print had smudged whole passages into indecipherability. To further obscure the tale, pages were missing throughout, and those that remained attached to the budget binding had been inserted in a confusingly capricious order.

I had tipped my friendly rickshaw-*wallah* with the last of my coins, so I paid for my slim, but incomprehensible, volume with a note. However, in my dizzy fever I gave my "buk sellah" 500, instead of 100 rupees. By the time I realised my inattention, he was nowhere to be seen. I was livid with myself for being so careless, and furious with him for not acknowledging my mistake.

I petulantly kicked off my shoes and climbed up into my upper bunk, feeling very sorry for my situation. Sick, weak, taken advantage of. Poor thing.

I huddled up against my rucksack in an effort to contain incendiary emotions born not only from my own negligence that had enabled the young vendor to cheat me, but my whole upbringing. I was coming to believe that, in my youthful innocence, I had allowed myself to be seduced by an image of an India that did not exist. I had been duped by tales of elegant comforts and exotic luxuries that had merely been a mirage, an illusion fashioned by previous generations on nothing more than the enforcement of colonial privilege and the vile deception of an imagined racial superiority, in which I now felt I had unwittingly played a part.

Suddenly, the book-boy reappeared in the cabin.

"Your change, *sah'b*," he said, offering me 400 rupees in carefully flattened notes and a conscientiously written receipt in an elegant hand.

I stared at the paper in his outstretched palm, unable to articulate a suitable response in my shame and embarrassment. I had automatically expected the worst of him. I had assumed him to be a scoundrel, like the other scurrilous urbanites who filled the rickshaw ranks, hotels and tourist-centred streets, all trying to scratch a basic living in an over-populated country oppressed by social divisions and all-pervasive corruption.

"You sad, *sah'b*?" he asked, eyebrows bonding in concern.

I told him I was fine.

"Be happy, *sah'b*," he smiled.

And waited until I smiled back.

Jiwan was quiet, still and apparently unharmed.

"Where have you been?" Jyothi asked. "You've been gone for days!"

Bindra wrapped the little boy tightly in her shawl, whilst Kushal and Darpan Magar quietly prepared a fire and made him a tunic from a length of the woollen cloth they carried.

"Where are your clothes?"

Jiwan shrugged.

"What did the *ban jhankri* feed you?" Jyothi persisted.

"*Syauharu*," came the whispered reply. "Apples. He gave me cut apples on the backs of his hands."

"Were you in his house?" Jyothi pressed.

Jiwan rocked his head from side to side. "In his cave."

"Was it dark?"

Jiwan rocked again.

"Were you afraid?"

Jiwan looked up at his mother. "I cried for *Ama*." Bindra pressed her face to his. "So he showed me *Ama* in the shadows. He said, 'Here is your *Ama*'."

Bindra was puzzled. "What else did he say?" she asked gently.

"He asked if my tears were for *Apa*" he replied.

"Your father?" Bindra was surprised.

Kushal Magar drew close and sat with them as Jiwan continued. "So he showed me *Apa* in the shadows. He said, 'Here is your *Apa*'."

Tears welled in Bindra's eyes.

"What else did the *ban jhankri* do?" Jyothi eagerly enquired.

"He taught me," came the solemn reply.

"Were there crows, *bhai*?" Kushal Magar asked, looking intensely at the little boy.

Jiwan nodded and rested his head against his mother's chest.

Kushal Magar remembered well the crows. Over thirty years before, a *ban jhankri* had taken him one morning as he had worked in the paddy with his parents, up near Turzum *basti*. The little red man had appeared at the dark tree line and had beckoned for him to come. It had been the *ban jhankri* who had taught him the mantras with which he now healed, comforted and initiated change in the many who came calling at his open door.

Yes, Kushal Magar remembered well the crows, the emissaries of Shiva and Kali, the Bringers of Knowledge. The *ban jhankri* had repeatedly tested his memory of the mantras imparted to him through their recitation under extreme duress. The young Kushal Magar had suddenly found himself being torn and cut by the beaks and talons of a mob of screeching birds. He had fought this way and that, but still in their cruel, black hundreds they had ripped into his tender flesh. He had screamed for help from the quietly observing *ban jhankri*.

"*Phalaknu!*" the little red man had repeatedly ordered. "Say the words!"

It had only been as he had fixed his memory on the newly imparted mantra that the crows had vanished. For, in truth, they had been but the shadow of crows.

I woke in the night, dripping with perspiration and shivering on my upper bunk. I had called out her name.

A baby was screaming below and a rank, biley smell filled the compartment. I laid the sandalwood soap from my bath-bag under my nose, then wrapped a vest around eyes and ears to dull the noise and the pulsating electric light, which the colicky child was switching on and off without restraint.

In the morning, I woke with a choking start, as though smelling salts had been discourteously rammed up my nostrils. The sun was only just breaking over the strangely pointed mountains and yet the air billowing through the windows was already scalding. I rolled over to discover the source of the nauseating stench. The infant had been allowed to relieve itself all night directly onto the floor, which was now awash.

With bent knees lodged against the ceiling, I struggled to dress as quickly as I could. I swung myself from the top bunk, straight out of the compartment door and into the corridor, without once letting my feet touch the ground. It was an immense relief to realise that the shakiness of my fever had largely passed. I had regained command and clarity of thought. A positive indication, I believed, of an imminent recovery.

I braved the communal carriage toilet, to find it to be no more than a hole in the floor, through which I could see the dash of tracks below. Despite its gaping size, numerous previous occupants had managed to miss their target. The floor and walls crawled with busy insects, the air fluttered with a menagerie of winged beasts. I washed my face and torso as best I could with the hot trickle of brown water that oozed from the single tap, whereupon the flying insects stuck to my skin, sending me into a frenzy of futile flailing.

Twice I walked up and down the train corridor, passing my compartment. I no longer recognised it. In the twenty minutes I had spent peeling wings and legs off my chest, arms and face, the cramped cabin had filled with strangers. A family of six was sitting on my upper bunk, gleefully rifling through my rucksack. I stood at the door and gaped as they passed around my socks, sun-block and journal for the other passengers to examine.

With teeth tightly clenched, I dredged through the foul swillings on the floor to gather my belongings and repack my bag. The father of the newly arrived family unashamedly refused me space on my bunk. Instead, his wife offered me one of my own bruised bananas. I still could not face the thought of food. Nor did the idea appeal of an unattractive verbal battle in incompatible languages to win back my seat in such a reeking and confined space.

I spent the remainder of the journey crouched on my heels in the corridor. Hugging my ravished backpack. Muttering indecorously.

Bindra relished the warmth of the fire as she watched her boys sleeping. Kushal Magar offered from his bag more *chiura*, the beaten rice commonly eaten in the hills that swells in the stomach and quickly eases hunger. She smiled in gratitude and tendered a bandaged palm, onto which he carefully piled a portion of the dry, cream-coloured flakes.

"So what does it mean, *dajoo*?" Bindra asked, as she began an arduous chew.

"Your Jiwan has been chosen as a *bhui putta jhankri*," Kushal Magar explained. "One who has 'broken through the ground'. One who is 'self-born'. For he has had no mortal guru."

Bindra continued chewing.

"None in the Himalaya can match their skill or knowledge of mantra, the Words of Power. None are more able to help others find the means by which to heal themselves," the kindly *jhankri* impressed. "It is a great and difficult gift. We can only wait and see what he chooses to become."

Kushal Magar threw a little more *chiura* into his mouth. He knew well the challenge of such a call, although he never spoke of it. He knew he would never marry. He knew he would never have children. It was the price he paid, for the *bhui putta jhankri* had no selfish desires.

Kushal Magar was no longer a man.

He was Knowledge.

♆

It was almost dusk as the train finally approached Delhi.

For forty minutes, in furnace heat, we crawled through an interminable landscape of wretched hovels, in which every tree had been sacrificed for fuel, every plant and every root consumed. Macilent figures swarmed like frenetic ants through a rotting carcass of rancid warrens and foetid dens. Scraggy cows and scrawny buffalo clogged the alleyways separating miserable shacks, amongst which they produced paltry quantities of germ-infected milk and runnels of liquid sewage.

The stagnant ocean of tin and plastic, rag and dung opened around a feculent pool that hummed in a haze of flies. Inhabitants squatted to relieve their bowels on the banks of these nefarious black waters, as others waded in to wash themselves with clay and ash, and raise cupped palms to parched lips.

I found myself unable to accept the loathsome scenes of abomin-able human misery, repeated mile after mile, along the railway tracks that pierced the nation's congested capital city. This was not the India of my father that I had come to find, surely. Not the India of bed-time elephant and Maharaja. Not the India of Grandmother's Uncle Oscar, Theo and Tagore.

Again, I found myself disorientated, angry, hurt.

At New Delhi Station, I climbed down from the train and pressed my back against a wall. I beckoned to an exquisite little girl who was bleating "*Aam!*" and placed a coin on her dirty palm, in return for a rotund mango. Her one dark eye looked at me and blinked. The other was scarred and shrivelled in its socket. I smiled at her. She blushed and scurried away.

As I watched the child vanish into the surging throng, an inexplic-able alarm began to pierce my chest. An engulfing sense of vulner-ability and isolation. A new and frightening fragility.

I no longer knew where I was trying to go, or for what purpose. Wherever I went, I would not find Priya.

I was suddenly overcome by a pressing need to remember the last words she had spoken to me. A pressing need to assure myself that our ultimate interaction had been meaningful. The declaration of a love that could not be dimmed by distance, unalterable even in eternal separation.

But what if those parting words had had no significance? The booking of a hair appointment? Her sister's choice of college? What if that last exchange had merely been a reference to the ordinary triviality from which a comfortable life is constructed?

I now struggled to excavate any memory of Priya from the compressed layers beneath which, in an instinctive effort of self-preservation, I had buried her. I now fought to find the least echo of her words, the least shadow of her face. But the abrupt violence of her senseless deletion from my life had silenced all recollection.

I crumpled forwards, winded by a new and fierce guilt. A realisation that, just as she had been ripped out of the future we had determined to forge together, her hand wrenched forever from my own, I too had been complicit in her eradication by silencing her voice within me, erasing her image, attempting to extinguish her memory.

"Priya!" I heard myself gasping at the surge of faces that pushed past me.

"Priya!" as the world began to blur and slide.

♆

Bindra woke just before dawn. She automatically put out her bound hand to find her two sons.

No Jiwan.

Bindra struggled to sit upright.

In the twilight, she could see him sitting around a new fire with Kushal Magar. He was now wearing oversized clothes the kindly brothers had been taking as gifts for nephews at their family home. They were talking in low voices. She tried to listen, but could not hear. It sounded as though they were chanting together.

Today, they had to continue their slow journey to the Plains. They must gather more *iskusko jara* and *tarulko jara*. They must collect more ripe papaya and clean water from the tumbling stream.

She looked back to the firelight. Kushal Magar was now on his feet and circling Jiwan in respectful blessing. Bindra looked on in puzzlement. She wondered what had happened to her son in the *ban jhankri*'s cave. She wondered what he had become.

Bindra looked to her feet, which were to carry her far today. She had no pain in her curled toes. Even the open blisters and deeply embedded stones did not hurt. Only her swollen knees, hips and lower back ached. But she had her boys. She shared their laughter and their songs.

Bindra had neglected the bandages on her hands since leaving the Tibetan doctor and his cheerful wife. They were loose and filthy. She began to gingerly unwrap her senseless fingers with her teeth, but as the cloth fell away she wrinkled her nose at the smell and gasped at the swelling. Bindra was astonished to find that the left hand was now unresponsive and entirely closed. She sat and stared, unable to accept that the stinking mess of flesh she had exposed belonged to her.

"*Bahini*," Kushal Magar said by Bindra's side, "you will get bad fever. We must give you *pisaiko hardi*, good turmeric paste, to heal your fingers. And neem leaves to ward off delirium. They'll be more palatable if you add a little sugar and black pepper, when next you can."

Jiwan helped the kindly *jhankri* to rummage in one of his bags until he drew out a small clay pot, bound in cloth. He gently applied its rich yellow contents to the deep wounds where fingertips had once been. Not once did Bindra flinch.

"I asked Kali Ma for knowledge – and burnt my fingers!" she chuckled awkwardly at herself. "Now I must take from her tree, *Neemari Devi*, to protect me from a fever my own inattention may bring!"

"The knowledge you are seeking you already have," the gentle *jhankri* replied, as he tore strips from a cloth for clean bandages. "All true knowledge is within. You need only to recognise it in yourself."

Bindra nodded her head from side to side. She knew this to be true.

"You know, *bahini*," he continued, "we make real the things for which we most yearn. There is no destiny, sister. Every choice you have ever made has determined your present path."

Bindra smiled. This was their way, in the Hills. Not the pre-destined fate taught by the Brahmins. Not the unchanging *Karma* and *Samsara* of the orthodox *Bahun* priests and Buddhist lamas. Not a life borne passively to pay off the "spiritual debts" of some previous life. Bindra knew that any loss of harmony was not the reaction of a watchful, chastising god. It was the product of her own thoughts and actions. A consequence of the way in which she chose to respond to whatever the natural ebbs and flows of life may bring.

Jyothi stirred and sat up. He was shivering in the cold morning air.

"*Ama*, can we go home today?" he yawned.

"Not today," she sighed, with a smile. "We have Ancestors with foreigners' medicine to find. And a whole new world to see!"

⍦

For five hours I stayed where my knees had buckled and I had slumped to the floor, against a spittle-splattered wall in New Delhi Station. In some self-castigating reaction, my fever had returned with a vengeance and I had been rendered barely capable of movement or speech. For five hours I watched through eyes made keen by searing temperature, as an entire sub-continent seemed to hurry past.

Black-skinned peasants from the south, curly-haired, broad-nosed, bewildered. *Bhil* people dressed in mirrored clothes of scarlet cotton, far from their lake island villages in search of work. Tired, determined parents bearing all they owned in loose bundles, shepherding children who carried still smaller siblings in their arms. Ancient porters in tatty red jackets, official brass badges bound to gangling arms that strained to drag cumbersome carts piled with post and luggage. Workmen, stripped naked to soap sinewy limbs at hydrant taps that spewed brightly between stationary trains.

Slum scavengers, beneath sacks on hunched and bony backs, combing the tracks for fuel to burn, rubbish to sell, morsels to eat. Tin trunks atop tall soldiers, wooden rifles across shoulders, hand in hand, cuddling in corners like lovers. Pilgrims with saffron beads and bowls, vermilion handprints pressed between sharp shoulder blades. Wandering holy men, uncut hair drawn back to reveal brows painted with the sign of their *sadhu* sects, narrow necks garlanded by flowers, long staffs clasped in torous fingers.

Of all these storybook people, it was the *hijra* who most puzzled my fever-fired mind. Devotees of the cockerel-riding goddess Bahucharji Mata, these ritually castrated men were dressed in gaudy saris, their henna-tinted tresses tumbling across broad shoulders. Eyes boldly daubed with shadow and kohl, pert pouts brazenly scarlet-stained. A cache of tawdry necklaces languishing across breastless chests, downy forearms jingling with iridescent bangles.

A little slum boy was the first to notice the feverish, fallen foreigner. He peered at me from between the mountains of cloth-bound freight, wincing in his curiosity. The serious-faced child drew close enough for me to stretch out a clammy hand and offer him the mango. He cautiously gathered shuffle-speed and confidence, and eventually grasped the fruit with a look of triumph on his face.

For hours little Jai and I sat together on the floor, as the jostling mobs hurried by, oblivious. Nobody noticed the defeated traveller sitting slumped and shaking, or the dirty urchin grinning at him and clinging to his fingers, as though they were old chums who shared a secret.

ψ

Bindra had never before stood so far from home.

The air was hot and heavy, the view before her disorientating. From left to right, as far as she could see, there were no forested hills, no mountains. Only flatness.

"What is this place, *Ama?*" Jyothi asked.

"It is what they call the *Madesh,*" she muttered in reply. "The Plains that lie where our Hills end."

"Well, I don't like it!" Jyothi stated categorically. "It looks like the edge of the world!"

Jiwan, whose hand he held, said nothing.

Bindra had regretted having to say goodbye to the Magar brothers amongst the cold, damp trees. They had shown such generosity and understanding. She would never forget. They had taught her in their kindness.

But that had been long days ago, amongst people she knew, in a place she loved. Now Bindra stood on the brink of a different world, of which she knew nothing. A world into which she, with her brave little boys, now felt compelled to step.

ψ

When next I awoke, Jai had vanished back into the swarming hordes. He had left the gift of an empty, well-chewed biro in my hand.

I tried to move, but found I could neither stand nor lift my backpack. My joints were ablaze and bubbling. My head a vault of molten magma.

I fought to focus fast-liquefying eyes on the station clock. My train to the heat-relieving north was due to leave in just two hours and I still had no ticket. I tried to stand again, but the world blurred into a vacillating smear and my face struck the filthy floor.

I lay still, panting heavily, unable to pull my arms from the tight rucksack straps. My fevered mind drifted back into heat-born visions and my sweat-wet eyelids closed. I had begun to believe that I was going to die on the concourse of New Delhi Station. And no one would notice.

Suddenly, a cool hand rested on my forehead. I looked up, startled.

"*L'Inde, c'est merde!*" a pale young man muttered, as he knelt in front of me.

Patrice from Strasbourg freed me from the shackle of my rucksack, propped me against it, then disappeared without a word. He returned with bottled water, an oily bag of vegetable *pakoras* and a clutch of bananas. I insisted that I could not possibly eat. He ignored my protestations and insistently force-fed me, unperturbed by my constant heaving.

Within an hour, revitalised by the first nourishment I had taken since leaving Dalba days before, I was able to stand and, with the support and humour of my accompanying French Samaritan, who insisted upon carrying my luggage in addition to his own, commence the tedious process of buying a ticket.

Queue at Window 20 for application form. Move away to fill in same.

Queue again at Window 20 to have form checked and scribbled on for no apparent reason.

Queue at Window 12 to have form scribbled on again and price calculated.

Queue at Window 18 to pay amount.

Queue at Window 20 to collect tickets and have original form retained.

Grasping my ticket in triumph was my last memory of New Delhi Station. The fever was such that I retained no recollection of boarding the train, or climbing into my berth. Nor do I remember any grateful "*Saluts*" to Patrice. I assume it was he who made my bed, undressed me, placed a wet flannel over my head, tucked a stock of bananas in my bath-bag, two bottles of water by my side and tied my rucksack securely to my leg.

When I next awoke, it was half past five in the morning. The train was still and quiet. The air, cool and fresh. I cautiously pulled myself upright to discover that, as though by some miracle, the fever had lifted.

The train had come to the end of the main line at Kalka, towards Kashmir in the north and Tibet in the east. It was here that I had to transfer to a squat, pre-war train on a narrow-gauge track, which was to take me high into the thickly forested mountains and hill stations of what had once been known as the Eastern Punjab. It was in these little, toy-like carriages that I was to ascend into mountains that had once been the home of Kipling's Kitty Mannering, young Cubbon, the Cussack-Bremmils – and my father.

Chapter Nine

Bindra could not withhold her cry as the end of the leather-bound stick struck again between her shoulders.

"Please, not my back, brother! Not my back!"

The soldier mockingly imitated her cry. "Then get moving, jungle woman!" he shouted in Bengali. "This is army property! And you, *khanki*, are trespassing!"

Bindra tried to pack her few provisions into the carrying cloth as quickly as she could. The soldier grew impatient and lashed out with his foot. The last two papayas, saved for their journey to Kakariguri and the *Gad Sup Hat* Ashram, span towards the undergrowth.

He kicked again. His foot caught her arm and came down hard on the few remaining lengths of tapioca root. He purposely drew the sole of his boot across them.

"And take your chinky-eyed monkeys with you!" he spat, forcing Jiwan towards her with a stab of his stick.

Before Bindra could catch him, Jiwan fell onto the dry earth. Before Bindra could reach him, Jiwan had leapt straight back up and had turned to face the uniformed brute. He looked hard into the man's face.

"Jiwan!" Bindra called, as she clutched a painful, darkening forearm to her chest. "Come!"

But Jiwan was motionless.

"Jyothi," Bindra turned to her eldest. "Bring your brother!"

But Jyothi did not respond. He was watching Jiwan, who had dropped to a squat and was now drawing in the dust with a broad, confident sweep of his finger.

Bindra started towards him, but was halted by a deep, resonating chant. She was astonished. It was coming from Jiwan. Even the soldier seemed transfixed.

Jiwan stood up. He carefully stepped into the centre of the pattern of intersecting lines he had marked out on the ground. He placed his small hands into carefully positioned *mudras*, manual gestures used to focus latent forces in both body and mind.

"*Hshraing hshklring hsshrauh* . . ."

The booming sounds coming from her little boy shook Bindra. She sensed a gathering commotion and looked up. The sky had filled with crows.

"Kali Ma!" Bindra gasped. "Dark Mother! What child is this?"

A swift flash of khaki and the guard struck Jiwan to the ground with a single blow. Bindra cried out in furious alarm and fought to reach her son.

The Bengali spat at them, cutting through the carefully scored lines in the earth with the heel of his boot, and hastily marching back towards the safety of barbed wire, parade grounds and procedure. The guard hut door slammed shut.

Bindra gathered Jiwan into her arms. His ear and cheek were bleeding.

"What have you done?" she whispered. "What knowledge has the *ban jhankri* shared with you?"

She turned to look for Jyothi. He was staring beyond the fence, towards the guard hut, onto which every silent crow was now alighting.

ψ

The fifty-five-mile journey from Kalka to Shimla took six hours. The view from the train had quickly transformed from Kali-armed cacti on stony hills to the dark malachite of mountain pine. Along the way, passengers and post were collected at Victorian village station stops. The further we climbed, so the faces of the new passengers changed from the sun-scorched Caucasians of the Plains to the Mongoloid features of the mountains, each broad cheekbone and almond eye hinting at our proximity to Nepal and Tibet.

The temperature dropped by the hour, as the century-old engine strained its weary way skyward. The clean, bracing air soon soothed all sense of fever. The chatter of silver monkeys, the glistening song of *koel* cuckoo and the rainbow blaze of parrots squabbling amongst the trees brightened my heart. My body had begun to regain its stability. My mind had begun to reclaim its calm.

Until just forty years before, my father had lived in these forested hills. I thought of him as a child, as *chota sahib*, full of hope and life, scaring the servants with his plasticine scorpions and proudly saluting the passing cavalry with his home-made sword. Saving *annas* to tip the snake charmers and mourning his dogs that died of rabies. Running from the monkeys on his way to school and hiding from the dilated gaze of ash-strewn *sadhus* as they wandered past the garden gate.

At that moment, the snow-capped heights of what my father had known as the Punjab Himalaya came into view above the treetops. I gasped in astonishment at my first sight of the very cloud-borne ridges I had spent years examining in the faded sepia of my grandfather's books. I pressed my nose to the cold glass in wonder at the ranges so loved by my father, as the mountain peaks to which he still longed to return, the pines and sapphire skies of which I felt I too was a part, merged into a single, kaleidoscopic blur.

A jovial Punjabi left two female companions sitting on the compartment floor and squeezed next to me on the single wooden seat. He put his arm around my shoulders and waited. He said nothing until I had wiped wet eyes and reinstated the well-trained reserve of my imperial roots.

Kamlesh was travelling with his young wife and her sister for a week's holiday in the Hills. He had come to say that they all thought I looked "a very nice young man indeedly – all handsome and loving."

For the last two hours of the journey, Kamlesh and I maintained a comfortably superficial discussion of our contrasting lives and

"Ooohed" at the view. The two women would not join in. They stayed on the floor, where they giggled and fluttered their eyelashes at me, blushing as though too chaste to interact with any foreign man and quite innocent of their game.

🔱

Kakariguri town was dirty and crowded.

Nobody noticed the two children walking beside a woman in a torn *chaubandi cholo* blouse, tatty *pharia* sari around her waist, *majetro* shawl bound about her head and shoulders. It was common to see impoverished mountain women wandering down here, lost, in search of work.

Bindra felt heavy and flat in the hot, still air. She had never been to this low altitude before. She had never felt this weight in her lungs, this density in her head. She led Jyothi and Jiwan to the shade of a large tree. They sat together to share the little remaining mountain water in the bottom of their canister. Nothing would ever taste as clean again.

A passing convoy of garishly painted lorries spewed yet more dust into the already congested air. Bindra clutched a corner of her shawl to her mouth and clung to her boys, as though they might be blown away by the black, choking exhaust fumes. She shuffled them around to the back of the tree, away from the traffic, and made an effort to brush down their grimy features.

"Is this our new home, *Ama*?" Jyothi spluttered, spitting on the ground to rid his mouth of diesel-coated grit. He looked up at her, baring his crunchy teeth in a grimace.

"We're not at the Tune-Snake-Hand Ashram yet," she began, struggling to quell the anxiety that threatened to consume her.

"Well, I don't like this place," Jyothi stated emphatically. "There's no forest here for food. It's too hot. And the air is grey!"

"But your big sister lives here!" Bindra offered in compensation, as much for herself as for her sons. "We'll see where Jayashri-*didi* lives and she'll give us hot *chiya* and *aloo dum*. We'll share the love we have for her in our hearts. Then the dust will seem like a friendly greeting, and the heat like the warmth of a kindly welcome. You'll see!"

Jyothi looked her directly in the eyes. "*Ama*, I want to go home!"

Bindra stroked his face with her bandaged hands. "After we find Jayashri, I must ask for medicine from the Ancestors. Then we can go back to the Hills," she smiled reassuringly. But even as she said the words, she could feel they were not true.

They were sitting opposite a long line of low bamboo huts with palm-leaf roofs that lined the roadside. The front of each house was open to the billowing dust, yet busy with bands of carpenters, second-hand rubber merchants, coir dealers, poultry sellers, their apprentices and customers. Jyothi wandered over to look at the newly carved domestic shrines and tables, the towers of old lorry tyres, the mounds of coconut shells next to robust coils of rope and piles of neat matting. He peered through the slats of round baskets stuffed with sweltering hens that were pecking each other to baldness. He rubbed his foot on the ground in search of worms he might push through the gaps to distract the birds from their claustrophobic insanity. However hard he rubbed, he only found more dust.

"*Paani*!" Bindra called after him. "Ask for water!"

She watched Jyothi approach a group of young men smoking under the plastic canopy of a nearby tea-stall. One stood and filled a bucket from an irrigation ditch that ran behind them.

Bindra gasped and struggled to rise to her swollen, rag-enwrapped feet. She moved quickly, but could not reach Jyothi before he had been drenched in thick, brown liquid and the indolent crowd had exploded in a roar of amusement.

As she hobbled towards them, the tea-stall quickly fell silent.

"*Bas! Bas! Aage ashbena*!" a young man commanded in Bengali. "Stay away! Don't you dare come any closer, *khanki*!"

Bindra did not understand his words, but she understood his meaning. She had so quickly forgotten.

"I just want my son, younger brother," she announced, reaching out towards Jyothi, who was trying to wipe stinking mud from his eyes. "He didn't mean to bother you. I just asked him to fetch us water. We're strangers here, *bhai*, and did not mean . . ."

She stopped still.

"Jyothi, come straight to me! Now!" she ordered, with uncharacteristic urgency.

The young man had bent to grasp a stone.

$$\Psi$$

Seven thousand feet above the sea, Shimla spread across a broad, crescent-shaped ridge. The cosy hill station had once been known as Simla, in the days when it had been the summer capital of British India, the "Abode of the Little Tin Gods" to which armies of administrators, their clerks, wives, mistresses and extensive households had trekked in order to escape the cruel incalescence of the Plains.

I stared out across the red-roofed Victorian chalets of its suburbs. I scanned the tin-topped clutter of its bazaar that clung to the steep, south-facing slopes. I peered up towards its castle-like public buildings and the terraced shops that lined the broad, central boulevard of the Mall. I squinted towards the tower of its parish church rising to the east and looked for the High Raj splendour of Viceregal Lodge to the west, where my father's parents had once enjoyed a "moonlight revel" of freaks, fortune tellers and baked potato stalls. Shimla was indeed an extraordinary sight.

Bedtime stories had led me to believe that upon arrival at the train station, strong-legged *jhampanis* would be awaiting my custom. I had long been assured these merry, bantering men would have primed their double rickshaws, with two sturdy fellows to push and two to pull, eager to whisk me along the narrow, winding paths that ascended into the town. But there was none. A rusting jeep, with a surly young man at the wheel with an absurd price on his tongue, was the only transport on offer. I chose instead to make the precipitous climb by foot.

I commenced my ascent with enthusiasm, but in far too few strides calf muscles began to protest at the relentless incline and lungs began to heave in the thin mountain air. It was, therefore, with slow deliberation that I trudged my passage through the crowded warrens of the bazaar. I hauled my way up flights of stairs and urine-sprayed passageways between buildings, in the hope that one might lead me to the Mall. I wheezed my way past grandsons and great-grandsons of the grocers, oil-sellers, curio-vendors, priests, pickpockets, and native employees of the government once known by Kipling and my grandfather.

I paused to survey the pierced wooden screens and carved balconies of the eccentrically piled buildings amongst which my heart now palpated. Some were only supported in their semi-vertical positions by the haphazard addition of precarious, childlike constructions of bamboo scaffolding. I recalled my father telling me that it had been in these now dilapidated hovels that courtesans had once discussed the supposed secrets of Empire.

I panted onwards, lugging my rucksack along the verandah-like "side walks" and alleyways of the "native quarter", until, at last, I reached the town's main street. In my father's day, all vehicles except the Viceroy's had been banned on the clean and quiet Mall. So had all dogs. And natives.

I peeped through the darkened windows of the Gaiety Theatre, where once audiences had disrespectfully roared at the strictly male-only productions of Shakespearean tragedies. I walked around the bandstand, where once patriotic anthems had sounded on Regent Street brass. I passed Scout huts, General Post Office, tea rooms, second-hand bookshops, clock tower and Town Hall. It seemed to me that I had walked into a much-decayed Epsom or Dorking, a Surrey market town on Bank Holiday, in which the entire population was tanned, beshawled and smiling.

I sat on a garden wall and watched children in prep school uniforms riding home on ponies, led by devoted servants. I leant against the Tudor Porch of Christ Church tower and watched little boys play cricket, where once the Protestant ruling classes had exchanged banalities in their Sunday best.

I scanned the hillsides, dotted with cottages and bungalows, their original weather-worn names of Chertsey and Cheltenham, Harrow and Hutton Henry still decipherable above honeysuckled porches and wild-rosed gates. The temperate climate had allowed for the laying of lawns and the planting of fruit trees around the summer residences of the town's British founders. However, as I was discovering to be the way of much of modern India, all had been left to decay and rot. Many of the old houses and hotels were fast collapsing. The gardens lay overgrown and desolate, the orchards diseased and barren. Herbaceous borders had turned woody and prize blooms had long gone to seed.

A young, short-bearded Kashmiri porter approached me and asked if he could suggest a hotel. Wary and mistrustful after my experiences in Bombay and Udaipur, I declined. I had decided to stay in the YMCA, which I anticipated to be cheap and clean. He emphatically insisted that I had made a bad choice and that he would accompany me to prove it.

The building we approached must have formerly been a grand mansion that had stood in extensive grounds. The rotten mahogany doors, the grimy decorated floors and collapsing central staircase gave mere glimpses of what this house must have once been. My Kashmiri companion collected a key from the front desk and took me to a room on the upper floor.

It was the fine cornices that first caught my attention as I stepped through the door and tripped over one of many shattered clumps of ornamental plaster, which lay scattered across the wooden boards. As I brushed off my hands, my earnest escort insisted upon brushing off my knees. This intimate moment evidently broke our mutual reserve, as he took it as a sign that he could now hold my hand. He only let go when I laughed out loud, in sheer delight, as he told me his name was Dilruba, "which, sir, has for its most finely meaning 'Heart Throb'."

Returning my gaze to the room, I stared in puzzlement at the ceiling rose that dangled precariously on taut tufts of horsehair. I sighed in despair at the elaborate marble fireplace, piled high with soot, rubble and empty Coke bottles, the yellow-stained sheets and the all-pervading stench of blocked lavatories. I needed no more convincing. My new-found chum had been entirely honest in his judgement. I conceded. He could now guide me instead to the one hotel in the town he had strongly recommended. "Heart Throb" was thrilled and immediately restored his hand to mine.

The Municipal View was an ugly, concrete shoebox that stood high above the town. However, my room was large, the bedding acceptable and the price within my limited daily budget. Even the bathroom was clean and promised hot water for an hour every morning. Although I was the only guest and the eighteen-year-old proprietor just happened to be my Kashmiri's cousin, I agreed to take the room. The young manager was thrilled at my custom. As he left me to unpack and wash, he advised that I "be keeping windows well indeed closed shutly, sir, for rascal monkeys cause much havocs and guest displeasures."

I expressed my thanks for his warning, turned the key behind him, and immediately opened the door onto the balcony. I stepped out and inhaled the crisp, enlivening air with a forceful gasp. Before me spread an astonishing view of the Elysium and Summer Hills.

And beyond them all, the great white peaks, range upon range, sweeping into infinity, of the mighty Himalaya.

$$\psi$$

"She's not here!" the young woman barked.

Bindra had taken hours to find the house. It lay well off the road, beyond an abandoned tea garden. Her exhausted, but uncomplaining, boys had stopped to pick a few leaves. They had been cheered by the hope of a flavoured brew before nightfall, but the bushes had been left unclipped for far too long. Their foliage was overgrown and bitter.

"Then what time is she back?" Bindra asked politely.

"She won't be back. She's not here, I told you! Never has been!" came the curt reply, in strongly accented Nepali.

Bindra was confused. Jayashri had started her life as a maid over a year ago. She had been taken to Kakariguri, to the home of this chicken farmer, by a woman who had come asking for children to go into service. She had promised good food, education, clean clothes, even wages. She had promised that Jayashri would be allowed home to visit once a year, in the hot season. Bindra had waited, but she had not come.

"Then where is my daughter?" Bindra tried again. "In whose house is she working?"

The young woman curled her lip. "I don't know who your daughter is, nor do I know where she is. What I do know is that she's not here!"

Bindra would not be deterred.

"Then where is Mrs Mukherjee?" The woman had already turned away. "Mrs Mukherjee, who brought my Jayashri to work in this house?"

"Never heard of her!" came the irritated reply. "Never been any Mukherjees here!"

ψ

Behind Shimla's incongruously neo-Gothic church rose Jakhu Hill, some thousand feet above the town. I climbed its steep, thickly wooded slopes, dark with pines and deodars, but soon had to pause. I sat on the forest path to the ancient temple, breathing in the sandalwood that floated through the Himalayan cypresses from the shrine dedicated to Hanuman, the Monkey God.

I peered back down the hillside and thought of poor cousin Dill and the steamroller that had crushed out his life as he had tried to save an unwary local, somewhere below me in 1923. If only Grandmother could have known that I was here. If only Priya . . .

I stopped myself.

No more "if onlys", I had vowed. Never again that single, self-destructive clause of the unreal past. Pointless.

The deluge of despair that threatened to defeat me was swiftly dispersed by the arrival of a mob of merry schoolboys. Smartly attired in royal blue blazers and caps, they clustered around me with a communal wish to practise their English. They wanted to talk about cricket, Milton and Wordsworth. Uninhibited by the petulant narcissism so common in Western adolescents, they spontaneously recited favourite passages from *Paradise Lost*, then in unison *"wandered lonely as a cloud"*. In turn, I recited a passage of Tagore, much to their surprised delight, only to expose my easy sentimentality by sharing out the bag of cashews I had procured in the Lower Bazaar. They leapt at the opportunity to milk another credulous tourist, and so, in response to their tireless entreaties, I handed over the last of my British coppers for their "collections".

Satisfied to have made a new, foreign friend – or at least an exploitable benefactor – and content with the gifts in mouths and pockets, they collectively waved goodbye and scuttled off home "for tea". As I watched their cap-topped heads bob back down the hill path, I wondered at the legacy of Empire that would maintain the rigours of pre-War uniforms and classical curricula, whilst allowing roads, buildings and any level of civic efficiency to slip into oblivion.

I strolled back towards the Mall and made for a small temple dedicated to the hill goddess Shyamala Devi, a form of Kali after whom the town was said to have been named. As I reached Scandal Corner, where *memsahibs* once gathered to exchange the salacious gossip for which these hills had been so well known, I walked straight into Kamlesh with his wife and her sister. The women giggled furiously and sauntered away to a fruit stall, casting long-lashed looks over their woollen-wrapped shoulders. Kamlesh took the opportunity to clasp my arm with unsettling excitement.

"I am loving you, Mister David," he announced.

I laughed and said that I thought him a fine chap too.

"No, no!" he protested. "I am loving you most deeply!"

The heat of his hand and the ardour in his eyes initiated a sudden, alarming realisation.

I called to mind that I was an intruder on a distinctly different culture. I thought of the farm boys in Gujarat, the soldiers at New Delhi Station, my new friend Dilruba and the unselfconscious ease with which he took my hand. I was coming to learn that both emotional and physical bonding between men had long been judged wholly natural and valid in India. "Heroic dalliance" shared between male companions bound by a deep and trusting friendship had long been deemed auspicious.

Back on the farmhouse roof in Dalba, Mukund had astonished me with talk of *Gandharva* marriages, in which men cohabited through a bond of love that required neither parental consent nor priestly ceremony. He had explained that this "celestial" tradition – named after mythical, irresistibly handsome musicians who possessed the secrets of the gods, with which they enlightened men in the arts of divine pleasure – had even been defended by ancient laws as a means to maintain individual stability and thereby social harmony. In Mukund's opinion, it had only been when a censorious British judiciary formally reversed these historic edicts that the Sub-continent had suffered a cultural blow of imperial, foreign "morality" from which it had yet to recover.

Kamlesh interrupted my hasty deliberations by grasping both my shoulders, to hold me squarely in his fervent gaze.

"Please be coming to my friend's house this evening," he pleaded. "My wife is being elsewhere, with no doubts."

I politely declined, in spite of the grin and raised eyebrows he proffered in excited anticipation. I claimed to be busy, although could not think of a single activity in this sleepy hill station that could so occupy my time.

"You are not understanding, Mister David," he pressed. "I am loving and respecting you. I am not laying one unworthy finger on you. Only as you are wishing. No jiggy-jig if you are not wanting, that I am promising. Please be having no fears."

I was struggling with the culturally appropriate response to such an offer, hardly daring to consider the implications of his bouncy colloquialism, when Kamlesh's wife suddenly screamed. A rhesus monkey had leapt on top of her, tearing a newly purchased bag of bananas from her hands.

While Kamlesh ran after the beast, waving and shouting in violent Punjabi, his sister-in-law fumbled to cover the gaping hole torn in his wife's long *kurta* with her own *dupatta* headscarf. While the onlookers laughed out loud and clapped their hands in delight at the entertainment, I took the opportunity to scuttle off in the opposite direction just as quickly as I could.

ψ

Nobody would stop to answer Bindra's question.

Some simply shrugged in response to her Nepali. Others kept a wide berth, pretending not to have seen her smiling to catch their attention.

At a busy intersection, she approached a man dressed in Western clothes. "Brother, where is the *Gad Sap Hat* Ashram?" she asked again. He tossed a coin towards her, but would not stop to listen. Bindra sent Jyothi to return it, but the man refused to take the money back.

Bindra led her boys to rest in the shade of a tree. The heat made the new skin on her back and neck prickle painfully. The lack of food and water was dulling her mind and clouding her sight. Jyothi and Jiwan had been quiet for a long time. She knew they were hungry and thirsty, and yet had never once complained since their arrival in Kakariguri the previous day.

The ringing of a bright bell caused Bindra to turn around and peer into a thicket of bamboo and banana palms that lay far off the road. Jiwan pointed directly at it and nodded, without a word.

The sight of a small Kali temple in the trees brought life surging back into Bindra's exhausted body. As they hurried towards the red *dhajo* temple flags protruding above the treetops, she thought she could hear the cheery, expressive intonations of their own Kalimpong Nepali.

They passed a single stall laden with all the usual *parsat* offerings of incense, scarlet garlands, *sidur* pigment, paper icons and metal *trishul* tridents. She smiled apologetically at the stall-holder and quickly led the boys towards the low steps. As they paused to brush the dust from their feet, Bindra noticed an elderly woman sitting on the ground. She showed all the ravages of long years of untreated leprosy.

"*Namaste didi*," Bindra smiled, respectively raising her hands to her heart in *pranam*.

The woman bowed her head in return and lifted a bowl between the shrunken stumps that had once been hands.

"Forgive me, *didi*," Bindra replied with regret. "We have nothing. Not even *chaamal* to offer you, not even raw rice."

The woman had only now caught sight of Bindra's bindings. She did not need to ask.

"No, wait!" Bindra suddenly beamed. "We have a coin. Jyothi, take it from your pocket."

Jyothi looked at her in disbelief. "But *Ama!*" he protested. "It's all we have to buy food!"

The Nepali woman raised her own arms to them in *pranam*. "*Bahini*," she croaked through a dry throat, "little sister, my children and husband are all gone. I've only one mouth to feed. You have three."

"A man dropped this coin and wouldn't take it back," explained Bindra. "So whether you have it or we have it makes no difference. Your hunger is my hunger."

The woman lifted her arms again. "No *bahini*, I need nothing from you. Just a prayer to Kali Ma. And *ahashis* from your little one."

"My Jiwan?" Bindra almost laughed. "You're asking for a blessing from my little Jiwan, as though he were your elder?"

The woman tipped her head and smiled with knowing.

Jiwan stood and confidently approached her. He bowed in *pranam* and muttered a long phrase under his breath. He drew the woman's thin, cotton shawl over her head, then bent forwards to whisper in each ear at a time. The woman bowed low in gratitude and touched his small, blackened feet.

Bindra was astonished.

"Come, *Ama*," he said, turning back to his mother. "Kali Ma awaits."

Chapter Ten

The sun had dropped behind the mountain peaks and with it the temperature of my room in the Municipal View. I covered my bed with the extra quilts provided, only to have to open the window to dispel the fungal mustiness.

I used the chilly bathroom for a moment and returned to find the room full of monkeys.

The charcoal-masked mob froze.

They stared at me with eyes wide, thieving fingers outstretched, suspended in compromising positions of pilfer.

My father's careful bedtime training flooded back into my mind.

Run in tight circles when faced by a crocodile.

Play dead with a cobra.

Keep face to face with a porcupine.

Remove your clothes and walk backwards if surprised by a bear.

But for monkeys?

My finest snake-hiss imitation induced mass panic amongst the guilty scoundrels. They scuttered straight back out of the window through which they had crept. However, despite the frenzy of their departure, they first managed to grab two pairs of underpants, nail-clippers, lip salve, alarm clock, dirty socks and tube of antiseptic cream, whilst scattering flurries of fleas across my bedding in their flight. I burst out onto the balcony in vain hope of restoring at least some of my accessories, but all were gone.

The distant glow of a full moon reflected across the snowy heights beyond my window, as I huddled down into damp blankets and reviewed the day to distract myself from my shivers. Mock-Tudor gables and collapsed chimneystacks. Unhinged garden gates and broken bay windows. I thought of grandparents, aunts and uncles in these hills. I imagined my father practising on his wooden tricycle along these forest paths, under the watchful eye of his turban-topped *khansamah*.

And in the darkness, the voices of my Dead-'n'-Gones seemed to whisper around the room, seemed to echo across distant mountains inside my head, as I closed my eyes and lay on my hands to stop myself from scratching.

$$\psi$$

"Tune-Snake-Hand?" the portly Keralan nun was mystified. "I'm sorry, but I have never heard of the *Gad Sap Hat* Ashram."

She beckoned the little family away from the edge of the road as another bus blasted by.

Bindra was exhausted, but nodded in gratitude all the same.

"*Didi*," she asked, "how do you speak such good Nepali?"

The nun smiled with satisfaction and explained that she had worked for some years amongst the tea pickers at Kurseong. She looked down at the two tired little faces blinking back at her.

"What is this place you are trying to find?" she asked with growing interest.

"There are Ancestors there," Bindra explained. "They have medicine to make me well." She had not meant to glance down at her hands.

"We want to go home," Jyothi added quietly.

The nun shook her head. "I'm sorry. I've just never heard of this Tune-Snake-Hand Ashram," she apologised, her Malayali accent at times impenetrable.

All of a sudden, her dense, dark eyebrows lifted in broad arches. She burst into giggles.

"No, no, wait!" she squealed, covering her discoloured teeth with a fleshy hand. "It's not *Gad Sap Hat* – it's the *Good Shep-herd* Ashram! And they're not Ancestors – they're Fathers! Catholic Fathers!"

Bindra joined in her laughter. But she did not understand.

⟱

The burghers of Kasauli proclaimed their town to be "The Cleanest and Calmest Hill Station". As I alighted from the bus onto the old parade ground, there was little to contradict them. Laid out before me were quiet, leafy lanes, dominated by a fine country church. There were handsome houses in well-kept grounds, smart army barracks and an intriguing array of pre-War shopfronts.

The journey from Shimla had been uncomplicated. There had been only one change at the decaying row of tiny shacks that constituted Dharampur, where the population had gathered to intimidate me with the steadfastness of their stares.

The final stretch of the journey towards Kasauli had been undertaken in a vehicle that looked as though it might have been driven across a minefield in a recent military manoeuvre. We had bumped and lurched our way through forested hills where strawberries, apricots and cherries grew wild. We had crossed deep valleys violently splashed with magenta rhododendrons and cut through by quicksilver streams. We had passed British bungalows with arcaded verandahs, and handsome "chummeries" where four or five bachelors once lived together and shared their servants. We had frightened skinny women who balanced foraged fodder on their heads, and skinny shepherds who herded skinny sheep.

Kasauli had always been spoken of by my father with the greatest affection. It had sounded to me more Narnia than his other homes at Risalpur or Sialkot, more Never Never than Khanspur or Murree. My greatest desire was to find the last house in which my father had lived, before the upheavals of Independence and the insanity of Partition.

In the cluttered tobacconist's, gob-stopper-stuffed with discoloured sweets in dusty jars, the chatty *dukandar* shopkeeper directed me to an old hotel on the Lower Mall, and its proprietress, Miss Holt.

I climbed the stone steps of the Hill Top Hotel and nodded to a tense *mali* gardener. He was busy deluging rows of potted geraniums on the verandah with two long-spouted watering-cans.

I had paused to watch a pair of long-limbed langurs negotiate the telephone wires, when a narrow glass-fronted door opened and the windfall face of a stooped figure appeared between the floor-length net. I was so taken aback to see a shrivelled Englishwoman high in the Hills that I was momentarily lost for words. She seemed unperplexed by my imbecilic expression and, in spite of it, offered her hand, simultaneously giving instructions to the *mali*, who was still fussing over the scented-leaf perennials.

"Dear boy," Miss Holt sighed wistfully, as though summoning vivid picture-book scenes of a secret life in another world, "I saw the Raj at its height. I lived through the Raj!"

Her voice was strong and retained the glimmer of a distant youth. It contradicted the crumpled body in its breakfast-egg-and-marmalade-toast-fronted cotton dress and cardi.

"The Raj was glorious, truly glorious," she continued, resting her palm on a plant-pot-piled reading table. "Everything ... beautiful. The likes will never be seen again by any generation, believe you me. I went to England once and was horrified. The seat of Empire maybe, but it was cold, grey and dirty. And all those sooty chimneys! I never went back. Now all my relatives are dead. Not one left."

I asked whether she knew of a house named Ketunky.

"Your family home?" she asked, pouting her sunken lips into a puckered scar. I nodded. "Once in a while, you people come on your sentimental journeys, in search of some grandfather's house or other," she tutted. "And every one of you is shocked and disappointed, because India is collapsing and so are your ancestral piles. However, Kasauli has changed little, except there's now half the population we had before Independence. And, of course, the whole place is falling down around our ears!"

She turned to shout at the *mali*, who had watered the geraniums so generously that they were now floating. "*Acha, memsa'b!*" he squealed, as he proceeded to tip up the pots to drain them, dropping sodden soil and flower heads all across the verandah floor.

The old lady rolled her eyes and took in a deep breath, "It's all so disappointing." She shook her head slowly, causing the pendulous skin of her wizened neck to drift from side to side like a lazy *punkah* fan. "Simla was glorious, of course. Every summer the viceroy and his council travelled over one thousand miles from Calcutta. He'd bring hundreds of his own attendants and guards, in addition to envoys, representatives, tradespeople and the like. It was like watching Hannibal coming up the mountain – without his elephants!"

Miss Holt had become animated with the commotion of her memories. She unconsciously began brushing down her worn clothes and straightening the unpressed Eton collar on her dress, as though she were about to be presented to Lords Willingdon or Curzon themselves. She raised an arthritic hand to sweep thin thrums of white hair from her face, and for a moment I caught a glimpse of a young woman looking out from her twinkling eyes. A bright, lively girl, still in awe of the grandeur and elegance of her youth.

"And the Viceregal Lodge, you've seen it of course," she continued, "five stories high, and all furnished by Maple's of Tottenham Court Road. Oh, my dear, the social life was so . . . eventful. Grand balls, the likes of which you couldn't possibly imagine. And eight hundred guests at a time!"

Over her head, I could see the *mali* getting himself into a proper pickle. His hands were full of mud and broken geranium stems. He seemed unable to decide whether to first re-pot whichever plants looked redeemable, or to clean the mess extending up his arms and across the verandah floor, which was now covered in dirty footprints, or whether to sneak past the reminiscing *memsahib* and make good his escape. Whatever his decision, it would not have made the slightest difference to her now. She was too far away in her reveries to have noticed the domestic disaster unravelling around us.

"My father owned Wildflower Hall, built on the site of Lord Kitchener's residence. It was a vast mansion, surrounded by pines. Beautiful. But it's all gone. Burnt to the ground. I refuse to go to Simla now. It's changed beyond recognition into a shabby mad-house. Frightful. All gone. Finished . . ."

She slumped, suddenly exhausted, and the twinkle went dark.

"India, the Land of Regrets," she mumbled, whiskery chin dropping onto her sunken chest. "Ruined. Ruined. Ruined . . ."

The old lady turned away, back bent almost double with the burden of bitter disappointment. She waved a hand weakly as though in dismissal, then withdrew through sallowed curtains into cloth moth-stippled darkness.

ψ

"*Didi*," Bindra continued. "Can you tell me where Mrs Mukherjee lives?"

The nun shrugged. "Which Mukherjee? It's a common name here."

Bindra could not answer.

"Well, what does her husband do?" the nun persisted.

Bindra knew nothing of the woman to whom she had entrusted her daughter. Mrs Mukherjee had spoken so nicely when she had come to the door. She had worn such a smart sari. Expensive. She had given biscuits to the children, handed milk powder to Bindra. She had talked a lot. She had made fine promises.

Bindra looked blankly at the stout woman in her strange blue dress with its matching lank cloth that hung around her thick, dark features.

"Mrs Mukherjee came to us nearly a year ago, asking for my daughter. My eldest, Jayashri," she began. "She told me good things. Jayashri would learn to read and write, and grow strong on good food. To be a maid is good work. Good training. I want that for my daughter. She is a good girl. She works hard. She is a kind and happy child . . ."

The nun's face had lost all spark of humour. She looked hard at Bindra. "Did this woman take other girls to work as maids?"

"I don't know," Bindra shrugged, listlessly. "But she offered more money if she could take my Jyothi too . . ."

A portentous alarm suddenly caused her heart to pound.

"Where's my Jayashri?" The violence in her chest was causing her to gasp for air. "Good food. Education. She promised!"

The Keralan nun looked grave. "You hill people are so trusting," she sighed, shaking her head, as though in tired despair. "You're as innocent as your own children. If you could but believe in Christ, He would welcome you with open arms into His Kingdom. 'Suffer them to come unto me,' He said . . ."

Bindra could make no sense of her. "My daughter," she interrupted. "Where is my daughter?"

The nun drew close and dropped her voice. Bindra could smell sour milk on her breath.

"I fear your little girl is now in Calcutta. Probably in Sonagachi district. Perhaps in Kalighat. These women come every year to search the Hills for healthy girls. And boys. Young girls. Pretty boys . . ."

The weight in Bindra's chest was crushing out the air.

"My sisters tell me there are almost 70,000 doing such work in Calcutta," the nun continued. "I've heard that 14,000 are brought in from Nepal alone, every year. Many are still children. How old is your Jayashri?"

Bindra did not want to believe that she was understanding the words through the distortion of their dense, Malayali accent.

"Jayashri has turned twelve. Perhaps soon thirteen . . ."

Again the nun shook her head. "I'm sorry," she said.

"*Ama*," Jyothi had taken hold of her arm. He was pointing towards the sky. "Look!"

Bindra's face turned up towards the blue. There were kites. Small paper kites, swooping and spinning.

She closed her eyes. "Dark Mother, what have I done?"

But the words were engulfed by the distant sound of her own voice, screaming.

ψ

A figure in flip-flops struggled up the steep hill path towards me. Beneath a plain shawl, I could make out the face of a handsome young woman. She had a feisty billy-goat on a string in one hand and a chuckling child astride her hip supported by the other.

I greeted her and asked, in Urdu, if she spoke English. She did not. "Ketunky?" I asked, as her son's eyes widened in horror at my strange white face and threatened to flood with frightened tears. The young woman nodded vigorously to my question and pointed back down the hillside up which she had climbed.

It all seemed strangely familiar. It was as though I had visited this place as a child. Perhaps it had been in that twilight region between wakefulness and sleep, my father's bedtime stories enlivening my eager imagination.

Was this not the path – stony and somewhat treacherous, wild forest to the left, British-built bungalows through the trees to my right – that I had seen in over twenty years of lucid dreams? Was this not the path down which I had vividly pictured my father being carried by two bearers on a wax-cloth and wicker *dhoolie* litter, his mother running behind shouting that they were trotting too fast and would drop him straight down the precipitous *khud*? Was this not the route along which I had imagined my father running to school, whilst scheming monkey hordes had bombarded him from above with a shower of fir cones, urine and worse?

A narrow track led me to the garden gate of a deserted bungalow. Monsoon and snow had stripped the red paint from the corrugated roof. Summer sun had blistered the window frames. Forest scrub had consumed the garden.

My heart was pounding, as though I were a young Pevensie finally ready to push his way to the back of the wardrobe.

I forced open the rusting metal and walked to the front steps of the verandah. The view that lay before me was exactly as it had been described over many years of childhood bedtimes.

I had found Ketunky.

And yet, never once had I imagined myself stepping alone onto this overgrown circular lawn, with its open views across deep valleys and dark mountains. This was a discovery Priya had made me vow to undertake with her, so we might together reveal the veracity of all those childhood stories on which I had been raised.

This was always going to be *our* adventure, to prove to both of us that for all the bright, breathless intimacy that was our own, we also shared a deeper, cultural connection.

I had planned to show Priya that it had been on this grass that my father had regularly had his hair cut by the dreaded *napi* barber, with shears so blunt their blades had not so much cut as plucked the hair from his scalp. I had intended to tell her that it had been around these borders that the family servants had placed little oil lamps every *Diwali*, their domestic Festival of Lights so enchanting my father as a child that the twinkling flames had continued to burn brightly in his memory for forty years.

I had wanted to tell her that it had been amongst these same flowerbeds that my father's pet dog had been mauled in the night by a leopard. He had found it before breakfast "without a face and with its head turned upside-down", a much-repeated phrase that had haunted my own upbringing, just as the memory of the gruesome discovery had haunted his.

I had anticipated making her grimace with the story that it had been from the verandah upon which I had expected us to sit together that my father's mother had once found a servant, his *dhoti* cloth raised high to expose thin legs covered in seeping sores. She had knelt before him to clean the wounds and apply antiseptic ointment. These benevolent treatments had been repeated for three days, but when his condition had not improved she had sent the man off to the doctor with a letter and a one-rupee note. Within the hour, an urgent summons had arrived from the surgery. The entire family and all staff were to attend the hospital directly. The servant had been riddled with aggressive syphilis.

I imagined that Priya walked beside me as I approached the house and rattled the doors. All were locked. It was as though my father's mother were still inside, clutching her *Flit*-gun for fear of spiders, humming wholesome hymns for comfort and hiding from the *loose-wallahs*. Such local rogues had regularly attempted to slip into the house stark naked and so greased with oil that, had they been disturbed in their burglarious transgression, no part of their anatomy could have been grasped in capture.

I shaded my eyes and peered through the small-paned windows, but all the rooms were derelict and dark. I looked into the sunless *bawarchi-khana* kitchen, where once my father's mother had kept an attentive eye on the staff, horrified by rumours that the servants used socks to strain soup, held mutton rissoles between their toes, and shaped fish patties in their armpits. I winced at the echoes of my grandfather's incensed splutters when a newly hired hand had attempted to impress by presenting a platter of mashed potato at dinner formed by his talented, though dirty, fingers into a menagerie of animals. The sight of a perky *aloo* elephant, smeary cobra and goggle-eyed monkey seated in a wallow of gravy beyond the braised pigeons and vegetable darioles had been too much for a seasoned *sahib* to tolerate. Angry voices had been raised, plates had been broken and at least one well-meaning domestic had been sent to bed in tears.

I chuckled aloud, as though I were telling Priya of the Christmas my father's mother had entrusted the icing of the cake to her Madrasi *bawarchi*. The cook had been proud of his spoken English and had emphatically stated that he needed no help whatsoever in its festive decoration. On the day, the cake had been carried into the dining room with great ceremony to be placed before the family and their guests, in the centre of the table. There had been a momentary silence before the entire company had burst into hysterics, to the bewilderment of the ever-obliging, but illiterate bearer. Inspired by a pretty, seasonal advertisement in the *Times of India*, he had pasted across the royal icing the confident cochineal legend: "Buy Littlewood's Pools".

I moved on to gaze into the patchwork shadows of the conservatory that had once been my father's playroom. Here, he had listened to the BBC's regular appointments with the plucky "Front Line Family" on the wireless, and first learned of rationing, blackouts, parachute-silk blouses and doodlebugs in a distant, unknown Britain. The door curtains of this room had been my father's theatre, his magic tricks and puppet shows deemed so amusing by an eager audience of servants that they had named him *joker-sah'b*. The geometric patterns of the Afghan rug that had once lain upon the playroom floor had been his giant game-board, across which my father's lead soldiers had boldly marched in tidy regimental lines, and his treasured Hornby train set had puffed its tireless circle.

I strolled to the side of the house and a row of derelict go-downs, the single-roomed huts in which the servants and their families had lived. There had been Burket, the well-liked *bawarchi* cook; Kondi Ram, the *khansamah* butler-bearer; Manu, the Pashtun *chowkidhar* watchman; Samir, the *mali* gardener; Harish, the *bhishti* water carrier; and Fakeru, the lowly *bhangi* sweeper, whose sole job it had been to deal with the "night soil" in his masters' "thunder box".

Despite the common practice of employing native nannies, my father's mother had adamantly refused to hire an *ayah* for her children. She had believed the rumour that opium was commonly secreted beneath such women's fingernails, on which their charges were expected to suckle at bedtime to secure for their nurse a night of unbroken slumber.

I peered into the windowless, chimneyless rooms of these go-downs, where my father had regularly sneaked to share meals with the servants' children. It had been on these dirt floors, wreathed in wood smoke and tempering spices, that he had developed his taste for all manner of native delights, which I in turn had inherited.

It had also been in these lowly quarters that, with no *ayah* in the household, the servants' wives had unofficially adopted the role of communal nanny. Upon discovering my father's insatiable appetite for sweetened condensed milk, these devoted and indulgent women had taken it in turns to proffer liberal spoons of the sticky, viscous pleasure until all his nascent teeth had been reduced to blackened matchsticks. The repetition of this chilling fact, with its unnerving image of carbonised incisors, had terrified me into an intimate relationship with my toothbrush from an early age, through which I had undoubtedly ingested an excess of baking soda and fluoride in my efforts to retain the pearly brightness of a youthful smile.

As I circled the house for a second time, my thoughts of tarnished teeth, toy trains and trusty staff became a constellation of curling pictures taken in these very hills, all now preserved in ancestral albums. Tea parties and church bazaars, Scout parades and Sunday School picnics. Solar topee-topped *sahibs* with their cricket bats, polo mallets and pig-spears. Broad-brim-crowned *mems* with their parasols, gossip and tennis-coach lovers. *Chota sahibs* and *missy babas* with their chatty pet mynahs and dog-collared monkeys. Smiling, confident, pale-faced generations, who had believed themselves omnipotent, now reduced to fading faces pressed between glassine interleaves.

Priya would have chided the mounting melancholy of my nostalgia.

"Come on! I'll race you to the church!" she would have laughed, delivering a pinch, then skipping ahead for me to catch her.

I left the overgrown garden of Ketunky and wandered up towards a tired tower. The great, ornamental iron gates of the entrance were so rusted that they could barely open. I breathed myself thin and squeezed through.

The building was near collapse.

"Untouched since the British left," a voice beside me apologised, "and only six Christians living here now." It was the vicar's wife, who indicated with an outstretched sweep of a thin, dark arm that I was welcome to explore at my leisure.

I wandered between rows of dusty Victorian pews, where once my father had sung "Jerusalem" and felt proud of King and Empire. I squinted through psychedelic shafts of glass-stained light at time-tainted paintings of Israelites and fishermen. I read every ornately inscribed brass plaque, in memory of Rutherfords and Driscolls, Eckersleys and Biggan-Smyths. All dead with disease and battle. Or too much tiger.

I stood at the altar rail and thought of my grandparents' enduring shame of having to attend a service in weekday dress, when rats had eaten all the fine bone buttons off their Sunday best. I turned to walk up the nave aisle, but it was scattered with hymn books and church records that dated back to the 1830s.

"Oh those scallywag monkeys!" the vicar's wife growled. "Old Nick's own terrors they are!" I helped her gather the torn pages, whilst trying to avoid the generous deposits the troublesome beasts had added to their mischief. "Come, I'll show you where these infernal imps climb in," she beckoned, directing me to ascend a precarious wooden staircase to a broad balcony.

High above the nave, she pointed to two broken panes in a neo-Gothic window, but I was not looking. Perched on the balcony was an ancient organ, of which I had heard my father speak. I ran my fingers around the corroded pump-wheel, at which he had once furiously toiled to earn a treasured Boy Scout badge, and looked about me in astonishment. The long-silenced instrument, its decomposing heart now rustling with rodents, was surrounded by towering piles of Victorian chests and Edwardian portmanteaux.

"Just old junk," my parochial guide explained, having followed my gaze, "left behind by Britishers from the old days – you know, before your Miss Kendal and our Mr Kapoor came here to film their *Shakespeare Wallah*."

Disturbed by nothing but indefinable paw prints and snake slithers, decades of dust lay in thick swathes. Between great latched boxes and crumbling leather trunks tumbled libraries of worm-mined books. Galleries of heavy-framed portraits of *pukka sahibs* and *mems*, faded sailor-suited sons and ringlet-draped daughters. I wondered who had stored them so safely there, intending to return. I tried to lift the cobwebbed lids, but all were firmly locked, their keys long lost.

I turned to ask more of the vicar's wife, but her slender arm now extended not a welcome, but a donations book and ready pen. I forced the joyless smile of a martyred saint and scrounged my pockets for token change. Grandmother's response would have been far more honest: the recitation of another of her rude rhymes about the clergy involving pigs and potato peelings, and a concluding "Amen!" in a pointed, plagal cadence.

As I pushed my way back through the gap in the gate, an old shop-board opposite caught my eye. It was Mullick's Haberdashery, a store that had also played its part in my bedtime stories. I crossed its well-swept threshold and entered a fusty interior, dimly lit and densely packed with old glass cabinets and shelves of faded boxes. I stood still and breathed in a giddy mix of naphthalene and camphor, stale incense and stewing tea.

A movement in the shadows suddenly made me start. An ancient man was silently rising from amongst rolls of woollen weaves that lay scattered on the cutting-table. He looked towards me with slow, deliberate eyes and wished me welcome in impeccable English. He enquired as to what might have brought me to this far-flung, foreign spot. I told him of Ketunky, of my father's love of Kasauli and my own childhood reveries. I told him of the surviving account book of my father's mother, which listed her weekly visits to this very counter, and of a paper bag of thimbles, printed with his name, that still languished in her sewing box.

"Manners?" he mumbled to himself, sifting through the dust of distant years. "The Captain Quartermaster's good wife?"

I was astounded.

"Ah, yes," he smiled. "An excellent customer, sir. Paid her bills and benefited every chilly toe in the district by teaching our women to knit socks with four fine needles. To this day, we still remember her very well and warmly."

ψ

"You have Hansen's Disease," the doctor announced. "Leprosy. The tuberculoid strain, to be precise." His voice was flat, devoid of expression. "It's bad luck for you, as the majority of us have a natural immunity to the germ. Do you understand? You people call it *Mahaa Rog*, don't you?" he yawned. "The Great Disease."

"Kali Ma," Bindra whispered, her mouth dry, her eyes sore from many hours of painful tears.

The nun had brought them to the ashram in a three-wheeled *vikram*. Bindra and her boys had never been in such a vehicle before. They had sometimes seen the little blue vans pass by in the town, hailed by pedestrians and crammed with as many as twelve passengers at a time. The nun had had to pay extra to the driver. No other passengers would join them. Bindra had cried the name of Jayashri all the way.

"You've had it for years, by the looks of you," the doctor droned, as he scribbled on a pad of paper.

"Not so long . . ." she muttered.

"Oh yes, many years," he insisted. "You know, you can carry the bacteria for two decades before the first signs show. You probably caught it from a member of your family. It's spread by droplets from the nose and mouth, or contact with open sores, and then can be activated by puberty or pregnancy. So who else do you know with leprosy?"

She heard his words, his strongly accented Nepali, but she did not understand.

"Your mother? Father? Are they lepers?" he asked with sudden impatience.

Bindra shook her head. Her mother had died beneath the feet of a wild bull-elephant. It had stamped out her life and that of Bindra's sister when they had been walking home one evening after working in the paddy. Bindra had only survived because the frenzied beast had knocked her into a ditch. She could still smell the *dana* in her nostrils, that sweet pungency that exudes from elephants when they are in rut and insane with lust. In the confusion of his grief, Bindra's father had abandoned her. Bindra had only been six years old. She had heard that her father had remarried, but no one could say where he had settled with his new family.

"Of course, it could be from your husband," the doctor muttered.

Bindra did not respond. It was evident that he did not really want to know.

"The disease settles in your lungs and nose," he continued, "then seeks out your cooler, peripheral nerves, you see. Makes them swell. Cuts off the blood supply. Kills them, if it's left too long." He glanced towards her feet. "You've been left too long," he stated blankly.

"Kali Ma," Bindra repeated under her breath.

"It often affects the skin first. Raised patches, with no feeling, no sweating?"

She nodded her head from side to side in tired affirmation.

"Loss of blood supply!" he announced. "Gradual loss of feeling in your fingers and toes? Weakness in the limbs? A rolling gait due to numbness in the outer soles? All indicates death of nerve endings."

She had no idea what the man was saying.

"And then you injure yourself. Starts with a small cut, a blister, a burn. But you don't feel it. You leave it unprotected. You don't keep it clean," he emphasised, as though in accusation. "It gets infected. Ulcers, gangrene, cartilage reabsorbs, fingers shorten, toes claw. Rot sets in." He waved vaguely in her direction with his pen. "Then we have a nasty mess."

He had still not looked up from his pad.

"Often affects the mucus membranes too, of course," he persisted with particular pleasure. "Starts with a snuffly cold, sinus pain. Then the face begins to collapse. Upper palate goes, nose caves in. Then we have to operate to open the airways, if there's time, to prevent suffocation. Most unpleasant for all concerned."

He was scribbling again.

"How're your eyes?" he glanced towards her, fleetingly. "The leprosy bacillus can attack the trigeminal nerve too. Lids don't blink, ducts don't produce tears. Leads to iritis, lesions. Horrible pain, apparently. Usually you go blind. And then there's the nephritis, inflammation of the kidneys. Very nasty. And if your husband has it, we'll have to check for testicular decay."

The doctor abruptly slapped his palms together, missing the intended mosquito, but knocking his pen and papers onto the floor. With irritation he repeatedly rang a shrill brass bell, which eventually summoned a lethargic orderly who restored them to his desk.

Bindra sat very still. She was confused and frightened.

The ashram unsettled her with its unpleasant, acidic smell and its collection of the brightest, whitest buildings she had ever seen. There were crosses and dead gods on every building, in wood and in paint. Even the doctor had one nailed to the whitewashed wall behind him, and another on his desk beneath a little plastic dome that had torn open its chest to expose a bleeding heart in which pulsated a little red light.

The Ancestors, or rather Fathers as they had turned out to be, were quite ordinary men as far as Bindra could tell. They all wore foreign clothes, although only one was a foreigner himself, with his pale skin, big nose, hairy face and clumsy body. He had smiled, he had been kind, but they shared no language. He had pointed her towards a low roof on long, wooden legs, where she and the boys had been given *daal-bhat* with bananas and water. Jyothi and Jiwan had swallowed handfuls of the thin lentil soup and steaming rice. Bindra had struggled to eat. The very thought of her eldest daughter had overwhelmed her body and mind with debilitating nausea.

The doctor returned to his aimless scribbling.

"You know there are plenty like you? India and Nepal have seventy per cent of all leprosy in the world," he grumbled. "You're just one of some two thousand new cases diagnosed every day – and that's just the official figure. Keeps the likes of me very busy!"

He spoke with pointed censure in his voice.

"Good news for you, however, is that, firstly, you don't have the lepromatous strain, which is far more contagious – and would probably kill you," he muttered as an aside. "Secondly, we can start you on M D T today – that's Multi Drug Therapy, the medicine to stop the bacillus. So let's hope we've caught it before the disease damages your face or kidneys."

Bindra had fixed on a word she had recognised. "You have *paraiharuko dabai*? You have the foreigners' medicine for me? To make me well?"

The doctor ignored her. "You'll have to take them every day for between six months and a couple of years. Most likely you'll be on some sort of medication for the rest of your life. My staff will have to keep an eye on you and check that you're responding, without any strong 'lepra reactions', which can sometimes be as damaging and unpleasant as the disease itself."

"You have the medicine that makes me well?" she repeated. She wanted to be sure that she had understood.

"The damage is done, of course," he said to the spiral-bound pad in his hands. "The nerves will never grow back and we'll probably have to amputate some of those worst infected digits. But for now just go to the dispensary . . ."

"Brother, I have no money," she interrupted, "but I can still work hard."

"No need for money. No work. This is all paid for," he announced. "See what we do for you people? In the old days, you'd just have been buried alive to redeem your sinful soul. You stay in the ward until there's improvement."

"And my boys?"

"Oh yes, I had a note that there were children," his eyes gazed blankly. "It's not hereditary – although the Americans would've once had you sterilised as a matter of course – but we'll check for infection there too. The Fathers can then put them into the school. They'll live in the boys' dormitory. We can't let them near you, in your state, now can we?"

But Bindra did not reply. She was losing herself in the whiteness of the walls beyond him.

With the roar of the bus as it pulled away for the slow journey back to Shimla, images of my father and his parents on these streets, in this church, these houses, schools and shops, crowded in. Kasauli had altered so little in half a century. And yet life had released my grandfather and uncle before their time, and had cruelly reduced my father's mother to an arthritic cripple.

As we wound our way down the steep, serpentine route, I looked for a hill path that cut up the *khud*-side. It marked the place where my grandparents' loyal staff had stood to weep their final farewells to three *sahibs*, a *memsahib* and *missy baba*. The inevitability of Indian Independence had finally driven my father's family to commence their long journey to Bombay, via Ambala and a pause in Pune, with a Cox & King's truck of trunks marked "Wanted on Voyage" for the Hot Weather leg, and "Cabin" for the Cold. Little could they have imagined the safe, dank domesticity of a red-brick semi named Westward Ho!, nor the interminable blandness of Bognor to which they were sailing with such urgency.

They had left Burket, Harish, Fakeru, Manu, Samir and Kondi Ram, their wives and children, wailing on the roadside for the loss of a family to whom they had been so long devoted, and with them the security of homes and salaries, and the stability of a united India. It had always haunted my father that he had abandoned those of his servants who were Muslim and their children with whom he had grown up, to walk towards the setting sun and cross the pen-stroke of a Boundary Commission cartographer. When settled beside Sussex shingle, he had never dared look at the images of burned-out trains and corpse-filled ditches that filled the papers and Picturedrome newsreels. He had always feared that he might recognise the charred face of a man who had once shined his shoes, the bloodied features of a woman who had palmed perfect chapati for his tiffin, or the terror-stricken eyes of a child with whom he had once shared his marbles and had considered a friend.

A well-dressed youth shuffled up beside me on the bus bench and introduced himself as, "nearly fully eighteen years in age and called by my goodly parents Ravikiran. Sir, I am Sunshine!"

He wanted me to buy his incense sticks, but I declined. I told him they made me sneeze.

"Ah yes," he nodded seriously, "I am seeing you are most gentle in your habits – both inly and outly."

Such was Ravikiran's confidence in this assessment that he linked his arm in mine and, as though by open invitation, cuddled into my shoulder. "So now tell me, Mister David," he grinned an eccentric arrangement of incisors, "tell me everything about the living of life in UK. Tell me how London is to see. And are you knowing Queen Elizabeth the Second?"

We chatted and laughed all the way to Shimla, whereupon Ravikiran gave me his address, requesting that I send him postcards of "Mrs Lady Di and Mr Big Ben".

I walked in slow motion through the ramshackle Lower Bazaar. I had discovered it to be the only way to cope with the altitude. I stopped to eat a bowl of noodles and plain vegetables, smiling at the thought that such a deed in the "native quarter" would have been forbidden to my father. For a moment, I allowed myself to imagine sharing this with Priya.

Fortified for the climb, I took a leisurely stroll up Jakhu Hill to give sweets to the schoolboys by the monkey temple. They were waiting for me. However, our pastille-sharing was brief, as an unseasonably cold wind rapidly began to animate the trees and pinch our noses. The boys postponed a competitive recitation of passages from Byron's *Childe Harold* for another day, and scurried off home.

I turned in early at the Municipal View. The night was especially dark. The moon and stars had been obliterated by dense clouds rolling across the mountains. It seemed I had been asleep mere minutes when I was woken by the furious screams of monkeys and the distant howling of wild dogs. I sat up in bed to switch on the light.

Nothing.

Shimla was without electricity. I was itching frightfully and in the pitch black could feel tender lumps on my arms and torso.

Suddenly the monkeys and dogs fell silent.

I held my breath.

The room ignited in an almighty flash and the mountains roared with violent thunder, as though the local goddess, with fierce weapons held aloft, were charging down Jakhu on her giant tiger, to wipe us all away.

I slipped from my bed to peer out of the window through the pounding rain. As lightning again split the skies asunder, I jumped backwards. My balcony was crowded with frightened langurs, huddled together, furrowing their bushy brows and cursing coarsely.

ॐ

"*Ama!*"

Bindra woke and turned her head. Jiwan was standing by her bedside.

She sat up.

"What are you doing?" she smiled in whispered reply, drawing him close. "They say you're not allowed in here." She pressed her nose to his hair and breathed him in.

"We don't want to stay in this place any more," he announced. "We don't like it!"

142

"But where's your *dajoo*?" she asked. "Where's Jyothi?"

"Outside, watching for the Fathers," he replied, indicating over his shoulder.

Bindra snuggled her nose against his cheek.

"But we can't leave yet," she sighed in apology. "The doctor says I must stay many more weeks, until my hands and feet are healed."

"But you are better, *Ama*!" the little boy protested. "You told me!"

Bindra held him close again. "Yes, the tablets make the sickness stop. But I must take the foreigners' medicine for a long time yet, the doctor said, to make sure it won't come back . . ."

"We cannot stay here any more, *Ama*!" Jiwan exploded.

She was surprised by the force of his insistence.

"We must return to the Hills in our dreams for just a little longer, my good, strong boy," she smiled, trying to diminish his disquiet. "You know, I too long to be back in our forests, collecting *iskus* and *tarul* together, with our snowy mountains in the sky above. I too miss the smell of *gundruk* drying in the sun, and *kinema* fermenting in its wrap of leaves. Remember the taste of sour *sinki* soup? And good, solid *churpi* as it melts inside your cheek? And how about the sweet song of *kalchura* on the roof at dawn, or the *jhankris'* drums at night . . .?"

"We cannot go back!" Jiwan announced with uncharacteristic intensity, unappeased by her reveries. "*Ama*, we can never go back to the Hills!"

"What do you mean?" she chuckled, unsettled by his unfamiliar passion. "You've not forgotten your sister, your little Jamini-*bhaini*, have you? She's still with the Christians at Ninth Mile. And we have yet to find your Jayashri-*didi*, to bring her safely home . . ."

"They will burn you again, *Ama*!" His eyes seemed to shine from the darkness of his silhouette. "I have seen it!"

Bindra faltered at the memory of the spiralling light. The flash of fire. The reek of flaming skin and hair.

"But, my son," she pressed, "we have nowhere else to go."

With effort, she lifted her legs from the bed and hugged him gently to her chest. Her hand touched his lower back. He flinched.

"Jiwan!" she gasped. "What's this?"

She ran her hand down his back. He flinched again. His shirt was stuck fast to his skin.

"You've been bleeding! Who's done this?" she cried aloud. "Who's hurt you?"

"We must leave this place, *Ama*," he began again, pressing his little body against her for comfort. "They make us kneel to the dead god on the wall. They say that we are *pa-paapi*," he stammered, "that we are wicked, because we give respect to *murti* images! They say that your sickness, *Ama*, proves you are *paapista paapini*! A cursed sinner!"

Bindra was astonished to hear such words in the mouth of her own child.

"But there is no sin, Jiwan!" she asserted. "Only lack of balance in our choices. Only lack of understanding . . ."

She heard herself say the words even as she searched for her own understanding, her head spinning in confusion, her heart pounding in fierce fury.

"We must leave this place, *Ama*!" Jiwan repeated, with no attempt to whisper. "This is not a good place to be."

"But, where else do we go?" she restated emphatically.

"*Ama*," he placed his hands gently on her cheeks and looked directly into her eyes, "we are going to Kashi!"

🔱

I rose early to discover that the plaster ceiling had split with the weight of the night's rainfall. My bed was soaking. Not only was I wet and cold, but also bearing a zodiac of bedbug bites.

As I left the hotel, I walked straight into the amorous Kamlesh. "My dear Mister David!" he cried in delight. "So here it is you are staying!"

I greeted his wife and her sister, prompting yet another round of uncontrollable twittering.

Kamlesh took my arm and turned me to one side. "Tonight I will be coming to the privacy of your own room, and will be showing all my true loving for you!"

Whilst Priya would have laughed until she cried, I responded by hurrying off to the railway office to book my passage out. It was time to say farewell to my father's family and start the great trek "up-country", across the Subcontinent, eastwards to Bengal, in search of the ghosts of my mother's.

It was time to follow in the footsteps of enigmatic Uncle Oscar.

It was late afternoon when I summoned my faithful, curly-haired Kashmiri to carry my rucksack to the station. I felt great regret at leaving Shimla and Kasauli, and did not relish having to return to the Plains so soon. As we made our way through the streets, we passed many of his barefooted colleagues. They were bent beneath huge crates, sacks, archaic typewriters and mattresses. One man had completely vanished beneath a double wardrobe, with only his muscular calves and thick ankles exposed as evidence of his presence.

At every step, "Heart Throb" smiled and laughed through his curly, black beard, and struggled bravely with his English. He revealed that he came from a village outside Srinagar, where he had had to leave his family, despite the fierce fighting between the pro-India and the pro-Pakistan factions in the city. He had been working for the season in Shimla in the hope that he might be able to afford to resume his teacher training back in Kashmir and one day support a wife.

I tipped Dilruba one hundred rupees at the train station for being entirely honest with me about the accommodation on my arrival and never asking for or complaining about money. He had only ever said, "You give me only as much as you believe I am deserving." At the sight of the rupee notes, he held my hand tightly and bent low, pouring gratitude. I took him by the shoulders and told him not to bow to me because he was my equal. He asked Allah to bless me with health and safety in my travels. As he walked away, waving and smiling, I knew he had taught me something in his calm dignity and sky-filled face, despite his days spent doubled over beneath other people's luggage and staring at his toes.

I sat on the platform, overwhelmed by Dilruba's reaction to a mere £1.50. I had to put aside the freshly fried, potato-packed *puri* and pickle I had just purchased from a station stall. For the first time since the Plains, I again felt overcome by nauseous guilt at my decadent origins, at the luxury of innumerable choices in my life which I had so mindlessly, irresponsibly squandered.

I wondered what Priya would have done.

The toy train soon tooted its readiness for departure, so I forced my rucksack into the crowded carriage, and settled into my seat. I tried to write in my journal, but my fellow passengers consistently peered over my shoulders. Some even boldly nudged away my arms for a better view of the page. These distractions, along with a blotchy biro, the jolt of the tracks and the discomfort of the wooden-slatted seats into which, due to a significant loss of weight, my newly acquired bum-bones dug, had turned my school-scolded script into a near unintelligible scrawl. This fact was brought sharply to my attention when two inquisitive passengers innocently enquired, "*Sah'b*, you Japanese?"

I eventually had to concede defeat. I put aside my book and instead leant my forehead against the glass. I considered the father I had found in these hills, where once he had been a stranger who had sporadically appeared at bedtime with tales of scorpions, rope tricks and tigers. I smiled at the child in his solar topee and Boy Scout garters, hiding behind his mother for fear that the servant girls might kiss his pink cheeks, or that the soldier guard who accompanied them to market might fall on his rifle and shoot them all dead.

Unexpectedly, as though some barrier had slipped away, I felt a connection to my father that I had never known before. We had lived so much of our lives apart, and yet here I realised that the nights he had sat at my childhood bedside had been extraordinarily influential on my perception of the world. I recognised, perhaps for the first time, the depth of his love and respect for me as his son. It was as though I was able to piece him together, as though the puzzle was now complete.

The dusk darkened with tempestuous cloud as my train continued to ease its slow descent towards Kalka. I watched as the mountains vanished beneath an impenetrable torrent of rain, their vast, suspended, indigo, island peaks momentarily silhouetted by furious bursts of brilliant topaz.

I was indeed forsaking Narnia.

Chapter Eleven

Dawn had not yet broken when Bindra, Jyothi and Jiwan walked quietly out of the Good Shepherd Ashram.

"Where are we going, *Ama*?" Jyothi asked.

"Kashi!" insisted Jiwan.

"My good, brave boys," Bindra smiled, "I don't know where we're going . . ."

"We're going to Kashi!" Jiwan announced again with untiring confidence.

"But, son, I don't know where Kashi is," she protested. "We speak of it in our tradition – but I don't know where to find it. Do we walk towards the rising sun, or towards its setting? Is it one day's travel, or one year's? You see? I don't even know where to begin."

Bindra knew the name of Kashi, the City of the Light of Liberation. She knew it from the tales of Skanda, the Spurt of Semen, divine patron of learning and hidden wisdom. She knew it as the place where Syambhuva and Shatarupa, the first named humans of this cycle of mankind, were said to have paid homage to the forces of their creation. She had described it to her children as the place at which an immeasurable laser beam, a *lingam* of light, once broke through the Earth's crust and illuminated the cosmos to reveal the underlying consciousness of which the entire universe is an expression. However, whilst Bindra knew of its mythical beginnings, just where the city of Kashi stood she could not say.

She paused at a junction in the dusty street. She looked from left to right, as though determining her bearings might help her decide what to do. She reached out her bandaged hands and drew her sons close.

148

Bindra felt utterly lost.

A distant glow to the east had begun to seep along the horizon as Bindra and her boys huddled together beside the empty road. In silence, they watched the darkness wane through a dust-sullied pallet of dirty mauves, pinks and oranges. They watched a solitary rickshaw appear from the gloom and pedal past lethargically, when Bindra's attention was caught by movement above the bamboo tops.

"Kali Ma," she whispered towards the raucous spirals of crows that were summoning the dawn. "I know!" she announced to her sons with sudden, new determination. "We'll go back to the Kali *mandir*! Someone there is sure to know where Kashi lies."

⑄

Upon arrival at Kalka, I disembarked the Shimla toy train and boarded the overnighter to Delhi. I pushed through jostling, good-natured crowds, grumpy porters and noisy vendors, only to discover that my pre-paid berth had not been reserved. According to the *gariwan* coachman, all sleeping compartments were fully booked and my name was absent from the list.

Until two o'clock in the morning, I was unceremoniously shoved from second-class bench, to filthy floor, to bustling corridor, until I could bear it no longer. I determined to search out the most senior conductor and implore him, on my knees if necessary, for a seat.

The portly, perspiring man became impatient and dismissive on my request, bellowing with unnecessary volume that the train was completely full, with "not one place for not one person!" However, it was hard to take his abrasive manner seriously when he had evidently spared no effort in his grooming to ensure his merkin-like ear tufts achieved their own perfection.

Indeed, the conductor may have noted my expression of genuine admiration for the coiffure of his hirsute auricles, as he promptly softened, conceding that he could possibly make one last check if I donated two hundred rupees to his outstretched fingers. I doubtfully, and somewhat begrudgingly, handed over the money, whereupon he swiftly turned and unlocked an empty compartment.

I did not wake until choking heat had parched my airways. I peered through tired eyes and grime-caked glass at the defecating throngs that lined the tracks. I forced open the window, inadvertently welcoming into the compartment the stench and dust that heralded my return to Delhi.

Upon arrival, I stepped from the train and plunged into the tumultuous tide. Before I had a chance to find my bearings, I was swept from the train door along the platform, up staircases, across footbridges, along corridors, through ticket halls and out into the street.

I stood in the road, trying to avoid being hurried into eternity by pollution-crazed drivers in their demon taxis and three-wheeled *tempos*. I turned to face the storming hordes pouring from the station entrance.

I was confused. At Shimla, I had been assured that I would arrive at New Delhi Station, from which I had originally departed, where my train to the east would be waiting for immediate connection. But, the station through which I had been so brusquely hurried was unrecognisable.

Rather than jeopardise my life by attempting to force passage back into the ticket hall against the single-minded, lemming sea of commuters, I pushed my way around to the side of the building. I blundered into an airless office, where a group of soldiers, sipping tea and holding hands, pointed me through an open door. Behind a paper-piled desk sat a fearsome little Fat Controller.

"Excuse me, sir," I began, with as much respectability as I could muster in my bedraggled state.

"No! No!" he shouted, waving me away.

I was not to be so easily dismissed. "Sir, could you please tell me . . ."

His eyes bulged to amphibian convexity. "Public complaints should be taken to the Grievances Cell for dealing with between 11pm and 6am!"

I attempted to explain the simplicity of my enquiry and that, until this moment, I had had no complaints whatsoever. However, the swollen veins on his temples were pounding and his short, plump fingers had become quite stiff, so I departed his presence before my polite request for assistance triggered an irreversible catalepsy.

ψ

The lamp-lit temple was bustling into life as Bindra and her boys approached along the tree-lined path. A small number of devotees were already circumambulating the shrine. The low hum of their repeated mantras gave Bindra comfort and restored her hope.

She led Jiwan and Jyothi to the steps, where they paused to brush the dust from their feet. "Once again, we bring nothing to Kali Ma," Bindra muttered to herself.

"*Ama*," Jyothi beamed, "I have uncooked rice and bananas!" He unrolled the little blanket he had tied across his shoulders and revealed its contents. Bindra was astonished.

"Where does this come from?" she asked, with concern.

"From the Fathers' kitchen!" Jyothi chuckled.

"However difficult things may be," his mother frowned, "we do not steal from others, neither in deed, word nor thought. There is wisdom in being able to accept that what we have is always enough. And lasting freedom when we surrender the desire to possess that which belongs to another – even when we think we are destitute."

Jyothi hung his head in theatrical shame.

She drew him close. "If we learn from our mistakes, then we are wise. If we choose not to, we are foolish. Choose the path of wisdom, my good, kind boy."

"But now we have *parsat* for Kali Ma!" he triumphantly announced, lifting his face to hers with a cheeky grin. And, proudly waving a banana, Jyothi scurried up the temple steps towards the sanctuary of the Dark Goddess.

ψ

Across the cavernous hall of the railway terminus, I caught sight of a faded sign that promised "Information". I clambered over tors of trunks and parcels, tiptoed between undulating hills of sleeping

151

bodies, slipped in generous splatterings of scarlet saliva – only to discover the desk was closed.

I asked various people for help, but no one was interested. Three times I was escorted by surly men to different platforms, only to endure importunate demands for money as a reward for their assistance. My patience had begun to wear very thin indeed.

A firm hand grasped my elbow and I turned to find an elegantly uniformed soldier beside me. He grinned and asked to see my ticket. He explained that I was at Old Delhi Station, not New Delhi as I had been told at Kalka. He walked with me to a platform, to my embarrassment moved people from a bench, and sat me down. Before I could thank him, he was gone.

It took a moment for me to realise that he still had my ticket.

I stood up in panic, but he had vanished back into the impenetrable crowds.

In my misery and anger, I could not think what action to brave next. The heat was rising fast and I was foolishly still dressed in my weather-wary hill station clothes. I wiped the spate of perspiration from my face and my handkerchief turned black. I took a gulp of warm bottled water and looked on enviously at the men and boys stripping at the standpipes with their communal bar of bright green soap.

A solitary woman approached me. Her tattered sari blouse exposed flaccid, nail-torn breasts, her face distorted by unimaginable terrors. She was evidently mentally ill. I smiled awkwardly at her, but she did not seem to see and wandered on. I watched her go, consumed with frustration at my incapacity ever to do anything more than spectate.

My eyes immediately caught those of an old man dressed in filthy rags. His nose had fallen into his face. His tongue lolled over toothless gums and distended lips. The remains of what had once been his hands rested heavily on the handle of a makeshift wooden trolley, on which he steered a crumpled woman. She had no fingers. No feet. No eyes.

I had never before seen human bodies reduced to such a pitiful condition. My father had told me of deformed beggars, of purposeful debilitations, of enforced amputations. But none of this was deliberate. This was disease. This was horrific.

The extraordinary vision cut a broad swathe through the crowds on the platform as it approached. People pushed and tumbled to get out of their path, snatching away luggage, plucking up parcels, clutching at children.

In a moment, they were before me. Two living, breathing corpses.

I bent to pick up my rucksack, to let them pass, then stopped. I stood up and looked back at the old man. In those deep, dark eyes was a dignity I did not recognise in myself. There was a peace. A stillness.

He smiled softly and I found myself transfixed by a depth of wisdom that starkly exposed the paucity of my own. In that moment, I felt that for my education, all my opportunities and indulgences, I knew nothing compared to this man who now struggled to stand before me.

I bent to place money into a tin the old woman held between her encrusted ankles. She suddenly came to life and offered *pranam* in my direction, as did he.

I returned a respectful bow to both of them.

"No, sir!" a voice cried out from amongst the crowd. "Stay back! They are lepers, sir! Lepers!"

The sun had illuminated the treetops when Bindra caught sight of a face she recognised. The woman slowly hobbled down the path, then slumped onto her usual spot at the base of the temple steps. She was panting.

"*Namaskar, didi!*" Bindra called out in greeting.

"*Namaskar, bahini!*" came the breathless reply.

Bindra shuffled along the step to sit closer, and offered one of Jyothi's purloined bananas. The woman touched her heart in thanks.

"*Didi,*" Bindra asked, "do you know of Kashi?"

The woman smiled and tipped her head to one side in affirmation.

"Then, *didi*," Bindra continued, "how many days' walk is it?"

The woman shook her head and laughed. "*Bahini*, Kashi is very far away! And it's not days, it's *many* weeks! Kashi is thousands of *kos* from here, far across the Plains!" She looked to Bindra's bound feet. "I'm sorry, *bahini*, but if you try to get there on those, you may never reach Kashi at all!"

Bindra nodded her head from side to side in resignation.

"*Tirthajatra?*" the woman asked. "You want to take a pilgrimage?"

Bindra shrugged. "It's my Jiwan, my little one . . ."

She turned to look up to the inner sanctum, where her youngest son now sat motionless before the image of Kali. Jyothi was rummaging through the palm thicket, in the hope of finding *iskus* and yet more bananas.

"Then you must go!" the old woman declared with conviction. "That child of yours has a path to follow. If it's to Kashi he says he must travel, then it's to Kashi that you must take him!"

Bindra's thoughts were suddenly very distant. "I have two daughters. Pretty girls, good girls," she said quietly. "I have left one up in the Hills. The other . . . I have lost." She looked up towards the circling crows. "How far is the city called Calcutta?"

"Also very far from here," the woman replied. "Far to the south, where the land meets the sea. It's a huge place, I'm told. Full of many great buildings, with cheap food, but too many people."

Again, Bindra nodded with resignation.

"Go to Kashi," the woman advised. "Trust Kali Ma and take your sons!"

"But, *didi*!" Bindra protested. "Look at me! Look at my boys! How can we walk so far?"

"Walk?" the woman laughed out loud. "Of course, you can't walk! You take the Pilgrim Bus! It leaves often in this season."

"But, *didi*!" Bindra repeated in protest, "I have no rupees to pay for a bus! And they would not take me!"

The woman laughed again. "*Bahini*, you think pilgrims, the dying and the widowed making their way to Kashi to welcome their end will care who or what you are? The Pilgrim Bus is very cheap. And as for money, sit here with me. It's a *puja* day. Many devotees of the Dark Mother will come, eager to give an offering to Kali Ma."

Bindra shook her head. "Forgive me, but I cannot beg, *didi!*" she gasped in dismay at the thought.

"Why? Are you better than our Lord of the Mountains, Shiva himself?" the old woman playfully retorted. "You know, one of His sacred names is Bhiksu, the beggar! Don't you know our mountain tradition teaches that one of the *ashramas*, one of the stages of life most suited to those of us living in these tumultuous days, is that of the *maagne* beggar? Even the *ranas* and *ranis* took time to wander in their lives, in search of truth. Yes, even our kings and queens found wisdom in living for a time from alms!"

Bindra chuckled. So often she had to learn the very lessons that she tried to teach her sons. It was time to put away her pride and learn new wisdom.

ψ

I had lost all hope of ever making my escape from Delhi before the heat boiled dry any residual moisture from my veins, when out of the milling crowd the grinning soldier unexpectedly reappeared.

He was clutching my ticket. He had only gone to confirm my departure time and platform.

I expressed my gratitude and relief with such immoderate emotion that he took my arm and ordered a eunuch to make room for me to sit down. I offered a distorted face of apology to the *hijra*, who pulled herself tall and, with a swish of henna-reddened locks and a flutter of kohl-caked lashes, went to join her "sisters". I had spotted a group of them earlier, working the platforms together. They had been vigorously slapping their palms in the faces of unsuspecting commuters. Unless handsomely paid, they had been noisily threatening to expose their unsightly, though undeniably unique, scars, while raining fearsome curses of misfortune upon the parsimonious.

The soldier hooked his little finger around mine for a moment and smiled broadly at the people surrounding us. I was evidently considered something of a catch.

A grinding, roaring hiss and the train pulled in. This was not one of the Reverend Awdry's bright and brassy "chuffas". Rather it was a monstrous tank, which seemed to have only recently returned from the infliction of some apocalyptic destruction. The crowds grabbed their cases, boxes, churns, water-pots and children, and ran to mount the carriage steps.

The soldier remained firmly by my side, insisting upon carrying the rucksack, until I had settled in my seat. He asked me to make a note of his address, with the plea that I visit his village one day to admire his ancestral fields, then wished a warm farewell and waited outside the window to wave me off.

I turned to smile and nod at the solemn young Sikh, the disease-scarred Hindu and the two expressionless businessmen with whom I shared the carriage.

Only the solemn young Sikh returned my genial gesture.

$$\psi$$

Bindra looked into the cloth she had laid before her. It was scattered with coins and handfuls of rice. She tutted to herself.

"*Ama-apa!*" she thought with unease. "If Mother and Father could see me reduced to this!"

"May you know freedom by never learning to scorn the dust," she recalled once being taught in blessing. "May you know freedom by never learning to yearn for gold."

Bindra bit her protruded tongue and shook her head.

Jiwan was still in the temple. He had been seated before the *murti* image of Kali for hours. This too troubled Bindra. Every day she wondered what had happened in the cave of the *ban jhankri*. Every day she wondered what would become of her serious little boy.

Jyothi had taken another banana from his cloth, when a scruffy monkey with a near-bald baby clinging to its back sidled towards him. He picked up a small stone and raised it above his head in threat, at which the monkey bared its teeth in resentment and scampered away.

"Son," Bindra said in a soft voice, "monkeys, bananas, stones and you are all expressions of the Mother. All forms of life are equal in their divinity. All are worthy of respect and compassion, whether man, monkey or mosquito. Would you throw a stone at me, if I were hungry?" she asked.

Jyothi was shocked. "Never, *Ama*!" he cried.

"Then in your life learn to call all men Mother before you hit them, curse them, steal from them," she advised. "Call all creatures Mother before you hurt them, hunt them, kill them." She drew him to her side. "My good, strong boy, choose now to gain nothing in your life by any thought, word or deed to the detriment of yourself or others. There is no more effective path to lasting peace. No greater gift of wisdom that, as your mother, I can give."

Jyothi wrinkled his nose and touched his head to hers.

"I'll try, *Ama*," he promised.

ॐ

To escape the commotion of the city was a relief, although the heat of the vast Gangetic plains of Uttar Pradesh proved unrelenting and unbearable. Despite the movement of the train, there was no breeze, no air at all. And my water supply was fast diminishing.

Across India's most densely populated state with a predominantly peasant population of over 166 million, sun-singed families threshed and winnowed sun-shrivelled crops in the sun-sodden fields. As the train slowed to change points and I fought off my urge to scratch the numerous swollen bites I had acquired in Shimla, I watched an old buffalo topple over in a field. I counted twenty-eight vultures shifting excitedly, stretching their wings and talons in eager preparation.

Eventually, from the awesome flatness of the Plains rose the tall spire of a roofless Anglican church, extensive time-tattered public buildings and dilapidated mansions. Nine and a half hours after leaving Delhi, we had arrived at Lucknow, once capital of the kingdom of Oude where, in the previous century, my Uncle Oscar and his Uncle Warwick had advanced their familial bond by shooting dead grylag geese and wild cattle.

By the time the train had heaved itself into the impressive, Mughal-style station, I was coated in a fine red dust, as was everything else in this Urdu-speaking city. I watched the cheerful mayhem of the crowded platforms from the safety of my open window, head flush with classroom memories of nawabs, sepoys and Enfield rifles. Beef fat, Residency and the haunting gore of a Cawnpore Dinner.

As the train pulled away from Lucknow, my compartment prepared itself for sleep. Upper bunks were unclipped and shoes removed, faces were washed and teeth rinsed. I watched entranced as the young Sikh removed his elegant *dastaar* turban, redressed his *kesh* uncut hair with his *kangha* comb, then rebound his head with clean, pressed cloth.

Three of my travelling companions had now retired to their beds. No such joy for me. The sombre businessman, who seemed bent upon hacking up his mucous membranes, had not yet arrived at his station and defiantly stayed seated on my bench seat, preventing me from lying down. My head was again splitting with the heat and my patience fast waning. When he left to use the toilet, the young Sikh indicated in energetic sign language that I should pull out my bed and quickly claim my stake before the miserable codger came back. This I did, only to have the said codger return to sit hard on my legs. To make his point, he then cleared goodness-knows-what from his throat, and spat copious quantities of it across my backpack.

Grumpily, I sat up again to stare out of the window, attempting to appease the tantrum threatening in my gut. Hazy through the film of dust clinging to the air like a mirage sea-mist, I watched a sultry dusk descend. The skies turned a livid opalescence as, across the paddy fields, sapphire kingfishers winged their way home. Sacred cows wandered nonchalantly towards bamboo thickets and coconut trees. Scrawny children ran behind belligerent buffalo, rallying them on with sticks and bleating cries. I watched as a family of ebon goats skipped across a well-worn path into their wicker-work pound, whilst their young keeper leant against a lonely tamarind and breathed songs into his wooden flute.

Grandmother would have loved this, I consoled myself. She would have said it was a Tagore poem come to life before us, the sunset *"hiding its last gold like a miser"*.

The train had now slowed to such a lethargic pace that I could see, seated in a clearing, an attentive village gathered around a white-haired elder who seemed to be unfolding the deeds of demon-defying deities. I was certain that he was still recounting the doings of long-dead heroes, even as the bruised sky darkened into night. As ibis, heron and egret left their muddy ponds. As peacocks hid themselves amongst the sugar cane and a crested serpent-eagle silently winged towards the gaping moon.

ψ

Bindra had slept for many hours, despite the clamour in the bus.

She leant forwards to relieve the pressure on her back and peered through heavy lids beyond the dust-encrusted window. Still too hot. Still too flat.

As every withered tree, bullock cart and low mud hut passed by, she repeated, "I have never been so far from home . . . I have never been so far from home . . ."

Bindra placed a gentle arm around her sleeping boys and let her eyes drift close, in search of glittering streams, dark forest and distant snows.

ψ

It was early morning when the Sikh unwrapped a parcel of *chat* snacks. He automatically handed me two small oranges, a savoury pastry of whole black peppers, and a condensed milk sweetmeat. I was touched by his spontaneous generosity and, although he could not understand a word, thanked him heartily. I recalled my father telling me that Sikhs were admired in his day for their practice of tolerance and respect for all. They were still known for welcoming any visitor to their *gurdwara* temples with the offer of shelter, food and a place to rest or stay.

My other travelling companions were not to be outdone. The remaining businessman gave me a fermented-lentil cake to be eaten with a spicy *achar* and a fresh, green chilli. The sullen, pox-marked Hindu handed me a banana, even though, as I indicated to him, I already had my own.

As I swallowed my last mouthful, the Sikh indicated to his bare wrist. I shook my head. I did not own a watch. He in turn shook his head, smiled and, for my benefit alone, announced, "Varanasi!"

Eighteen hours after leaving Delhi, I had reached my destination.

Bindra woke with a start. She sat up.

The bus had exploded into frantic life. Luggage was being lifted from racks, boxes from floors, babies into arms.

Jyothi was beginning to stir, but Jiwan was already wide awake.

"Look, *Ama*!" he announced with a look of triumph on his face. "We are in Kashi!"

Chapter Twelve

The train station at Varanasi was teeming. All around me, pilgrims in their multitudes were bursting from the confines of innumerable railway carriages, spilling out beneath the beehive-shaped, Nagar temple towers of the terminus's theatrical exterior.

I was accompanied to the taxi stand by the usual rabble of rickshaw-*wallahs*, hotel touts-cum-pimps, cannabis sellers and beggars. It was no little relief to be able to finally slam the door of the old Ambassador and ignore the chorus of keenly knocking knuckles beyond the glass.

My driver, Vipin, was impressed by my efforts at "kitchen" Urdu and seemed to warm to me immediately. There was enough in common with his Hindi that we could maintain some semblance of an intelligible exchange. I had picked out a cheap hotel, down by the river, which promised a courtyard garden. Vipin, however, did not approve.

"No, no, Mister-sir!" he cried, suddenly revealing his English. "Most nasty place! Dirty, smoky hippies. No, no! Not nice for nice Mister-sir like you!"

Memories of dishonest drivers in Udaipur blew noisy horns in warning, but I dismissed them. I sensed that Vipin was different. When he suggested that he could take me to a private, friendly house near *Asi Ghat*, where rooms were clean and food was "most goodly tasty", I happily agreed. When he drew up at the end of a dark lane, too narrow for cars, and pointed me towards an old and well-kept building facing the river, my heart sang.

An elderly woman and a plump child were undertaking morning *puja* at the family shrine to Hanuman, as I climbed the steep front

161

steps. The woman bowed to me and graciously pointed towards the front door. I removed my shoes and entered.

The interior of the house was beautiful, every pillar finely carved, its decorated floors well polished. Windows were shaded by carved latticework and, at every turn, domestic shrines bore exquisite images of gods and consorts lovingly disfigured by generations of devotion.

A pot-bellied man dressed in pristine *kurta pajama* offered a courteous welcome, and a clean and airy room. It was perfect. When he led me out to my own balcony overlooking the river, I laughed with joyful astonishment. I had seen this view in my dreams. To my left, the vast, sweeping curve of the Ganges with its supernal bluff of temples, mosques and palaces. To my right, a misty Maharaja's citadel, boat-moored mudflats and an infinite wilderness beyond.

It was hard to believe that I now stood in Varanasi, one of the world's oldest inhabited cities. The Islamic and British rulers of India had called it Benares. Others still called it Anandavana, the Forest of Bliss. But most favoured of all remained its ancient epithet – the City of the Light of Liberation.

Kashi.

ψ

Jyothi and Jiwan clung to their mother as Bindra struggled to keep up with the pilgrim horde. Their companions had almost broken into a trot as they neared the banks of Ganga Ma, despite limps, senility and debilities.

"Kashi! Kashi!" Jiwan chuckled in triumph, beaming at every passer-by.

Jyothi was silent. He was intimidated by the crush of bodies and buildings. He had never seen so many people before.

"Stay close!" Bindra kept calling. "Stay close to me!" as on and on they hurried. Although to what, she could not say.

ψ

Having washed and changed my clothes after far too many days, I commenced my long-awaited initiatory stroll along the *ghats*, walking across great sweeps of steps and platforms that slipped beneath the surface of India's most sacred river.

I found the sun much higher and hotter than I had anticipated. With my father's warnings about sunstroke, my Grandmother's tales of aunts wasting to hollow shells and cousins going mad in the noonday blaze, I moved away from the water's edge. I made for the shadowed labyrinth of the old city and found myself entering another world.

The *pucca mahal*, the ancient heart of this City of Shiva, boasted one of the highest population densities on the planet. So tightly packed were the decaying, multi-balconied buildings at the centre of the antique metropolis, that I discovered there were no roads. There was also no sun, for centuries of rebuilding had plunged some of these dark thoroughfares a full six feet below the level of the houses. Many were too narrow to accommodate the meeting of even two pairs of broad shoulders, and yet I found many lanes to also be a *gali*, or market.

The mildly nauseating tang of rancid milk, the rows of terracotta bowls balanced on every available step and sill, announced the curd market. The shady routes blocked by herds of lethargic, foraging cows heralded the vegetable district, whilst the dominating pungency of jasmine indicated that a flower market was near. The turn of a crumbling corner and the stupefying explosion of butterfly brilliance that dazzled the mind and stole the breath, even amidst the deep shadows of the urban chasm in which it lay, declared that I had stumbled upon the quarter of the city's renowned sari sellers.

It seemed that at every carefully negotiated step, yet another bell-heralded, incense-clouded temple arose. The air rang with chanted tributes to the tiger-riding Durga. The sounding of conch shells to the supreme yogi, Shiva. The beating of drums for the all-consuming Kali. The desperate propitiations of the goddess of smallpox, Shitala, bringer of fevers. And everywhere I rested my ever-widening eyes, *lingams* ancient and new, deep within inner sanctums and suspended around dark throats.

All day I drifted, entranced. Not until dusk did I realise that I had eaten nothing and that the sun had gone.

I was making my way back to the boarding house when I came across a group of shaven-headed widows dressed in their emblematic thin, white saris. They had gathered along the water's edge to light *akash deep*. I watched as they suspended their sky-lanterns on bamboo poles and muttered mantras to the waning day in hope that they might guide their departed husbands across the "river of rebirth".

I lingered until all had finished their *puja* and had wandered back to the charity houses in which they awaited the lighting of their own pyres, before I approached the cluster of suspended lights. I looked to the mist of insects that billowed in the guttering glow of the *akash deep*, and placed my hand from heart to bamboo pole.

"For you, Priya," I whispered.

And, for a single moment, dared to believe that she might hear.

⚶

Bindra had lost sight of the chattering crowds with whom they had shared their gruelling bus journey from distant Kakariguri. Every few, stumbling steps she looked down to ensure that both her sons were still beside her.

The streets here had grown so narrow and twisting that she had found herself disorientated. And all the time, Jyothi's plaintive cry, "Where are we going, *Ama*? Where are we going?"

Bindra had seen no Hill faces since her arrival. There would be no one here to understand her tongue. No one to understand her entreaties for assistance or advice.

"Stay close!" was all that she could say. "Stay close to me!"

Pressing on through the warren of dark and bustling passage-ways, the narrow strip of distant blue above suddenly split asunder the fortress of blackening walls. All at once, Bindra's eyes seemed to melt in the shimmering iridescence of mighty Ganga Ma. The choked lanes burst open onto vast, stepped *ghats*, pouring their chaos down stairs and platforms that tumbled into the waters, their foot-smoothed stones crowded with milling devotees and silent dead.

Stiff with rigor mortis and wrapped in cloth, a ceaseless stream of corpses was coursing through the congested lanes, around which Bindra was negotiating her sons. Bodies borne at unnerving speed on the shoulders of friends and family. Bodies balanced across planks and bicycles. And yet there were no tears, no wailing, for such sentimentality is only thought to prevent the knot of individual existence from unravelling back into the universe of which it is but one expression.

Such vibrant life and visible death colliding at the very brink of solid heaving earth and shining flowing water, afforded this place an extraordinary quality. The air was heavy with ash, every breath intoxicating with the sickly smeech of sandal, ghee-drenched wood, hair, flesh and bone. And yet, here there was a curious lucidity, an inexplicable clarity, in light, in act, in every thought.

"You see, *Ama*!" Jiwan announced, with a look of wide-eyed elation. "In this place, we are neither here nor there. Neither in this world nor the next!"

Bindra looked down at his face, shining brightly in the reflection of the water. She could find no words with which to respond.

She could only look down at him. Shining brightly.

ψ

I woke long before dawn and scurried down to the muddy banks of the river. I quickly found the low, narrow boat with its friendly oarsman whom I had met the previous evening. Sudeep's family had been boatmen on the Ganges for generations. With his dashing smile, his gentle nature and insistence that I pay him only what I considered his service worth, I had confidently hired him.

Sunrise on the sweeping, four-mile stretch of Varanasi's central riverfront was utterly astonishing. The city's palaces and pillared pavilions, mansions and temples, domes and cupolas, minarets and *shikharas* rose as an immense, tiered precipice from the eighty or so *ghats*. Never before had I been so acutely aware of India as the world's last remaining great, ancient civilisation. Whilst the Egyptians, Phoenicians, Greeks and Mayans had risen and fallen, India's millennia-old customs and practices survived intact. I had already found myself utterly enchanted by its wondrous, and at times terrible, beauty.

I watched in captivated astonishment as innumerable flower-bearing pilgrims gathered at the water's edge, intensely employed in their oblatory ablutions. The air pulsated with mantras of consecration and liberation, mixed with the pounding of cloth against *dhobis*' stones, the low of buffalo and the percussive pop of skulls bursting open in the flames.

Naked *sadhus* gathered for communal *sadhana*. Masseurs and barbers plied their trades beneath broad bamboo parasols. Zealous young cricketers hit driftwood "balls" with driftwood "bats" and muscular wrestlers practised their ancient *garadi* tradition, for which the city was so famous. Whilst, in the waters, pilgrims and locals of every age anointed then submerged themselves amidst all the debris of urban life, inestimable *pujas* and the recently departed.

Not until breakfast, back at the lodging house, did I see the newspaper. The day before, the crowded passenger train on which I had been travelling had tumbled to its terrible end. The neglected, Raj-built bridge that lay beyond Varanasi had given its last, tired ruckle and had collapsed into the river below.

As I scanned the sobering statistics and the front-page gore, I found myself smudging the newsprint at the thought of the smiling Sikh, the kindly businessman and the pox-marked Hindu, who had so generously and unknowingly shared with me their last breakfast.

ॐ

The previous night, Bindra had led her boys well away from the oppressive crowds, to the quiet of a broad stretch of worn stone near *Lalita Ghat*. They had boiled rice and the last of their daal on a little fire built from the swathes of refuse that cluttered modern Kashi's sacred heart.

Bindra woke at dawn. She placed her hand in blessing on the sleeping heads of her two sons and lay still to watch fishermen, pilgrims and tourists moving slowly on the dark waters.

As the sun began to rise above the distant trees on the far shore, she made her way down to the river's edge to wash. No sooner had she entered the shallows than she caught her breath. She had heard Nepali. She scanned the *ghat*, but could see no one but a solitary, naked *sadhu* busy with his morning *puja* to Ganga Ma.

Again she heard a whisper of the cheery, chatty tones she knew so well. She looked up. High above the great river wall stood a wooden temple, shaded by a single spreading tree.

Bindra hurried back to the boys. They had only just begun to stir.

"*Au! Au! Yaha hamro sathiharu cha!*" she called with excitement, "Come on! We have friends here!"

Together, they clambered a steep flight of stone steps until they reached the temple compound.

"*Namaskar dajoo!*" Bindra bowed in eager *pranam* to an elderly priest, who was sitting on the ground with two young novices. The man bowed in courteous return, indicating with a nod of his head that they were welcome to enter.

"*Ke ramro!*" Bindra declared, "How beautiful!" as she surveyed the highly decorated building that rose before them. She eagerly led her sons to the entrance steps of the temple, but the doors were closed. Bindra bowed in respect and touched the base of an ithyphallic image of Shiva by her side.

"*Ama?*" Jyothi was staring with curiosity at the stone *murti*. "Why is Lord Shiva's *laro* sticking up?"

Bindra smiled. "Firstly, it tells us that this temple is of our Hill tradition." Jyothi rocked his head from side to side in recognition. "But most importantly, his *thankieko laro* upright phallus indicates the unchanging stability of universal consciousness. The true power of continuous creation, ever-ready to express itself."

Jyothi looked bemused.

"You'll learn to understand in time," Bindra assured him.

Jiwan was already circumambulating the temple, so Bindra and Jyothi followed in their own clockwise route. When they caught up with Jiwan, he was staring at a graphic carving of explicit, erotic play.

"What are they doing, *Ama?*" he innocently asked.

"Exploring the limitless truth within themselves," she smiled, her head sparkling with sweet, bright memories. "And the truth in us is the truth of the universe . . ."

A noise behind them caused Bindra to turn. It was the priest. He touched his heart and bowed towards her.

"Sister, you have wisdom," he said with quiet respect.

Over his many years in Kashi, the old priest had encountered all manner of disease, despair and death. It had taught him to approach all life without fear or judgement. "Come and sit with me," he offered in gentle invitation. "My students will prepare *haajri*. Share it with us."

Bindra grinned in delight. He had used a colloquial word for the morning meal only heard in the Hills from which they had come.

ψ

The air was sweet with buttery ghee and fragrant sandalwood. The smoke from the pyre drifted across the Ganges and around family members overseeing the incineration of their loved one. A middle-aged man approached the flames with a heavy stick. With a single blow, he struck the charcoaled head, splitting it in two.

"That is the eldest son," a voice said to me in melodious English, "releasing the soul of his father."

I turned to face a small, plump man, with a betel-nut-stained smile.

"It equally ensures the *Aghori Babas* don't steal the skull as a begging bowl!" he grimaced theatrically. "There are many *tantrikas* around *Manikarnika Ghat*," he explained, indicating for me to survey the soot-blackened buildings surrounding us. "They do *sadhana*, their active practice, on the cremation ground after dark."

Ramesh was one of the "untouchable", yet wealthy, *dom* caste, who oversaw every aspect of the funerary rites. He was eager to share with me the details of his work, for a hefty fee. I thanked him, but expressed my preference for undisturbed observance.

"I have my own farewells to give," I offered in discreet explanation, unwilling to engage.

He nodded in apparent understanding, yet still he lingered by my side.

"You see my brothers sieving the smouldering ashes?" I did. "They are searching for jewellery or gold-based dentistry. Such finds will pay for the ritual incineration of the destitute."

I was impressed, but still unwilling to hand over cash for this information. He was becoming agitated.

"I have been in a *flim*!" he announced, his forehead trenching in frustration at my unwillingness to hire him as a guide. "French foreigners made a *flim* about the *Dom*!" He seemed aggravated at my indifference to his celebrity. "I have been in a *flim*!" he shouted at me. "A movie *flim*!"

The overseers of the funeral pyre were staring up at us through the drifting smoke. I bade him farewell, ignoring his vehemently outstretched palm, and made my way towards a quiet length of riverfront, to sit alone at the water's edge.

It was the permanent presence of death, exposed here as an inevitable, even essential reality of life, that had brought me to Varanasi. I had felt compelled to confront this certain end, that I might better comprehend the loss of those lives that had been integral to my own.

And yet, I had feared to face this perpetual truth, as though the grief from which I had attempted to escape might here consume my sanity. I had anticipated that the flaming pyres might too candidly expose the pointlessness of every thought and action, lay bare the futility of being. I had even feared that fires fed by smouldering flesh might finally scorch my own precarious hold on life.

Instead, I had witnessed an acquiescence to man's inexorable end that had brought me unexpected comfort. In facing the inborn dread of death, I had found nothing left to fear. To my surprise, on these river *ghats* it had not been despair that I had revealed, but rather an affirmation that the vast ocean of life demanded more than just the dipping of a trepidatious toe. Its infinite depths were to be plunged into, its inestimable fathoms sounded, its boundless waters drunk.

The sudden ringing of a temple bell drew my gaze. A spreading tree and the sight of a carved wooden temple with a pagoda-style roof tempted me to seek out the steep steps that would lead me to its shade.

As I sheltered my eyes from the sun's reflection on the river wall, a little boy peered over its top.

We smiled at one another. And waved.

$$\psi$$

"Do you know of the *Aghori*?" the priest asked in his eastern, Hill Nepali.

Jiwan did not.

"They're an *achara* sect of wandering *sadhus*, who live an extreme tantric path. They seem to make great efforts to upset the *Bahun*, the orthodox Brahmin priests!" he chortled.

Jyothi had joined the young acolytes in their kitchen, to watch them scrub the cooking pots, in the hope of leftovers. Jiwan sat with his mother, captivated by their kind host's talk.

"How do they upset the *Bahun*?" he asked with excited curiosity.

"Well," the priest began, "as part of their chosen path to liberation, the *Aghori Babas* mindfully break all taboos. This they do in order to examine their attachment to the mistaken belief in a 'self' that is separate from all the same forces of creation and dissolution of which our limitless, multi-dimensional universe is an expression. You understand?"

Jiwan shook his head in puzzlement.

"Well, the *Aghoris* fearlessly provoke rejection and contempt in others, simply to test their own detachment from the notion of duality . . ." the priest attempted.

Jiwan sniffed his nose and pursed his lips.

"When I say duality, I mean all those judgements we make on the world and ourselves, according to our particular culture," the priest persevered, in careful elaboration. "Like the idea of what is good and bad, or beautiful and ugly. The idea of what is spiritual and sensual, or clean and unclean. The idea of what is divine and mundane, or sacred and profane. You see? All those divisive limitations with which a society obsessively defines itself – and yet which are only determined according to its particular habits and sensibilities at any one point in its history."

Jiwan rocked his head tentatively.

"The problem is," the priest persisted, "that in dividing up every aspect of experience into 'acceptable' and 'unacceptable', 'right' and 'wrong', we lose all sight of the underlying, unifying truth – and thereby lose all sense of who and what we really are."

Bindra smiled broadly. To see her son attentive to the teachings of their mountain tradition afforded her great comfort. She could almost believe they were home.

"So what do the *Aghori Babas* do to test themselves?" Jiwan pressed.

"Oh, well, they wear no clothes, of course," the priest continued selectively, chuckling again at the thought of the extent of social defiance he had witnessed amongst these ash-caked *sadhus*, shouting foul abuse at passers-by and sexually stimulating themselves in public. "They also carry a skull – preferably that of a conservative *Bahun* – which they use as a food bowl and for collecting alms," he added.

Jiwan's eyes were wide.

At that moment, a group of excited, travel-worn Nepali pilgrims pressed up against the gate and rang the heavy temple bell to announce their readiness for *puja*. The priest beckoned them in, then turned back to Jiwan.

"You know, the *Aghoris* practise their *sadhana* below us, here, on the burning *ghats*. They have open *lingam* shrines dedicated to Shiva in his wrathful form – Shiva as Kaala Bhairava, whom we Nepalis call Bhairon."

As Jiwan ran to have a look, the priest dropped his voice and turned to Bindra.

"However, *bahini*," he almost whispered, "the reason I mention all this is that a well-known *Aghori Baba* has a clinic here. He's a good man. He offers free medicine to those with . . . your trouble. One of my boys will take you to him tomorrow. I can promise he will help you."

Bindra's heart swelled with inexpressible relief. She stretched out her bound hands to touch the kind priest's feet, then looked to share the news with her boys.

Jyothi was still collecting leftovers in the temple kitchen, from which he intended to assemble their evening meal.

Jiwan was peering over the top of the river wall to scan the *ghats*, in search of naked *sadhus* and fierce gods.

Down below a foreigner stood squinting.

Jiwan smiled at his strange, pink face. And waved.

ψ

By the time I had reached the gate of the little wooden temple, I found it clogged with pilgrims. I peered over their dark heads for a moment, but felt uneasy at my intrusion. I decided to return another day, so turned away and wandered into the comparative coolness of the bustling *pucca mahal*.

It was not until late afternoon that I returned to the river *ghats*, where prayerful pilgrims were still dipping in the dark waters. Washermen *dhobis* were still beating iridescent cloth on glistening stone, whilst bony buffalo and their keepers wallowed in the scum-topped shallows. Priests were still intoning Sanskrit *slokas* beneath bamboo parasols, whilst the continuous pyres billowed grey phantoms of cremation ash across us all.

As the stifling heat promised to ease, misshapen shadows began to emerge from alleyways and stairwells to sit against the river walls. The destitute and disabled, the diseased and disfigured. I felt unable to ignore them. I had clean sheets and a generous, home-cooked feast waiting for me at the far reach of *Asi Ghat*. This extraordinary city, suspended as it was between sky and earth, life and death, now forced me to dispel all reserve and caution. I determined to speak to as many of these wraith-like figures as I could on my slow journey back to the indulgent comforts of my guesthouse. Despite the deficiency of shared language, I resolved to learn something of their lives and sat with every one of them.

I met men who had turned to the wandering life of a *sadhu* due to elephantiasis of the scrotum, their taut and shiny, balloon-like swellings exposed to me beneath grimy *longis*. I met expressionless children with dead eyes, riddled with ringworm, their stomachs distended. Congenitally crippled bodies pulled on simple, wheeled boards by younger siblings. Blind women who rocked and nodded to their own eerie, nasal laments. Boy prostitutes with henna-dressed hair, who offered to drop to their knees and "sing" for me in the ruins of an abandoned palace, in exchange for a few coins.

And then a little woman with two malnourished boys, sitting on a ragged shawl, below the wooden temple. Her wounds drew swarms of black flies and sniffing, licking pye-dogs in their packs. Leprosy. She looked away as I crouched to speak to her. She seemed ashamed to look me in the face. Her state was appalling, the stench foul. As she understood that I was no threat to her sons, her eyes began to brighten. It was evident that she needed simple nursing care. However, as darkness fell and the small crowd that had gathered began to intimidate her children, a little money for good food and medicines was all that I could offer. She protested. So I left it with her smiling, waving sons.

The *diya* lamps were already lit when I eventually reached the guesthouse, the air already scented with *dhup* incense. I had missed the evening *puja*.

My hosts seemed relieved to see me home, and were quick to assert that an unofficial curfew for outsiders was advised. It was common for visitors, whether foreign tourist or domestic pilgrim, to become lost in the maze of the *pucca mahal*, they explained. Indeed, some who ventured out after dark, they wished to impress on me, were never seen again.

I tried to clear my head as I sat alone for dinner, taking care to savour every mouthful. I tried to clear my head as I made my way to bed, relishing each soft pillow and clean sheet.

I tried to clear my head all night long, struggling with myself to find one moment that felt like sleep.

✿

Bindra had a bed again.

White washed walls, scrubbed floors, medicine. And not one dead god hanging above their heads.

They had either *daal-bhat* lentils and rice, or *tarkari-roti* vegetables and flatbreads, with good *dahi* curd, to ease their hunger, and sweet *chiya* tea to start the day. Jiwan and Jyothi were even permitted to sleep together on a cotton-stuffed bedroll, on the floor beside her. And no one beat them.

The Nepali priest encouraged the boys to visit the temple as often as they pleased. When Jiwan asked to be taught to read and write, he happily accepted such an enthusiastic pupil. Some days Jyothi would return from helping the novices in their chores with surplus food that had been donated in alms. It was thus that Bindra tasted mango, cucumber and okra for the first time in her life.

The smiling woman doctor told Bindra her wounds were in a poor condition. They would have to cut off fingers and toes to save her limbs from spreading infection.

Bindra did not mind.

The doctor had given her a large pack of silver-wrapped medicines for her to keep. And as she had talked, the kindly doctor had looked her in the eyes. Not once had she scribbled on her pad of paper.

✿

It was with great regret that I had to take my leave of Varanasi.

At midnight, I took a taxi to the railway station. It was time, before my limited funds expired, to continue my journey eastwards to the jungle-clad foothills of Uncle Oscar's Kanchenjunga, which lay some twelve hours away.

I woke as the train rattled through the Hindi-speaking state of Bihar, infamous as one of the most corrupt and lawless in all of India. Across the barren fields, small villages of grass huts crouched desiccating in the sun. I wiped the dust from my eyes and peered down into the dry Gandak River, where an army of women and children were busy breaking stones.

The bare living that could be scratched from rice-growing offered little sustenance to Bihar's hungry population of eighty-four million. Many had simply turned to the more profitable professions of banditry and smuggling. I had already noticed that Bihar was frequently reported in the Indian newspapers for unceasing atrocities. For its notoriously undisciplined police and the systematic blinding of prisoners. For bride burnings and torture.

How incongruous this all seemed when it had been from Bihar's city of Patna that the great king Ashoka had once ruled his peaceful and prosperous kingdom, and at Pawapuri that Mahavira, founder of the principal tenets of Jainism, had attained *Nirvana*. How incongruous, when it had been at Bihar's Bodhgaya that a prince named Siddhartha had once sat beneath a *Bo* tree and found the "enlightenment" of Buddhahood.

At Baruni Junction, two men joined my compartment. Neither was willing to acknowledge me. I turned my attention, instead, to the platform, which was crowded with fried-peanut sellers offering their wares mixed with spices, chopped onion, green chilli and slices of lemon, served in paper cones made from gaudy magazine pages. There were vendors of salted cucumbers, juicy coconut slices, oranges, cashew biscuits and chewing tobacco. There were makers of omelettes, *pakoras*, *puchkas* and *paan*, whose younger siblings persistently flicked the air with water in a vain attempt to keep down dust and drive away flies.

Inside the train, *chai* and *kaufi* sellers scurried along the carriage corridors, each trying to out-cry their competitors. Fleshless boys with grass brushes vigorously swept the compartment floors in the hope of a few rupees, sending dirt and dead bugs billowing into the air, and robust cockroaches scurrying into corners.

My water supply was largely depleted and I had counted upon buying more at the station. However, out here, in this most desolate region which foreigners purposely avoided, amongst all these hawkers with such a variety of fare, there was not one vendor of bottled water. I was desperate.

Suddenly, a mendicant gang forced decaying limbs between the bars of my open window, the foul, chaotic stench of putrid flesh awakening in me an instinctive, animal alarm.

Leprosy!

With indescribable horror at the suppurating stumps thrust towards my face, I looked into the beseeching eyes that stared back at me. Defying all reason, I wanted to reach out and put my arms around them.

Instead, I fumbled to drop pathetically few coins into the tins that hung from scabby wrists. When I handed out the last of my bananas, my companions reprimanded me and shooed them all away.

As the train moved off, one of my fellow travellers donated his soap and signed for me to go and clean myself immediately. When I returned, I discovered the other man had not only removed his shoes to sit in my window seat, but was washing his own hands and face in the last two inches of my only drinking water.

Hair stiffened into sedge by scalding dust, mouth parched and lips cracked into a drought-crazed crust, I slumped into a corner. Despite the intensifying stench of stale sweat and stinking socks in the compartment, which seemed to cause the very air to curdle, I deepened my breath in an effort to exhale the memory of leprous wounds and extinguish the pleading eyes that still stared within my pounding head.

I looked down at my own firm, fully fingered hands to find that I was shivering with shock.

$$\Psi$$

Bindra woke. She looked at the dim glow of the early dawn reflecting on the ceiling and smiled. She felt well today. Even her back was more comfortable to lie upon. She turned to peer at her boys, to mouth a blessing upon them for the new day ahead.

Only Jyothi lay sleeping on the bedroll.

Bindra sat up and awkwardly swung her legs over the edge of the bed. She was not yet permitted to walk. Not until the newly stitched stumps where toes had been were fully healed.

"*E* Jyothi!" she whispered, not wishing to disturb the others in her dormitory. He opened heavy and resistant eyes.

"*Hajur*?" he muttered respectfully, "Yes, *Ama*?"

"Where's Jiwan-*bhai*?" she asked with urgency. "Where's your brother?"

"Oh," he yawned, scratching his head with one hand, his ear with the other. "He's gone."

"Gone where?" Bindra gasped.

"Jiwan-*bhai* has gone to the burning *ghat*, *Ama*," he replied sleepily, "to become an *Aghori*."

Chapter Thirteen

My train had been scheduled to arrive in the early afternoon, far north of the Ganges River delta and Calcutta at the Bay of Bengal. I had wistfully fancied that I would take the first transport up into the mountains and reach Darjeeling in time for dinner. However, the train did not reach New Jalpaiguri station until shortly after ten at night.

In the days of the Raj, the gregarious Bengali had been derided for his gentle, optimistic disposition and small stature. His colonial masters had not only dismissed him as "effeminate", but had denounced him for lacking that most essential of "manly" restraints, which they had believed would save him from going blind, insane, or growing hair on the palms of his hands.

"Effeminate" was the last adjective on my mind as, through the darkness of the station forecourt, I was besieged by a mob of taxi drivers, hotel touts and rickshaw-*wallahs*. It was now all too familiar.

I quickly returned to the safety of the station building and enquired at the *chauki* police office as to how I could reach Darjeeling before midnight. The *dufadar* constable regretfully informed me that all buses and the toy-train steam railway, which took a full seven hours to make its perilous ascent, had completed their last trips for the day. My only option was to stay the night.

I stepped back into the riot of the forecourt and considered what to do. Despite the lateness of the evening, the heat was sweltering. However, I had no opportunity to acknowledge just how tired and thirsty I was feeling, for the touts and drivers lunged towards me, each grasping hand determined to glean some income from the solitary foreigner, by dragging me, against my will if necessary, into the urban misery of the town.

My mind was set. I had to procure a taxi willing, at such a late hour, to make the circuitous fifty-mile journey into the mountains.

The mention of Darjeeling, and the clamant mobs vanished. Nobody would agree to drive me.

I was approached by a boy who seemed bright, resourceful and fascinated by the colour of my skin, which he asked permission to touch. In return for my concession to his exploration of my forearms with grimy fingertips, I asked him to seek me out a driver directly. He flicked his head to one side in cocky affirmation and confidently led me across the car park to a vehicle, at which he indicated I was to wait.

I had almost lost my confidence when the boy returned out of the darkness. He was in the company of two cheerless men, both of whom looked as though they had been newly woken from deep slumber. They were not too drowsy, however, for much intense and noisy bartering, at the close of which they had agreed to take me to Darjeeling for what ultimately remained an extortionate price.

My attempt to climb onto the back seat turned into a tussle, as I insisted that I was to keep my backpack with me and not have it stuffed into the boot. Their repeated objections had been unnecessarily aggressive.

I settled back for the long, slow ascent to an altitude of some seven thousand feet. And yet, as we turned out of the station forecourt and began towards the town, I found myself tense and alert.

My instincts were vociferously asserting that all was not as it should have been.

Bindra did not know what to do.

The clinic staff had adamantly refused to allow her to walk out of the ward. The stitches on her feet, where gangrenous toes had been removed, were far too fresh. She must take her medicines, they had told her. She must wait.

Bindra's agitation was preventing her from any rest. She had thought of sending Jyothi to the cremation ground, to search for Jiwan, but was afraid he too would not return.

Bindra sat on her pillow in an attempt to peer over the window sill into the *gali* lane beyond. She could see nothing, so shuffled to the end of her bed to get a better view of the corridor. Why would Jiwan walk away without a word to her? How could he choose to leave with such ease?

Was this, then, the path on which the *ban jhankri* had set her little boy, all those many weeks before in that distant forest? Was this the path foreseen by the woman at the steps of the Kali temple in the palm thicket? Was it for this that Jiwan's daily lessons at the wooden Shiva temple had been preparing him?

Bindra lay back on the bed and closed her burning eyes.

"*Ama?*" Jyothi said softly, as he cuddled up against her side. "Was Jiwan-*bhai* born to be an *Aghori*? To live on the cremation ground, without his clothes?"

"Not 'born to be', my son," Bindra replied, her voice tired and tight. "There is no destiny. Not in the way the *Bahun* priests describe."

She was searching for a way to explain it even to herself.

"The truth is we determine our own futures," she began. "You see, ours is a limitless universe of infinite possibilities. From these we make our choices of how to think, feel, react, to be, every minute of every day. These are choices that ultimately determine the experiences we call our life."

Jyothi wiped his nose on the back of his hand, but stayed quiet.

"It means we have great power over the passage and experience of that life," she continued, "for if we change our choices, we change our 'destiny'."

Jyothi's thoughts took time to become words.

"So," he tentatively began, "if Jiwan-*bhai* believes he can be an *Aghori*, if he chooses to be an *Aghori*, then that's his 'destiny'? But if he believed he could be a paddy farmer and chose to be a paddy farmer, then that would be his 'destiny' instead?"

"This is why we must make our choices with awareness, with responsibility," Bindra affirmed. "We need to ask ourselves whether our daily choices lead us towards greater freedom, joy and truth, or towards greater contraction, pain and self-delusion. This is what our *puja* teaches us, whether it be to Durga or Lord Shiva, Kubera or Kali Ma. The symbols of all our rites and traditions remind us to reconsider the choices we are making every day of our lives."

Jyothi was listening intently, trying to understand.

"As you grow older, my brave, strong boy," Bindra continued, "you will learn to see that the person you are and the life you lead are the results of all the choices you've made so far. Instead of blaming others for the way we feel, the way we are, we must take responsibility for it ourselves."

"So are you choosing to cry tears now, *Ama*?" Jyothi asked, with concern.

"Yes, son," Bindra replied, wiping her eyes again on the sheet and laughing gently at herself. "I suppose I am."

$$\psi$$

The two men drove in silence through miles of twisting, unmade back streets.

I was slow to realise that they had been taking me in repeated circles. I leaned forwards to ask why we were still in the town. They pretended not to understand.

Minutes later, the car was brought to a hasty halt in an unlit alleyway. The driver switched off the engine, whereupon both men hurried from the car.

I watched them vanish into the darkness.

I waited.

And I worried.

Just as abruptly as they had left, the two men returned. They slammed the doors, started the engine, and we were off, without one word of explanation. Not until we passed beneath a solitary street light at an intersection were their faces momentarily illuminated.

Only then did I realise that the men now driving the car were not those who had driven me into the alleyway.

As the two heads silhouetted against the windscreen remained stationary and silent, I quietly rummaged in my rucksack for my single defence: the Deluxe Tinker Swiss Army Knife. I drew it from its wrapping and clasped it tightly between my legs.

The vehicle bounced on and the scant glow of the town quickly faded into impenetrable darkness. As the scent of jungle seeped through the glassless windows, I breathed deeply and slowly, preparing myself for the worst, while hardly daring to contemplate just what the worst might be.

For almost an hour we drove through deep forest, along a rough, winding road, overhung with tropical trees.

Suddenly, the hair on my neck prickled with foreboding.

My fists instinctively tightened.

The driver braked.

The man in the passenger seat swung round and savagely thrust a short, blade towards my face. He broke the breathless silence with the scream of "Dollars! Dollars!"

I did not pause to think. I swiftly raised my solitary defence and levelled it at his throat.

"No dollars!" I replied firmly.

To the surprise of us both, I found myself smiling broadly at the surreal absurdity of the situation. Smiling broadly that I was threatening two violently inclined bandits with an inadvertently extended corkscrew.

My two would-be assailants began to jabber at each other at ever-heightening pitch.

"*Tor matha gooe bora!*" the driver spat, evidently furious with the unexpected turn of events.

"*Tor gesai boto nai!*" his accomplice retorted.

In response, the driver punched him squarely in the face.

The ensuing scuffle on the front seat gave me my opportunity. I flung open the door, grabbed my rucksack and leapt headlong into the undergrowth, trying not to laugh out loud at how ridiculously

Bulldog Drummond, late of His Majesty's Royal Loamshires (Hurrah! Hurrah!), it all seemed.

The engine immediately started up.

With my open door swinging, and the Bengali obscenities still exploding from the front seat, the car turned and swerved its way back towards the dusty miseries from which it had come.

I stood up to watch the rear lights of the vehicle disappear into the darkness. And dark it was. There was no sight of moon or stars above the forest canopy. The jungle was quiet, except for the gentle movement of a cooling breeze. The quote *"Life rustling in the leaves, death moaning in the grasses,"* suddenly came to mind, unsettling my nerve. Curse those schoolboy recitations.

I knew Darjeeling lay high in the mountains above me, but the Queen of the Hills was at least another hour or two's drive away. I did not much fancy my chances on foot, nor did I know what inhabited these jungles. I had once read that the Bengal tiger still claimed the lives of, on average, thirty people a year. I had no wish to join a guidebook statistic and certainly had no intention of becoming a macabre anecdote for my nephews or nieces, however much it might bring them their friends' eternal respect.

I decided instead to wend my way down the centre of the road, my knife, and now the vicious-looking horse-hoof scraper, open at the ready. I had noticed flickering lights amongst tall, straight *saal* trees some miles back. I would make my way to the gates and barbed-wire fences of what had appeared to have been the neatness of an army base.

I felt sure the two startled soldiers were meant to raise their wooden rifles and shout the standard playground, "Who goes there? Friend or foe?", as I approached the perimeter fence. Instead, they remained holding hands and simply blinked in silent astonishment at the appearance of my wraithlike features in the darkness.

My cheery "Good evening, gentlemen!" stirred them to invite me into their guard hut, where they sat me on a wooden stool. They automatically threw a blanket around my shoulders, despite the heat, and offered a steaming cup from their canister of tea, whilst I breathlessly spilled my sorry tale, to which they made suitable noises of outrage and sympathy.

After a hurried discussion between themselves in animated Bengali, one of the young soldiers ran out into the night. He promptly returned behind the wheel of an open-top jeep, where-upon Corporal Rao announced that the least he could do, consider-ing his fellow-countrymen's dastardly behaviour, was to deliver me safely to Darjeeling.

ψ

Bindra woke herself with her own panting sob.

She had thought she had been searching for Jiwan on the riverbank, and amongst the mounds of *dhobis'* washing. Searching in the piles of cremation ash, and in the heavy darkness of the water.

Bindra closed her eyes again, but could not fall back to sleep. She could not accustom herself to the heat of the Plains, nor the quiet of this city at night. No thrum of insects in the trees. No *jhankri* drums. No jackals in the darkness.

She moved her arm to give Jyothi's head a little more room on the bed. He did not stir. She skimmed her eyes back across the ceiling, to find the pale *cheparo* lizard that scuttled on its dainty toes, above her.

Bindra had requested an audience with the *Aghori Baba* who had founded the clinic in which she lay. She had wanted to thank him. Again and again, to thank him.

She had wanted to ask her unseen benefactor to find Jiwan amongst his ash-strewn kind. To bring him back to his brother, to return him to her arms. But the *Aghori* had been visiting his guru in the mountains for many months. Nobody could say when he would return.

Bindra closed her eyes and her head began to drift.

She was back home, oiling her daughters' hair. They were laugh-ing as brightly as snow on the mountain peaks. *Gundruk* boiling in the *tasala*, *makai* maize cobs drying on their poles. All those she loved gathering together at the *shaktiko roukh*, taking it in turns to place *saipattri* marigolds around its roots.

Suddenly, the tree burst into violent flame, consuming flowers, bark, leaves and goddess.

Bindra backed away, to find that she was all alone.

No Kailash. No children. No hands.

Bindra woke with heart pounding and brow wet. Gasping for air, she carefully pulled herself upright, without disturbing Jyothi.

Bindra cried out.

Standing by the side of her bed was a small, naked, silver-grey figure, with red stripes drawn across forehead, arms and chest.

"*Ama, ramro cha,*" Jiwan whispered. "Mother, all is well."

And he was gone.

Chapter Fourteen

I could see nothing of Darjeeling. The town was not only suffering a total power cut, but had disappeared in dense fog.

The chatty soldier drew up his jeep in front of what he promised was the Planters' Club. To express my gratitude, I handed him the taxi fare I would have spent. He grinned broadly, touched the notes to his heart, then wished me a gracious farewell and vanished back into the gloom.

Without the headlights of the jeep I was suddenly quite blind. The main gates of the Club had been firmly chained for the night, so I felt my way around the outer wall and cautiously entered an unlocked door. The fathomless black of the interior burst into shimmering shadow as a Nepali servant lifted a glowing oil lamp high above his head. The *darban* doorkeeper could not understand a word I said, so made a phone call and handed me the receiver. It was the manager.

"Sir, you are very late," the fatigued voice pointed out astutely.

I apologised and asked if there might be a vacant room for my use. He replied that he would be pleased to allow me to stay, even though he had already retired for the night. I asked whether the price included breakfast.

"Oh my, sir!" he exclaimed. "You are driving a hard bargain, but for you I'll say most certainly, 'Yes'!"

The sleepy-eyed servant led me down a broad, open verandah, and up a rickety wooden staircase to my room. He lit two candle stubs, stoked up a coal fire, bid me goodnight and disappeared back into the mist. Exhausted, I dropped onto the bed as heavy rain began to patter over the skylights.

So here I was at last, in the club to which Great-Uncle Oscar had belonged all those years ago, lying on a bed in which "Hindoo Uncle" – as he had signed himself on the photographs he had regularly posted home – might also have once sought sleep.

The bedroom was large, yet still cluttered with colonial furniture. I had my own *en suite* sitting room, in which stood a dusty bureau, an empty plant-stand, and an open-cane three-piece, set around a badly torn green-baize card table. I had my own Victorian *gussal-khana*, with a porcelain flush-toilet and washbasin made in Aldershot, and a gargantuan, grimly stained bath tub, with heavily encrusted chrome taps, made in Birmingham.

I unpacked my essentials and threw more coal onto the fire. I bathed in four inches of tepid brown water, which was all the tap enamelled "hot" eventually managed to produce, then snuggled deeply into chalky sheets, beneath a damp eiderdown. A Yuletide roaring in the grate, thermal long johns, scarf and woolly socks, yet still I shivered with the cold. It seemed impossible that, just hours before, I had been limp and panting in stifling heat.

I blew out the candles by my bed and vigorously flailed limbs in all directions in an effort to warm myself by friction, just as Grandmother had once taught me in my chilly bed in Sussex. I quickly drew the blankets around my chin and curled up to watch flaring embers in the grate flicker phantom battles across walls and ceiling.

"Just look at me now, Grandma!" I said aloud, as though she were sitting in the lumpy armchair, ready to enchant me with another ancestral tale. "All tucked up in Uncle Oscar's very own Planters' Club, with Darjeeling outside my windows! Who'd have thought?"

I waited, as though for her reply.

"*Your breath like the full moon in the summer night shall hover about my dreams, making them fragrant,*" I smiled, quoting Tagore to the empty room.

And still I listened for "my Johnny Sparrow" until, as sleep swiftly stole away all thought and memory, I was aware of nothing more than raindrops slipping down the chimney to make the fire hiss.

⟱

Bindra was awoken by crows. She turned her head to find an untidy row of black feathers sitting on the sill of the open window.

"Kali Ma," she whispered towards them from her bed. "What have you brought for me today?"

There was no response from the six steadfast stares.

"I don't know that I'm yet ready for more learning," she murmured in admission. "I don't know that I'm yet ready for more wisdom."

She had first learned of wisdom from her grandmother. Bindra had lived with her after her mother and sister had died beneath the elephant, and had grown to love her dearly.

Bindra's grandmother had never been into the town. She had lived her entire life in the mountain hut in which she had been born. Even when she had married a Nepali from lower in the Hills, she had defied custom and refused to move in with her husband's family. He had stayed on his ancestral farm, and she had stayed in her mountain hut. Bindra's grandfather had visited his new wife once a week initially. However, when she had given birth to a daughter, instead of a son, he had abandoned them both and had taken a more compliant, conventional village woman with whom to raise a family.

Bindra's grandmother had not believed her husband's excuse about the birth of a daughter. Amongst their people a daughter was a blessing, a goddess incarnate. They had not held to the misogyny of the orthodox, patriarchal traditions of the Plains.

Bindra's grandmother had known too well why he had really abandoned her. She was a *bojudeuta*, a "Grandmother God".

Others had preferred to call her *bokshi*.

Witch.

⟱

At seven in the morning, I woke to find a Nepali room-boy opening the curtains and tying back the skylight blinds. He introduced himself as Yashu, wished me a chirpy "Fine morning, sir!", then left me to rouse myself with a hot pot of ginger brew, which he had laid out with great care on the bedside teapoy.

I attempted some semblance of a wash in the granular, brown trickle proffered by the bathroom taps, dressed, then wandered down to breakfast. The fog had returned after the night's rain, thwarting all hopes of any views from the balcony of the snowy-peaked Kanchenjunga.

A smart, Tibetan-looking doorman showed me to the single laid table, informing me that I was the only guest in the Club. Impatient to begin my search for some evidence of Uncle Oscar's life in these tea-clad hills, I pressed him to know at what time the Club Office might be manned.

The doorman shrugged. "Perhaps after breakfast, sir. Then again, perhaps not."

As he wandered back towards his post, an elderly, Nepali *khitmutgar* servant approached with some effort on his arthritic limbs. He bowed with undisguised discomfort, took my order and laid a heavily stained napkin across my nippy knees.

The dining hall in which I sat was floored in Burmese teak, thick with decades of wax polish. Between the alcove windows, with their accommodating inset seats, stood pristine stone fireplaces. The Brunswick blacking of the grates gave the room a delicate taint of asphaltum, linseed oil and turpentine.

Set into one wall stood display cabinets, congested with past members' tarnished trophies. They dated far back to the time when sport had been a near mania in British India, an antidote perhaps for the grinding boredom inherent in the disciplined formalities of the Raj. Cups for polo and cricket, badminton and tennis. Medals for *shikar* and archery, jackal hunting and pig-sticking.

Mounted above the picture rail, my only companions' glass eyeballs stared down with contempt, each decapitated chinkara and blackbuck, muntjac and cheetah leaking sawdust and hung on hooks, having proven to former generations that they had indeed dominated all animals. And foreigners.

The wild rattle of a wooden screen made me start. Breakfast had arrived. I watched my elderly *khit* slowly wind his way through the dining tables with their matching sets of sub-William Morris chairs. He gradually set before me cornflakes, toast, poached egg, marmalade and hot milk, then proudly indicated towards the large opening in the wall from which he had collected the tray.

"Our fine buttery hatch, cut into the dining room in the old days to facilitate a more efficient service, due to complaints of insufficient attendance at table being made. It is, sir, to your satisfaction?"

I assured him that it was. His clipped, pre-war vowels had been faultless.

As he poured my tea, I wondered why I found such satisfaction in the faded elegance amongst which I now so delightedly sat. Had the prized modernity of my generation so banished all hints of gentility from our tediously sanitised lives, that it drove us to seek out the cosy reassurance of nostalgia? Even on this, my own sentimental journey, I had become acutely aware that I was doing little more than grasping at ghosts, ultimately dependent upon my own imagination, my own terms of reference. Kipling, Forster, Waugh. Jhabvala, Merchant, Ivory.

In truth, the tablecloth spread before me was no longer starched or pressed. The years of tea, coffee and Colman's mustard had patterned the cotton in stains no *dhobi*, however energetic, could erase. Decades of unwiped vases had left a myriad of concentric ripples across the bare tabletops. The cruet had been left to tarnish, the cutlery all belonged to different sets. The leather upholstery had worn through so long ago that it now exposed horsehair and cotton flock, torn scrim and rusty spring.

I recalled, from delving into my Grandmother's treasured box of mementoes, that there had once been a time when the breakfast menu at the Club had offered plain or parsley omelette with a variety of grilled offal. There had been bacon and tomatoes, sausages and mashed potato. Patties of meat, best steak and mutton hash. Eggs boiled, poached and "rumble-tumble".

But now all choice was gone. The cornflakes were stale, the butter rancid. The greasy milk was speckled with ash, the Bhutanese marmalade served in its shop-shelf jar.

And yet, whilst battling with incinerated toast, I seemed to catch an iridescent sparkle thrown across the room by cufflinks and tie-pins. The lustre of pearls and precious stones resting softly across pale throats, wrists and fingers. The scent of skin doused in Rowland's Kalydor, "Friend of the Complexion, Solace of the Flushed, Last Hope of the Freckled".

As I picked crystallised ants from the sugar bowl, I seemed to sense the rub of gum-stiffened cuffs and collars on old *koi-hai*. The tintinnabulation of silver on fine imported china, as *pukka burra sahibs* and *sakt burra mems* tucked into Oxford sausages, mutton pillau, salmon loaf and Brown Windsor soup. Walnut blancmange, guava fool, mango mould and Taj Mahal jellies.

The tireless talk of tea crops, Cold Weather tours and tiger shoots. The ceaseless flow of *billayati-pani* pink gin sodas and Murree beer. The orotund toasts to Queen Empress, King Emperor and the confident delusion of an eternal *Pax Britannica*.

༓

Bindra often longed to speak to her grandmother.

The *bojudeuta* were highly respected in the Eastern Himalaya for their knowledge, secret arts and wisdom. People came from all around for medicines and advice, understanding and answers.

As a child, Bindra had assisted her grandmother. She had gathered plants for pounding in the wooden *okhli musli* pestle and mortar to treat sickness and bestow second sight. She had collected tree bark for crushing on the *silauto* grinding-stone, to make a poultice that would heal wounds and mend broken bones.

She had bartered for *putkako maha*, the rare, intoxicating insect honey that cured all infection, and its *kut* wax that proved such an effective antidote for snakebite. She had sought the bitter, black *bikuma* plant that was the only remedy for the deadly, yellow poison of the ghost-like *kapat* insect, and fetched yak's milk *churpi* that, when dissolved in plant oil, could dull the pain of grief.

Bindra had seen many people come. Infirm men, sick women, diseased children. There had been young *repas* and aged *lamas* from the monasteries. Gurkha soldiers from Deolo camp. Even a personal maid of the Queen Mother of Bhutan who had scurried in one day with a secret trouble, when her mistress had been staying in her hot season palace.

Bindra had watched her grandmother's visitors walk away from their hut with ease, when they had been carried up the hill path in crippling paralysis. She had seen them laugh out loud with fearless joy, when they had arrived weak and drawn with devastating suffering. She had seen her grandmother's ministrations enable women to sing as they gave birth to their children. She had seen men struggling against Lord Yamantaka's inescapable noose of death smile softly and embrace their end in peace.

Over the years, Bindra had watched the constant course of visitors bow to touch her grandmother's feet upon departure. She had seen them, in their gratitude, lay before her rice and daal, *atta*, milk and mustard oil, yet never once did she demand a fee for her remedies or request money for her wisdom.

And yet, it was only Bindra who saw the ensuing pain and fever, exhaustion and debility, the fits and phantom labours endured by her grandmother when others hurried home to show their miracles.

It was Bindra alone who knew the hidden price of the *bojudeuta*'s healing.

ψ

The broad verandah of the Planters' Club was bedecked with mounted skulls, hat stands, three-tiered plant holders, marble-topped tables and long-sleever chairs with drink pockets in the arms.

I peered through the door labelled "Billiards" and found a large, empty room painted in a restful shade of soot-stained, buff Kosmo. I looked into "Bitters" to find red Keystone walls, frayed *moonj* matting and a sleeping servant tucked against the skirting. I popped my head into the red velvet plush and guinea-gold brass of the

"Lounge", and discovered a jumble of sagging armchairs and lumpy sofas in need of reupholstering.

The walls of the "Reading Room" were a madman's map in old distemper, its warren of wormy bookshelves packed tightly with web-laced tomes. Flyleaves listed previous borrowers, with return dates from the days of the Queen Empress. All Lord this and Lady that. The signature of a Bonham-Carter, Yeatman-Biggs and Wrangham-Hardy. The flamboyant scrawl of a Ptolemy Carew-Hunt and the ever-so-thrilling W. F. Maguire-Luzeo-Péppé.

I disturbed dense dust to discover not only an extensive miscellany of reputable British writers – from Shelley to Stoker, Scott to Sackville-West – but all manner of Anglo-Indiana. The classic *Curry & Rice* by Captain Atkinson. Major Shadwell's all-essential *Economy of the Chummery, Home, Mess & Club*. The spirited rhythm and rhyme of Aliph Cheem's satirical *Lays of Ind*, on which I had been raised, with all those childhood favourites of the sullen Humptee Dumptee Frumtee Chundrer, the liberal Baboo Humbul Bumbul Bender, and good Rajah Kistnamah Howdie Doo.

The red-nosed Tibetan librarian, who sat behind a paper-piled desk, expressed delight at my interest in the damp-mottled volumes with the faulty beam of a tooth-depleted grin. She was evidently eager for me to borrow a book, just to have the rare chance of using her crumbling rubber stamp and arid ink pad, to enter a title and author into her mould-stained "books out" ledger.

The Club office was still not open. I returned to the verandah and looked down towards the town. It remained thickly enshrouded by an impenetrable fog. I decided to wait a while before venturing beyond the garden walls, so summoned a smiling servant for a blanket and settled down in a wicker armchair on the verandah. I would pass my misty morning in the company of the borrowed edition of Sir Henry Cunningham's *Chronicles of Dustypore* and a pot of scalding ginger tea.

The servants thought me *paagal* mad to be sitting out in the dank cold. And yet, alone with my book and with the town submerged in all-obscuring cloud, I could imagine that it was still 1920. I could imagine that Uncle Oscar was out there, in the bazaar, purchasing supplies for another campfire meet with his ferociously hedonistic planter chums, all ready to sit around open flames on elegant sofas and comfortable chairs hauled through deep jungle by an army of attendants.

I could have imagined that it was still 1920, except my flight of fancy had fundamental flaws. The paint of the Club was peeling, the windows all unwashed. The wicker and cane had been allowed to split, the floors left un-soda-scrubbed. The puffings of muslin in the rooms were long unlaundered, the damask and chintz untouched by flannel and bran.

I could have imagined that it was still 1920, except hidden traffic blew impatient horns beyond the garden walls, whilst the *mali* gardener, indolently weeding a herbaceous border, sported Adidas trainers, a baseball cap and over-sized polyester slacks.

Ψ

Bindra had been just eight years old when her grandmother had first taken her to the old cave temple above Lapu *basti*.

They had arrived long after nightfall. In their carrying cloths they had wrapped *toriko tel* lamp oil, *batti* wicks, *dhup* incense, *sidur* pigment and *tori* mustard seeds. They had been laden with *parsat* offerings of *phalphul* fruit, *chamal* rice, *kapur* camphor and *supari* betel nut. Once settled, they had chanted together in the darkness, until sunlight had illuminated the peak of the Kanchenjunga.

They had spent all the next day sitting at the rock face. Bindra's grandmother had given her plant-infused water to drink, on which had floated scarlet hibiscus flowers. She had gently blown smoke from burning moss and dried herbs into Bindra's lungs that had made her sigh. She had bathed her in the fish-churned temple pool, from which rose Lord Shiva's weather-wasted *trishul* trident.

She had sat Bindra in the warmth of the sun, as she had slowly circled her, moving her hands in carefully chosen *mudras* to focus her intention and express her purpose. She had muttered indiscernible mantras as she had gently marked Bindra's young body with indelible symbols of supreme, universal union.

All day long, Bindra's grandmother had methodically taught her. She had given her knowledge that, when applied in daily life, she had promised would lead her to the wisdom for which she yearned.

As dusk had fallen, Bindra's grandmother had initiated her with her first mantra. She had told her that she was to repeat these Words of Power every day. Firstly, as the sun rose from behind the mythical mountain in the east, called Udaya. And then again, as the sun set behind the mythical mountain in the west, called Asta.

In time, Bindra's grandmother had imparted a second mantra to be whispered into the ears of each of her future children as they married. And finally, a third mantra, to be whispered into her own ears at the moment of her death.

Bindra had imagined that she would be an old woman herself before she would use the last. And yet, she was only in the third month of her womanhood when called upon by the *jhankri* to whisper the Mantra of Severance into the ears of her grandmother. To share the final breath. To bury a cloth-bound portion of charred flesh beneath the river sand.

And then to feed the crows.

The damp of Darjeeling had reached the hollows of my bones. I put aside my book, sifted the last dregs of tepid tea, and left the verandah to try the Club office once again. The door was open.

The ill-lit room was chaotic, clogged with bureaucratic excess. A stocky Nepali peered at me over a swelling sea of official forms in quadruplicate. He pushed files of flavescent papers and dried-out typewriter ribbons from a swivel chair. He cut a swathe through the jumble on the floor with his feet and bade me join him.

I explained that I had come in search of my Uncle Oscar. He listened intently and with sufficient interest that I felt able to ask if I might examine the old Club records. He was delighted to oblige and began to rummage unsystematically through drawers and cabinets.

Above his deliriously cluttered desk hung a faded photograph. However, this was not the likeness of the usual smiling, bespectacled Gandhi, or tightly buttoned Nehru. Rather, this was an English woman, who in her lifetime could easily have been mistaken for a young Larry Grayson. As to this *pukka mem*'s identity, or the reason for her pride of place, the office-*wallah* was about to enlighten me, when he made a cheer of triumph. He had finally uncovered three leather-bound volumes of minutes dating back to the Club's establishment in 1868. Thrilled and impatient, I hurried to my room with the books, having been allowed to borrow them for "just as long as you do be guesting with us".

Page after page was inscribed with the name of Uncle Oscar. I yearned to have been able to run to a telephone and share every word with my Grandmother.

At the regular reminders for him to pay outstanding Club bills she would have chuckled, as at his complaints to the sub-committee regarding the tinned plums in syrup, which he had found "utterly inedible", and the kippered herrings, which he had deemed "quite unfit for consumption".

She would have approved of his recommendation that electric light be introduced into the Club building, but would have given an explosive snort at his vehement resistance to the suggestion that women be admitted any more than twice a month, and then only to dinner or the public salons.

At Uncle Oscar's support for Colonel Roberts, who had protested against the posting of a sham telegram regarding the bombing of Alexandria, she would have yawned, but, being a talented musician herself, would have cheered his decision to punish members of a drunken rugby scrum who had damaged the "lounge" piano.

She would have dismissed his judgement on the bold accusation by Mr Bahrer that, one evening after cards, Mr Leg-Jacob had committed an "ungentlemanly assault upon his person in the Reading Room," but would have applauded Uncle Oscar's persistent requests for the importation of tins of Jordan's Chocolate Imperials, and for the delivery of Italian sweetmeats and wafer *biscotti* direct from the celebrated restaurant of Signor Angelo Firpo in Calcutta.

And at his repeated appeals for the prompt shipping of a volume of Art Poetry, by "The Very Gay Company of the Seven Troubadours of Toulouse", Grandmother would have stretched her eyes wide and cried, "Pot Herb!"

ψ

The row of silent crows perched on the ward window sill was undisturbed by the sudden agitation in the corridor.

Bindra sat up. She strained to listen to the excitement of voices beyond the open door.

Jyothi rubbed his eyes.

"*Ama*," he croaked through an unmoistened throat, "is Jiwan back?"

Bindra stroked his face with the softness of fresh bandaging.

"I don't think so, my gentle, loving son," she replied with regret.

Bindra peered towards the corridor.

"But something new is coming that will bring changes for us." She glanced towards the crows as one began to bob. "Something that will bring new wisdom."

Jyothi quickly sat up and pressed his face hard into his mother's chest.

"I won't leave you, *Ama*!" he declared with fierce insistence. "I'll never leave you!"

Bindra tightened her arms around him.

"And one day, we'll all be together again," she insisted with a determined smile. "Jayashri-*didi*, my good boy Jyothi, Jamini-*bhaini* and Jiwan-*bhai*. Back in the Hills, back in our home ..." She suddenly, desperately needed to believe that her words could come true.

Again noises in the corridor. Voices.

Bindra looked up.

In the doorway stood a man with a single length of black cloth around his loins. His hair and beard were uncut and matted. His skin was caked with ash. His chest was heavy with long strings of gnarled *rudraksha* seeds. His eyes were full of sky.

"*Babajyu!*" Bindra gasped.

The *Aghori* had returned.

Chapter Fifteen

Settled on an old sofa in my private sitting room, with a smoky fire blazing in the grate and a chilling fog beyond the windows, I leafed through the musty pages of the Club minutes and felt my "Hindoo Uncle" drawing closer.

Oscar had been one of eight children born to well-to-do Anglo-Swedish parents. His father had boasted descent from no less than two red-headed royal mistresses, a noble illegitimacy the family proudly asserted through the liberal use on letterheads, rings and curricles of their crest of a broken lily rising from a crown. A collection of much-treasured Rococo and Gustavian silver bore witness to this august, if illicit, lineage, for snuffboxes, teapots and tankards engraved with regal seals had been given in dowry by kings to compensate lovers discharged in their gravidity. Oscar's parents had also retained a number of fine portraits depicting the imperial family, including an oil painting of the dashing Karl XIII, his left eye discreetly incised, it was claimed, for use in espionage at Stockholm's copper-topped palace.

Oscar and his twin, Olivia, had been born in 1857, the year of the Indian Mutiny that had initiated the violent end of the Mughal Empire and the founding of the British Raj. However, despite his Scandinavian ancestry, Oscar had taken his first breath far from Nordic intrigue and palatine paramours, on the southern crest of Crouch Hill, in London's fashionable Northern Heights. He had been named after the popular and humane King Oscar II of Sweden, with whom his mother had danced at a celebratory ball to mark the royal engagement to Princess Sophia of Nassau. Eleven years later, on the morning of their shared birthday, Oscar had lost his twin sister to cholera.

Oscar had been educated at a boarding school for the sons of gentlemen in Oxfordshire, before taking a position – arranged by his mother's cousin and based on little more than a vague knowledge of rose pruning, the maintenance of toy engines and the care of sick pets – with the Upper Assam Tea Company. At the age of twenty, and with the "glamour of the East" upon him, as he had put it, Oscar had sailed from London's Victoria Docks for India.

Oscar had first paid his respects to an uncle at Lucknow, then had travelled on to Calcutta, where he had taken a train to Goalundo, close to the junction of the Ganges and Brahmaputra Rivers. There, he had boarded a paddle-steamer and, thirty-three days later, arrived at Dibrugarh, near the Burmese border.

In time, Oscar had become manager of the tea-garden, and when, in 1883, a proposal had been made to build a railway into Upper Assam, he had offered a successful bid for the contract to supply the sleepers. It was thus that Oscar had made his fortune, just as his Swedish grandfather had in Britain half a century earlier – one with Germanic crosscut-saws and Scandinavian *skogshuggarer*, the other with Nepalese sawyers, Assamese elephants and *mahouts*.

In those days, the tea companies had forbidden their managers to marry until the age of thirty, in order that they might afford a standard of living worthy of a *sahib*. A polo horse was, naturally, far more important than a wife. It was, therefore, quite normal that Oscar had taken an Assamese mistress. The result was the beautiful and captivating Theo, of whom my Grandmother had so wistfully spoken.

Oscar had later moved west, across the Dooars from Assam and up to the temperate climes of Darjeeling, in order to manage an extensive tea-garden in the hills below the town. It had been there that the family legend had been carefully silenced.

However, my Grandmother had whispered to me that Oscar had once contracted dysentery from his plantation workers. She had hinted that he had been nursed back from the brink of death by a tribal princess, who subsequently bore him children.

If there was any truth to this tale, I had come to reveal it.

If there were indeed descendant generations, I was here to search them out.

ψ

The *Aghori Baba* smiled broadly as he approached the bed. Bindra placed her bandaged hands to her heart and bowed her head in *pranam*.

"*Namaskar babajyu*," she greeted him in respect, reminding Jyothi to join her.

"*Behenji, aaj aap kaisi haiñ?*" he said to Bindra, respectfully asking how she felt today. She did not respond. "*Aap Hindi bolte haiñ?*" he tried, asking if she spoke Hindi.

Bindra laughed shyly. She had guessed his question. "*Ma Hindi boldaina*. I don't speak Hindi," she replied.

"*E bahini!*" the *Aghori* grinned. "Sister, of course you are Nepali! I live many year in mountain with Nepali people. I speak *ali ali* little little."

Bindra immediately burst into anxious, animated life.

"*Babjyu*, my son is on the cremation ground where he's joined the *Aghori Babas* and I would go to find him myself but I cannot yet walk and I fear to send my Jyothi as he speaks no Hindi and does not know this great city . . ."

She was barely taking a breath.

The *Aghori* put up his hand to quieten her.

"*Behenji*," he said softly, "sister, what you ask me?"

Bindra held her breath for a moment, but could not hold back new tears. In a single sob she burst, "Where is my son?"

"*Behenji*, you no need fear," he offered in confident assurance, his eyes tender with compassion. "Sister, I send and find him. No problem."

ψ

Mr Sengupta shook my hand warmly and offered the worn, green leather of his most comfortable chair. He sat back into his own seat, smiling benevolently. Billowing cigar wraiths haunted the air around him, clinging to his tweed cap and moleskin waistcoat, nestling into the burrows of his neck-scarf and the folds of his face.

Word had reached the Club office that their single guest had once counted family amongst their number. Mr Sengupta was intrigued and promptly offered to arrange an appointment with a Mr Duppa.

"This chap claims to be in his nineties," he explained, "and is exceedingly knowledgeable in matters of tea history. This Mr Duppa was once a planter, you know, in olden times past."

Mr Sengupta paused to slowly draw on his pipe.

"As for his longevity, you must be most naturally wondering," he continued with smoke-shaped syllables. "Well, this he attributes to his not eating of meat, but," he suddenly dropped his voice and craned his short neck towards me, "it is thrice that I have seen him dining on a fine Club sausage! Pinch of salt, young man!" he grinned through tobacco-tinged teeth. "Pinch of salt!"

I stood to shake his hand in grateful farewell, when Mr Sengupta placed into my proffered palm a piece of paper on which he had carefully inscribed an address. As I stepped back into the dense fog, he suggested I study an old photograph in "Billiards", which he felt certain would prove of interest. I thanked him again and hurried back along the verandah.

Above the sooty mantle, against the smoke-stained wall, hung a heavy-framed print of the Club Committee. It recorded a formal gathering of starch-fronted *buckram-sahibs*, in 1928. And there was Uncle Oscar! He was seated with arms folded, his face a portrait of solemnity and distance, seemingly unaware of the photographic occasion to which the other twenty gentlemen had risen with appropriate pomposity.

"Please be excusing, sir," a soft voice said beside me. I turned to meet the cheerful eyes of my Nepali room-boy standing in the doorway. "Mr Sengupta-sir is asking that I am guiding you-sir into bazaar."

I was puzzled. I had no intention of doing any shopping.

"Yes, sir," he continued with an unfalteringly mischievous grin, "bazaar is where we are finding Mr Duppa-sir. He most olderly.

Such an olderly man you-sir never before seen! Not even anyone so olderly as he!"

Yashu followed me up to my room, where he insisted on helping me with my coat, scarf and woolly hat. As we ventured out into the blindfolding mists, he asked if he could take hold of two of my fingers, "to be most sure I may not be losing you-sir," he impressed with earnest sincerity.

Darjeeling was not unlike Shimla, sprawling over a ridge and spilling down the hillsides in a complicated maze of interconnecting roadways, footpaths and narrow flights of stairs. The town itself was a jumble of Victorian cottages, villas, hotels, schools, churches, temples and small shops, all of which were disintegrating, slipping down the steep inclines and further into oblivion with every season. Surrounded by fast-diminishing forests, the town nestled beneath the Kanchenjunga range of the Himalaya, tempting Plains-weary tourists with the promise of views to Sagarmatha, the Head of the Sky, as my ever-attentive Yashu called Mount Everest.

I had asked Yashu to first take me to purchase a gift of sweets for Mr Duppa. He clasped my index and middle fingers tightly and led me straight to an extraordinary survivor of the Raj, named Glenary's, a bakery that faithfully adhered to the old recipe books left by the British. The elegant, Edwardian glass cabinets that lined the old shop were heavy with jam roly-polys, scones, tea buns, chocolate cakes, handmade confectionery, and all manner of Billy Bunter-worthy fare. I indulged in a bag of soft-centred chocolates to sustain us both on our foggy excursion, and a light fruit cake for my anticipated hosts.

As we stepped back into the street, a pair of urchins waved and grinned at me. I knelt down and offered them each a sweet. Their slanted mountain eyes widened in disbelief and they burst into a giggly gabble of chat. They nibbled at the dark coating and peered at the gooey sweetmeat within, showing each other and me their discovery. Never had I seen two children more grateful for, or as excited by, a bag of chocolates.

I looked up to find an elderly Buddhist monk standing over us, his grin as broad as those of the sticky-lipped boys. He indicated towards the children and chuckled away to himself in Tibetan, which earned him an exploratory rummage in the paper bag for his own moment of un-monastic indulgence.

As Yashu and I commenced our descent into the rabble of the bazaar, he pushed his fingers between mine to take hold of my whole hand, and I found myself smiling.

I was falling in love with these mountain people.

ψ

The *Aghori Baba* stayed beside Bindra as the nervous Bihari nurse unwrapped the heavy dressings on her feet and hands. He tutted in concern.

"Much hurt to your feet, sister," he grimaced to Bindra. She nodded her head from side to side in resigned silence. "But now you eating good medicine, no problem."

"*Babajyu*," Bindra asked, her mind far from the poor condition of her remaining clawed toes and unhealing ulcers. "Is my Jiwan safe? Safe with the *Aghori Babas*?"

"Very safe, sister," he smiled in answer. "No problem."

"But I know of the *Aghori Babas*," she persisted, "I have heard what they do. Such a life is not for my Jiwan. He is a gentle boy. He's too young for such a life on the burning *ghats*."

The reputation of the *Aghori* was well known, even in the distant seclusion of Bindra's beloved Hills. She knew they directed their *puja* to Kaala Bhairava, Shiva in His fiercest form, to whom they offered a handful of scarlet blooms drenched in their own semen. They called Him Kapaleshvara, the Lord of the Skull, He who Assimilates All Existence, for Bhairava was not "fierce" in an ordinary sense, but rather an expression of the natural cycle of dissolution in the cosmos.

"Lord Bhairava is 'fierce' only to those who identify themselves merely through the limitations of the material world," her grandmother had once taught her. "To look into His face exposes the absurdity of our judgemental attitudes and worldly attachments, the futility of our obsessions with social conformity and habit. And as for the *Aghoris'* life on the cremation grounds, how better to acknowledge that we do not take our worldly wealth with us! That social station and prestige are worthless!" her grandmother had impressed on the young Bindra. "Such a life amongst the remains of the dead reveals that as the fear of death is exorcised, so the fear of life is dispelled."

Bindra suddenly could not bear to think of her little Jiwan amongst the taboo-breaking *Aghori Babas*.

"*Behenji*," the *Aghori* looked into her eyes, drawing her back from the dark anxiety in which she was losing herself. "Sister, no need for fear. No problem."

ψ

"Young chap," Mr Duppa announced, "I'm as old as the century! I had an English father, became a planter in 1919, and attribute my uncommon longevity to an unfaltering abstinence of salt, chillies, meat, alcohol and tobacco – in addition, of course, to the devotion of a loving wife."

I nodded with an appreciative smile, and thought of his plate secretly piled high with lamb chops.

We were sitting in an old wooden house handsomely furnished with Victorian mahogany and teak, its walls and floors draped in richly dyed cloth and hand-woven carpets.

I looked up to meet the eyes of Mrs Duppa, who had appeared in the doorway. She bowed in greeting and offered me a plate of spiced egg sandwiches. Like her kindly husband, she had retained a remarkable elegance, even beauty, despite the stains of age.

"Now, Mister David," he continued, "I am informed by the Club of your search for your Uncle Oscar."

I nodded, my mouth full of peppery deliciousness.

"We knew him well," Mrs Duppa added nonchalantly, thrusting a plate of sweetly scented sour-milk cake slices beneath my nose.

I was stunned.

"You knew him?" I spluttered, in such surprise that I momentarily lost co-ordination and inhaled my first mouthful of cake.

"Oh my, yes! You did not realise this?" asked Mr Duppa.

I shook my head, unable to speak as I was trying to dislodge the lump of creamy stodge now stuck in my throat.

"My wife's cousin, Premlal, married Lily. So you see, we are related! You know Lily?"

I shook my bewildered head.

"Oscar's eldest daughter. A most luxurious woman. She wore golden ear pieces, precious native necklaces and never used the same handkerchief twice. She also had a passion for pet rabbits, which was considered highly eccentric in these hills," he chuckled, sipping noisily at his tea. "Then there was Tuss, of course, who disappeared off to sail the seas with a parrot on his shoulder. Winnie was a wild one – called a 'flapper' in those days – who was always running away, until her pet monkey bit her and she died of lockjaw. The youngest daughter, Elinnie, was beautiful, intelligent, with a gift for music, and loved by all – but she went away and never came back. And last of all, Harry, who was named after me!"

My head was spinning. My Grandmother's clandestine whispers had been true. Tears began to run down my cheeks.

"Oh, how we understand your emotion at hearing our chitter-chatter of your old family, all now expired," Mrs Duppa nodded in sympathy.

A touching moment it may have been. However, the cause of my watering eyes was the cake lodged fast in my windpipe, which was now causing me to struggle for breath.

Mr Duppa continued, oblivious.

"Young Harry and his wife – also a Eurasian, as we mixed-blood of the so-called 'Domiciled Community' were once called – spent much time here with us. He was a freeman of independent means, so left for New Zealand, or some such spot that was British and sunny, and we unhappily did not hear of him again."

My distress at the prospect of having survived violence, disease and dangerous jungle in my journey across India only to lose my life to a surfeit of teacake, caught the attention of Mrs Duppa. She had, at last, begun to realise that my strained expression was much more than immoderate sentimentality.

Still Mr Duppa continued.

"Oh, but Darjeeling was magical then, of course. The Governor and his entourage would spend the six summer months here, if not at Simla, to escape Calcutta at its worst. They would stay at the Club, while the planters moved into the Elgin and Park Hotels. And such balls we had! The Darjeeling Gymkhana had a Burmese teak floor so perfectly sprung that we could dance all night and never once tire! And every day the streets were washed so as not to soil the *memsahibs'* white dresses, all ordered from European *dhurzi* tailors. They even had hairdressers brought in, just for the season, all the way from Paris! Can you imagine?"

I could not.

Rather, I had given up all hope for myself and had turned my concerns instead to the effect on my genial hosts of a discourteous demise on their chaise longue.

At that moment, the octogenarian Mrs Duppa leapt to her feet. She swung towards me with alarming speed and belted me across the back with a force that quite surpassed her age.

The incident seemed to endear me to Mr Duppa because, whilst they laughed and I apologised as a servant cleaned up the ejaculated soggy crumbs, he told me that in the future I was to call him Uncle Harry. He glanced at his pocket watch, then indicated to me that it was time that we go together into the bazaar. I obediently bade fond farewells to his sweetly smiling, powerfully dextrous spouse, who insisted I take with me a full tiffin's-worth of cake and sandwiches, which the maid had already bound in brown paper.

My new uncle took my arm as we walked back into the crush of the old bazaar, busy with all manner of mountain people from across the Eastern Himalaya. In his three-piece suit, wide-brimmed hat, and with a confident swing in his polished cane, he walked me straight to the home of a swarthy Tibetan. They muttered to each other on the front step, whereupon Uncle Harry announced that at seven the following morning, Gombu would drive me in his jeep, eastwards across the mountains, to a town called Kalimpong. There, I was to stay at a hotel called the Himalayan View.

"Ask the proprietor for directions to the home of Doctor Alex," Uncle Harry insisted. "None but he has the answers for which you have come."

ψ

Bindra was sitting up in bed.

The heat was unbearable. The air stagnant. Her head throbbing.

Jyothi had gone to the Nepali temple for the afternoon. He had promised to do *puja* at the *lingam* on her behalf. He had promised to bring back *sidur* to mark her forehead, to honour the divinity within.

Bindra shifted herself again. She had been warned by the doctor not to remain in one place for too long. The loss of sensation in her body risked her lying motionless for hours, unaware of the deficiency of blood in her veins, the ulcerating pressure on her bones.

Even so, Bindra could not stay still. These days she was constantly agitated until Jyothi was back with her, cuddled against her on the bed. He had not used his bedroll once since Jiwan had gone. She could feel his loneliness.

She wondered whether the *Aghori Baba* was really out on the cremation *ghats* searching for Jiwan. Was he looking properly amongst the crowds? Was he asking every *dom* that cremates the dead? Was he searching all the Bhairava temples in the city, and not just the *Aghori mandir* near Thatheri Bazaar?

Bindra wiped perspiration from her forehead with a bandaged hand. She scanned the other women with whom she shared the little room. Most were sleeping in the heat. None could speak Nepali. All had been ravaged by leprosy. She wondered where they had come from and what had brought them to Kashi. She wondered if they too had lost their homes. And their children.

Bindra stared into the haze beyond the window, searching for the promise of a breeze to ease her mind. She longed to be outside, on hillsides, in forest.

Bindra suddenly longed to be anywhere but here.

Back at the Planters' Club, I sat beneath a dilapidated gazebo in the garden to try to write the first letters home since my arrival in India. It was time to explain my sudden disappearance, both to my parents and to Priya's. I had been so consumed by my own grief, that I had not once considered theirs. I needed to apologise, to give account of myself, and it was not until now that I had felt able to begin to find the words.

I was still struggling with the opening lines of the first page when a young boy in a smart school uniform confidently approached.

"Uncle," he addressed me courteously, "will you play TT with me?"

I had no idea what he meant.

"TT, uncle! Tabletop Tennis! Will you play with me?" His polite pleas were irresistible.

Ambreesh from Calcutta passed a very long hour indeed beating me at every game, before we were abruptly interrupted by an anxious Yashu.

"Forgive my goodness, sir. Just to be warning of much possibly troubles in town," he announced in earnest. "For your sake, sir, please be keeping out from bazaar!"

Little Ambreesh shrugged his shoulders. He shook my hand, graciously thanked me for letting him win, which in truth I had not, and ran to find his parents.

I left the safety of the Club as jeeps began to invade the streets, grinding their gears beneath the weight of angry youths waving green flags and chanting "Gorkhaland! Gorkhaland!" Lorryloads of Gorkha National Liberation Front militants had begun to pour into Darjeeling to hear their leader, Subash Ghising, threaten to revive aggressive agitation for the creation of a new mountain state within the Indian Union. I decided to take my self-appointed valet's advice and slip away from the town centre.

I walked quickly along the Nehru Road, where shopkeepers were hurriedly pulling down shutters. I scuttled across Chowrasta, where

Gilbert and Sullivan had once rung out from the bandstand, but twitchy soldiers now gathered with rifles ready.

I reached the road for Observatory Hill as the mountains began to resound with violent ranting blasted through megaphones, demanding political independence from the Marxist state of West Bengal. Chilled by tales of riots, murders and bombings here just a few years earlier – all of which seemed wholly irreconcilable with these gentle-mannered, tolerant hill people – I decided to keep my distance and visit the Gymkhana Club.

The main doors of the old building were guarded by a stocky little Gurkha. He was unexpectedly rude and adamantly refused me entrance. I grizzled under my breath and was about to turn away, when he promptly softened.

"You're a Britisher?"

I replied that I most certainly was.

"Oh, I am apologising!" he burst. "I am much accustomed to barging Americans that I was not considering, until I was hearing of your fine speech. Of course you may by-golly enter," he offered in penance. "And in my friendly sorryness, I am giving you a marvellous jolly guiding!"

The Club was a rambling building, parts of which seemed to be fast approaching dereliction. My diminutive escort led me through the banqueting hall with its precarious musicians' gallery, and the library with its empty mahogany shelves. The numerous games rooms with their worn baize card-tables and ornate scoreboards from which all brass inlay had been meticulously picked. The panelled drinking salons with their cracked, smoked mirrors and splintered linen-fold panelling. The cavernous ballroom, the *moorghi-khana* "hen house" for the *mems*, and then the vast upstairs skating rink, once so popular amongst the ladies for all those inevitable "collisions" with eager bachelors.

I had to catch my breath at what must have once been an exquisite tiered theatre. It still had its original hangings, now suspended from their fixings in shreds. Painted flats were stacked in optimistic readiness for another season of Barrie and Shaw, but were now rotting to tatters in the scenery store. The auditorium had retained the ruins of once elegant seating, although the orchestra pit was now home to a pack of wild dogs.

My doorman reverently showed me into the old boardroom, still with its original long teak table, surrounded by chairs. He suddenly drew so close to me that I thought he was about to plant a kiss on my chin in appreciation for my nationality.

"I fought for our most goodly king in the War," he announced with emotion, "and am receiving a bally handsome pension from your fine marvellous country."

I assured him that I was delighted, and that his annuity was no doubt well deserved.

"But," he hissed, "the Britishers have not left this place, I am telling you! At nights when I am guarding they come!" His eyes widened and his lips seemed to pale in genuine fear. "If I am not attentive to my duties, if I am placing these chairs this way and that, in the willy-nillies, they come around when I am at my least expecting to push me so hard that I am left all tipsy-topsy!"

He quietly shut the door and led me, with exaggerated stealth, to the bottom of the main staircase.

"In day-time and night-time, those old Britishers come back, drinking in the bar their top Club whiskies," he whispered with intensity. "Now you are not believing perhaps, but many have heard their talking, their merry chinkling of glasses and creakly footsteppings." He gripped my arm tightly. "But one which gives me most the terrorful jeebies is a *pukka sah'b* who is walking down so jolly quiet and disappearing, oh my gollies, in this very same spot," and he indicated to the foot of the stairs.

I could have listened to his tales for hours, but dusk was fast descending and I needed to return to the Planters' before I was caught up in any riots in the darkening town below. As I thanked him for his kind indulgence, my retired soldier, evidently fearful of the coming night and the persistent ghosts of *sahibs* and *mems*, hugged me tightly in farewell, his head only reaching my chest.

"Be most forgiving, sir, but you could be my very son," he mumbled into my coat buttons.

ψ

When Bindra woke, the sun was low. The cooling air moved sluggishly, bearing on it the sweet incense of innumerable *pujas*. Jyothi was sitting beside her, in silence.

"*Timi thakay ko chau?*" she asked him. "Are you tired?"

No response.

"Jyothi?"

Nothing. She drew herself close to him.

"*Ama?*" he asked quietly. "Am I going to die?"

Bindra sat up, enabling him to rest his head in her lap.

"What a question for such a young boy!" she chuckled to disguise her unease at his uncharacteristic demeanour. Jiwan would ask such a thing. But not Jyothi.

She hugged him closer.

"You know we are all born and that we all die. Life and death, sickness and health are just part of the natural order . . ."

She paused to consider her words.

"That's why we see Lord Shiva as both bearer of the eternally creative *lingam* and as dancer of the *Tandava* that causes the cosmos to unravel," she continued slowly. "And Shakti may be expressed both as Annapurna, who nourishes life into being, and as Kali Ma, who absorbs it all back into its original, inert state. You see? Creation and dissolution are the two principal forces of all existence. One is not 'good' and the other 'bad'. They are both indivisible aspects of the same eternal process. Two ends of the same stick!"

Jyothi did not respond.

"Even the deodars, Lord Shiva's most revered cypress trees in our high Hills, rise and rise until they touch the sky, only to fall back to the earth from which they sprang," she explained. "Even the stars in their innumerable *crores* appear in brilliance, only to tumble back at the twinkle of an eye into the same darkness that gave them birth. We all come and we all go, like sun and moon, cold season and monsoon. It is the natural order," she repeated. "It is all as it should be."

Jyothi gently placed his hand on her arm.

"And what happens when *I* die, *Ama*? Where do *I* go?"

"Well," she took a deep breath, "*Bahun* priests with their laws and castes, and mountain *lamas* with their *Dharma* and Buddhas, believe each of us is born again in another body. Many times, over and over. They believe that if we're 'good', we're born as a pale-skinned Brahmin, or as a holy monk. And if we're 'bad', they say we're born dark-skinned, low caste – or as a woman!" she chuckled out loud. "But, of course amongst our people, it's different," she emphasised. "We don't hold to caste, do we?"

Jyothi shook his head.

"We see all men, all women as equal."

Jyothi rocked his head from side to side in agreement.

"We see all life, in all its forms, as an expression of Shiva and Shakti – consciousness and energy – in perfect union."

"So when I die?" Jyothi reminded her.

"When *we* die, all the elements from which we are made, including the knowledge we have learned and the wisdom we have gained, return to earth, plant and animal. To fire and water, air and sky. All back to the single, underlying source from which new life continually springs."

Jyothi now lay very still.

"So you see, we each have a responsibility to seek out good knowledge and learn true wisdom," she impressed on him. "Each life has a bearing on what comes after. Nothing and no one is lost. For, in truth, there is no 'death', no destruction, no end. Only absorption back into the ceaseless course of creation."

Jyothi listened hard. He listened for answers and understanding.

"My good, kind boy," Bindra assured him, "as you grow older, you will see how our gods and our *puja* all help us to understand this essential truth."

Jyothi put his arms around his mother and hugged her tightly.

"*Ama*," he whispered, "I hope I have life enough to learn."

213

With "Gorkhaland! Gorkhaland!" still ringing through the town, and half-sized Rambo-imitators storming through the streets in green headscarves, waving flags and tying banners to drainpipes, I was relieved to reach the Club without incident.

The fog that had enshrouded Darjeeling since my arrival had begun to dissipate in the late afternoon sun. I paused to look from the balcony across rooftops and market, wooded heights and dark valleys, but was quickly driven inside by an increasingly aggressive wind. I entered the room to find my bed prepared and curtains closed, the fire lit and bath towel hung nearby to warm through.

I pulled back a curtain as I undressed to peer out at the dying glow of dusk, when lightning blazed in silence across the distant mountains. I watched from my sitting-room window as the entire view of snowy peaks, forests and tea-gardens disappeared in a second ferocious flash that knocked out the town's power supply. In moments, Yashu arrived with an oil lamp and ginger tea. "Most mighty great big one coming, sir!" he warned and scurried off to the shelter of his quarters.

It appeared as though forest beasts were opening their heavy eyes, awakening to revel in nocturnal secrets, as little windows and doorways across the hills gradually began to glow with oil lamps and candles hung in jars. In mere moments, a thick, wet fog flowed in with criminal stealth. The lambent, amber eyes blinked momentarily and were gone.

The vociferous rhetoric in the town fell quiet. I looked up from my book and instinctively held my breath.

A roaring wind suddenly tore against the verandah, stealing away wicker furniture and plant pots, blowing in my double doors. Hail the size of Koh-i-noor diamonds volleyed furiously against the roof and windows. I forced a desk up against the doors to keep them shut, and withdrew to the safety of the bedroom and the comfort of my blazing fire.

With the battery raging on outside, I packed my rucksack in preparation for an early departure and the next stage in my search for Uncle Oscar. I attempted a hot bath, but once again there was no water in my taps, only bilious gurgles and a rusty sludge.

I retired instead to my bed, where I lay smiling at the ceiling, replete with fruit cake and ginger tea, a head full of chocolate-smeared ragamuffins, yellow-stockinged monks, and spectral *sahibs*.

"I'm happy here!" I said out loud, surprising myself.

I listened for an echo of the unexpected words as they pulsated through the room. I sought to seize the syllables as they rebounded from flaking veneer and peeling wallpaper, before they were absorbed by discoloured damask and unlaundered candlewick. I needed to be sure.

"I'm happy here!" I tried again. "And I'm here because of you. Thank you, Grandma. Thank you, Priya," I whispered into the flame-lapped shadows.

Another assault of thunder and Tagore was once again bright in my memory, like a heartfelt promise:

"In the gusty night when the rain patters on the leaves you will hear my whisper in your bed, and my laughter will flash with the lightning through the open window into your room."

I closed my eyes smiling and, despite the storm, sank into a sleep that remained unstirred until the crows announced a clement dawn.

ψ

It was dark when the *Aghori Baba* returned to stand by Bindra's bed. She withdrew her arm from around her sleeping son and eagerly sat up to greet him.

"*Behenji*, many friends is searching your son," he smiled.

"Jiwan!" she gasped in anticipation. "You have found my Jiwan?"

"Yes, yes," he assured her. "He's fine. Very fine."

Jyothi was immediately wide awake. "*Ama*, is Jiwan-*bhai* back?" he asked with excitement.

Bindra looked to the *Aghori* in hope.

"*Behenji*, be brave," he replied. "Your son is choosing his path. Not your path. His path."

She nodded. She knew.

"*Behenji*, your son is went away from Kashi. No more here."

"Went away?" Bindra was unsure that she had understood his awkward Nepali. "Jiwan has gone where?"

"*Behenji*, your son is went away to guru's guru. Far away, in Himalaya."

"But, *Babajyu*!" she gasped. "He's just a child! He needs his mother! He is not ready!"

The *Aghori* raised his hand to calm her.

"*Behenji*, nothing is belonging to us. Not our clothings, not our houses. Not even them we are loving. All is Shiva, all is one. Be brave. No problem."

Bindra could not offer *pranam* as the *Aghori* disappeared back into the darkness. Her arms were clinging too tightly to Jyothi. Her mouth was pressed too hard against his head as she fought to muffle her sobs.

Chapter Sixteen

The town of Kalimpong spread broadly around a narrow mountain ridge, at an altitude of over 4,000 feet. Its temperate climate and spectacular views of the Kanchenjunga had drawn the likes of Rabindranath Tagore, Helena Roerich, the Maharaja of Dinajpur, two dispossessed Afghani princesses, the Bhutanese royal family – and Uncle Oscar – to settle in the lush forests of its precipitous hillsides.

The three-hour journey from Darjeeling through the mountains revealed an astonishing landscape of peaks and forest, valleys and jungle, rivers and tea. The wild beauty of the uninhabited country beyond the windshield was in stark contrast to the suffocating crush inside the jeep. Ten adults were unceremoniously crammed into the suspension-less vehicle. A further six clung to the outside by their fingernails.

In my efforts to ensure an uninterrupted view, I had chosen to sit beside the driver, as had three others, all of whom were wedged onto the front seat beside me. A sudden, deep inhalation on my part could have cracked the ribs of a Buddhist monk or a Catholic nun sitting two passengers away.

At the jumble of wooden shops and houses of Teesta Bazaar, the jeep stopped. My fellow passengers exploded like spiderlings from the cruel confines of their nest, enabling me to hand over my credentials for scrutiny by bored officials. I sat in a military *daftar* office for over an hour, whilst humourless despots read and re-read my passport. They lethargically recorded my details in triplicate and eventually deemed my visa worthy of a smudgy stamp. I was now

217

permitted to remain in the sensitive border district for a non-negotiable fifteen days.

Over a rickety, army-built bridge and across the roaring, deep-green torrent of the snow-fed Teesta, we commenced our climb towards the hill station through a sub-tropical wilderness of towering ferns and giant palms.

Kalimpong town was disappointingly squalid, with none of the architectural charms of Shimla or Darjeeling. I asked a sober-looking young man for directions to the one hotel emphatically recommended by my magnanimous, new Uncle Harry.

"I am, sir, Sangay 'Tiptop' Tamang," the youth announced, "a faithful civil servant and most terrible pleased to be of your humble servicing."

"Tiptop" promptly marched ahead, one hand stopping traffic in our path with all the confidence of a village constable, whilst the other enthusiastically beckoned me to follow him up an interminably steep hill. My calves were dripping with perspiration under the strain of my cumbersome rucksack by the time we reached the hotel gates, where my smiling guide took his courteous leave and waved me down a gravel drive into an Eden of verdant lawns and secluded flower gardens.

"Mr McKenzie?" I enquired of the handsome, Anglo-Indian gentleman who approached in greeting. Beyond, in the shade of the verandah of a solid, stone-built colonial house, his wife nodded a gracious welcome. "Mr Harry Duppa has sent me from Darjeeling," I explained, wiping rivulets from my forehead and eyes.

It was all I needed to say.

In minutes I was showering in a spotless bathroom, which opened directly into the gardens, and unpacking in a teak-floored, whitewashed bedroom, tastefully furnished in old mahogany. I was flopping onto the freshest bed linen and softest pillows I had seen since home, sipping cold, sweet lemon juice and munching on home-made fruit cake, brought to me by my cheery room-boy, "Named Christopher, sir, and most goodly Catholic."

I had stumbled into paradise.

Ψ

Bindra was fascinated by the four neat stubs where her fingers had once been.

"Doctor-Madam is very pleased," translated the Nepali novice from the temple.

Bindra looked up. The doctor was certainly smiling.

The young man listened to the woman's refined Hindi and continued: "She's saying . . . that the disease is no longer alive in you, but you must continue to take your medicine every day . . . for many more months. You'll be given a complete supply."

"So am I cured?" Bindra dared to ask, with tentative excitement.

The doctor leaned forwards and tapped her polished nails on the desk to emphasise her phrases. The young man listened intently.

"Doctor-Madam's saying . . . not strictly 'cured'. You must continue with your regular check-ups until the disease is gone . . . until you are 'burnt out' (I don't know the Nepali for this term, *didi*)."

Bindra looked back at the deformed clumps that had once been her capable and hard-working hands. Hands that had planted seeds and milked her goat, oiled her daughters' hair and massaged her sons. Hands that had clung in love to Kailash and stroked the perspiration from the length of his spine in the still of night.

"Will they grow again?" she almost whispered.

The doctor intuitively replied.

"Doctor-Madam is saying . . . the disease has done its damage," the novice translated, with an apologetic wince. "Your fingers and your toes are gone, sister. They will not come back . . . nor will the feeling return. (I'm sorry, *didi*,)" he quietly added.

Bindra slowly nodded her head from side to side. She already knew.

"And . . . she's saying you must wrap your feet to protect them from cuts and blisters. You must clean and oil your skin twice a day, to stop it cracking . . . to stop infection and more disease."

Bindra nodded again, but wondered how she would buy oil. She had no money for food.

The doctor stood up.

"Doctor-Madam's saying . . . it's time for you to go now (let me help you stand, *didi*) . . . You must come back in two weeks for a check-up, then two weeks after that."

Bindra gingerly rose to her feet.

"This is your medicine," the young man smiled, handing her a silvered box of silvered cards, to which were attached tablets of different shapes and colours. "And here's a bottle of good oil for your skin."

"*Dhanyabad didi*," Bindra bowed in gratitude to the kindly doctor. "Thank you, thank you, elder sister."

As Bindra made her way down the corridor towards the ward, she could see Jyothi sitting on the end of her bed. He was anxiously waiting. But as his mother approached, he had his answer.

Bindra was smiling.

ψ

Washed, well fed and more refreshed than I had felt in many weeks, I left the hotel and strolled into Kalimpong town. I was clutching the piece of paper given to me by Uncle Harry, on which he had written the address of Doctor Alex. He alone, I had been promised, could answer my questions.

It was not a market day. The large *haat* square was virtually empty, its numerous stalls and stands little more than the playground of bare-footed children, scraggy chickens and mange-marked pye-dogs. A broad-faced boy ran with rosy cheeks up to me with a glistening grin and told me he was Pemba. I asked if he knew of a Doctor Alex. He eagerly rocked his head in excited affirmation, grasped my hand and led me through filthy streets, soliloquising in Nepali all the way.

The oppressive shadow of tall concrete and busy clutter of wooden cottages quickly gave way to the cool dapple of towering bamboo. At the base of Deolo Hill, my chatty companion stopped and pointed off the road. Pemba indicated that I was to descend a narrow, stony path that wound away into a thicket.

220

"Doctor Alex?" I asked, doubtfully.

He nodded in cheery confirmation and again pointed down the track.

Twisting through dense undergrowth and impenetrable clumps of bamboo, I could see a scattering of houses and bungalows tucked in against the hillside. From the Art Deco "sunburst" balcony of an old wooden building, a fair-faced woman watched my descent. I asked for directions and, with a broad smile, she directed me towards the lowest path. I could see her continuing to stare after me until the heavy foliage of the trees became intrusive.

As I walked past the second house, a teenage boy looked up in surprise. He was polishing a bicycle. Distinctly Anglo-Indian in appearance, he mouthed a shy "Hello" in greeting, blushed and slipped away inside.

I paused to chuckle in amazed delight at the sight of my very first live mongooses, energetically rough-and-tumbling on the lower lawn.

I looked back to the house into which the bashful youth had vanished and caught sight of three pairs of eyes staring at me through the crack of the door. The smile and wave I offered in greeting prompted a peal of ethereal giggling and the crack closed shut.

The bungalow at which I next arrived was surrounded by a well-tended garden of roses, camellias and fruit trees. The broad verandah was adorned with an abundance of geraniums in hand-thrown pots, mounted antlers and the once brightly feathered head of a shabby hornbill.

I knocked. And knocked again.

No reply.

A curious servant peeked around a corner.

"*Namaste*," I offered in greeting. "Doctor Alex?"

As she approached, I could see that the diminutive woman had a beautiful mountain face and a nervous smile. She was dressed in an adventurously patterned half-sari and blouse, her greying hair bound in thick cloth.

I asked again, "Doctor Alex?"

She shook her head and beckoned for me to follow. We left the garden and made our way through guava, luffa and banana trees, to a second bungalow. She indicated that I was to wait outside on the front step, whereupon she bowed and scurried backwards into the kitchen block.

I was looking for the mongooses when a small woman in a lavender cardigan opened the front door and demurely welcomed me in. She led me to the sitting room, sat me in a chintz armchair, then promptly left without a word.

In a minute, a serious ten-year-old entered, dark hair sharply parted and still wet with his mother's lick. He formally greeted me with a rapid nod, then sat on a stool at my feet, whilst maintaining total silence.

The woman in the cardigan soon reappeared, having changed into an elegant sari. She was attended by a pretty young girl, who was too self-conscious to look up at me. They were followed by a round-faced, pale-skinned woman draped in blue. With smiles, nods and quiet cluckings, they offered me hurriedly cut sandwiches of tomatoes, ginger root, curd and black pepper.

Two servant girls poked their heads around the door to see if it was true. When I offered them a sandwich-plumped smile, they ran away squealing.

The women let me finish my second plate before they probed the purpose of my search for Doctor Alex. I explained that I was on a quest for information regarding a member of my family. That Mr Duppa of Darjeeling had sent me. That I hoped to find a grave.

They all rocked their heads from side to side, but did not seem to understand.

Cashew cake was being sliced and sweet tea poured when a fair-faced older woman entered. I immediately felt drawn towards her. She smiled broadly in welcome, her eyes bright with life. Brief words in Nepali were exchanged between the three women, then in perfect English she asked me to repeat the reason I was seeking out Doctor Alex. I told my story again. Still it did not seem to register with them.

"I'm his niece, Cecilia," she explained, "and I regret to tell you that you are too late. Doctor Alex expired over a month ago."

I was shattered. Uncle Harry had been convinced that only Doctor Alex could answer my questions. Only Doctor Alex could reveal the full truth of the family secret. I was unable to hide my disappointment.

"You are a missionary?" the young woman in the cardigan enquired.

"Our maids are certain you are an English prince!" the woman in blue blushed with unexpected embarrassment at the candid admission.

I laughed and, for a third time, patiently explained the reason for my appearance on their doorstep. Slowly, a light seemed to dawn and they began to chatter excitedly to one another.

Cecilia turned to me with raised eyebrows and tentatively asked, "Please tell me, do you know Aunt Helena?"

My heart began to pound.

"My Grandmother was Helena!" I stuttered in confusion.

To hear her name! To hear it here!

"You knew my Grandmother?" I burst. It seemed impossible.

Cecilia caught her breath for a moment. "We never met, but . . ."

She suddenly turned to the others for another hushed exchange in Nepali. They all stared back at me, their dark eyes wide.

"What is the name of this relation for whom you are in search?" she asked.

"Oscar," I swallowed. "My great-uncle Oscar."

The three women blinked at me.

"If Oscar was your uncle and Aunt Helena was your grand-mother," Cecilia said with careful consideration, as she raised her arms towards me, "then you are . . ."

"Our cousin!" they cried in unison.

Chapter Seventeen

It was dusk when the old Nepali priest caught sight of two figures slowly climbing the temple stairs. He watched with curiosity as the boy gently attended to the ailing woman with every arduous step. As they approached, the child looked up and smiled.

"*E Jyothi-bhai*!" the priest called, peering at him in the bat-spun gloom. "You've brought your mother this evening!"

Bindra bowed as she struggled to catch her breath. She made her way to the top of the river wall, where she sat to wipe the perspiration from her face with the corner of her shawl. As the priest sent Jyothi to fetch fresh *chiya* tea, Bindra turned to Ganga Ma, the *Mandaakinii* Milky Way personified, which spread before her like a silver sea. She breathed deeply, searching for relief from a promise of a breeze in the stifling heat.

"*Om namah Gangadhar*," she whispered in respectful salutation to Shiva, He who holds the mighty Ganga in His hair, Lord of her lost mountains.

"*Bahini*!" The priest sat beside her and looked into her eyes. "Little sister, Jyothi-*bhai* tells me that the foreigners' medicine has made you well again."

Bindra rocked her head in confirmation. "So I've come for *puja*," she smiled, looking towards the temple doors. "I've been distracted for far too long. It's time to prepare."

"Prepare for what, *Ama*?" Jyothi asked.

He was holding a rough, clay bowl of hot tea towards her. Bindra directed him to place it on the wall. Jyothi and the priest watched as she struggled to secure its rim between the heels of her palms and lift it towards her mouth. She refused their offers of assistance. She was determined to learn.

Not until they had undertaken *puja* before the temple *lingam* and were sitting together in the still darkness of the inner sanctum did Jyothi repeat his question.

"*Ama*," he asked, "what are you preparing for?"

"My good, strong boy," she began, "this *lingam* represents Lord Shiva in his form of Pashupateshvara. Do you understand that name? The Protector of Animals, the patron of all Nepali people."

"Are we Nepalis *pashu* animals?" Jyothi asked with a laugh.

"Nepali, Indian or foreign. Cows, dogs or crows. We are all expressions of the same truth." Bindra's face was serious. "But *pashu* is not just 'animal'," she explained, looking to the milk-drenched *lingam* as it glistened in the lamplight. "If a man is *pashu*, it means he lacks true self-control. He lacks self-mastery. His body and mind are unstable and changeable, his actions inattentive and confused. His day-to-day life is a swollen, torrential river, which sweeps him along, like flotsam on the eternal currents of Ganga Ma."

Jyothi was listening to his mother's every word. He relished her teaching, even when he knew he did not yet understand.

"I am a *pashu*," she stated unequivocally.

"*Ama*!" Jyothi exclaimed in shocked disapproval.

"No, really, son," she chuckled. "These past months I've found myself distracted, my mind troubled and unquiet. I've let myself feel separate from others and from the world. I've been unable to rise above my fears . . ."

"*Ama*!" Jyothi protested again. "You've been sick! People have been unkind to you! Unkind and hurtful!"

"And that's why I had to come here this evening, to do *puja* to Shiva in his form of Pashupateshvara," she smiled. "This *puja* reminds us that we too must be protectors and friends, even of those who are blinded and controlled by their mindless habits, habits they use to feel separate from everyone and everything else. This we must remember before we judge others to be more or less of a *pashu* than we are. Before we see qualities of either balance or imbalance, wisdom or ignorance, in others, we would do well to first recognise them in ourselves."

Jyothi sat quietly and considered her words.

"So, *Ama*," he asked again, with greater emphasis, "what are you preparing for?"

Bindra beckoned him closer, to enfold him in her arms. She looked back to the flickering *lingam*, symbol of the underlying reality, the stability of an essential truth in a constantly changing universe.

"It's time to move on, my big, brave boy," she announced softly. "It's time to go to the mountains."

"To find Jiwan-*bhai*?" he asked with excitement.

Bindra nodded her head from side to side.

"Tomorrow, at dawn, we leave Kashi."

ψ

I sat bewildered and breathless in the tidy bungalow, fingers clinging tightly to the chintz armchair.

The puzzle was tumbling together in my head, piece by piece. My father, Grandmother and Oscar. Loving, lovely Priya. Kitchen Urdu, Johnny Sparrow, scorpions and red Wellingtons.

It felt as though all the years, with all their learning, confusion, joys and griefs, had brought me to this moment. To this old wooden bungalow, nestled deep in the lush foliage of this bamboo-dense hillside. To these smiling, silk-enwrapped women and their smiling, wide-eyed children.

Uncle Harry had not revealed that he had sent me to Oscar's grandson. He had not even hinted that the bungalows and houses on the hillside, past which he knew I would have had to walk in search of Doctor Alex, had been built on the estate to which Oscar had retired from the tea-gardens at Darjeeling. Nor had he disclosed that they were filled with his descendants.

An explosion of activity, and into the room piled not only yet more excited relations, but shining trays of hurriedly fried *pakhoras*, *puris* and salted tapioca root, with fresh tomato and burnt garlic chutneys. Platters of sweet and spicy *chat* mixes and delicious potato *aloo dum*, served with small, round, tongue-blistering *dalle khursane* pickled chillies. And then a tasty boiled cardamom cake, topped with drizzles of condensed milk, and unstoppable pots of creamy, *masala chiya* spiced tea.

In our mutual excitement, we had not noticed the setting sun. It was dark when I finally, regretfully rose to leave, despite their protestations at my return to the hotel.

"There is so much to tell!" Cecilia promised. "Stories to recount and questions to answer! But it's best that we share it when we're all together, in Grandfather-Oscar's house, at the top of the hill path. Come back to us in the morning, just as soon as you have eaten your breakfast," she insisted.

The women clustered beneath the dim flicker of the single light bulb that dangled on a frayed cord above the front door.

"Cousin, beware of *dakaits*!" Cecilia called, as they stood waving and nodding, clucking softly. "There are many bandits in these hills."

I thanked them all for their kind concern and followed their grinning boys, my new "cousin-brothers", who led me up to the road by the light of dangerously flaring rags on sticks.

Back at the hotel, I dressed for a late dinner out of habit, even though I had no appetite left to satisfy.

The proprietors asked if they might join me for dessert. I was as delighted with their company as they were intrigued to hear of my discoveries of the day. Indeed, they seemed to smile knowingly at its unfolding.

"So Uncle Harry was pure discretion until the very end!" Tom McKenzie chuckled.

"You know Mr Duppa?" I asked with unnecessary surprise.

"Everyone knows Uncle Harry!" Nerula McKenzie replied, spooning yet more Nepali *khir* rice pudding into my bowl.

"Uncle Harry was a planter," Tom explained, "as was I until recently. We few remaining Anglo-Indian planters are an intimate community."

"A law unto themselves!" Nerula interjected and they both laughed.

Tom glanced knowingly at his wife, who nodded. He then turned back to me. "You see the large oil painting?"

From a large canvas above the fireplace, a handsome Edwardian gentleman gazed down on us with benign confidence. He was dressed in an incongruous mix of tailored Harris tweed and a loose wrap of native cloth.

"My grandfather," Tom explained. "He took a native princess, Apu Dolma Mutanchi, as a wife . . . like your Uncle Oscar."

Again Tom and Nerula exchanged an expressive look.

"My Grandmother told me my great-aunt was a princess," I replied, with excitement that she had been proven right once again and that perhaps all my childhood fairytales had indeed been true. "Rather a coincidence though, isn't it?" I asked. "Two planters and two princesses?"

Tom chuckled. "Well, you see, two planters who were best friends married two sisters . . ."

He paused to let the light begin to dawn.

"You mean . . ." I began cautiously.

"Yes!" he grinned. "We're family too! In fact, at the last count we reckon you have about thirty-four blood-relations here, with at least another forty or fifty by marriage!"

I could not swallow the rice pudding.

"So," he chuckled, "we could say this first meal with us is, in fact, to welcome you home!"

༓

At first light, Bindra and Jyothi undertook their final *puja* at the temple. The priest expressed regret that Jyothi would no longer be taking his lessons. He had been a cheerful and helpful student, if somewhat undisciplined in his studies.

The novices, fresh from their morning *puja* in the sacred shallows of Ganga Ma, handed Jyothi a bag of food, which they had carefully prepared in gratitude for his untiring assistance with their chores. The priest insisted Bindra take a little bundle of rupee notes wrapped in old newspaper.

"You cannot walk, sister," he pressed, as she strongly protested. "You must travel by bus and train. But keep inconspicuous. Keep covered. Let Jyothi buy the tickets and you'll find no problem."

As Bindra and Jyothi entered the *pucca mahal* of the city's hidden heart, a fearful doubt began to press hard against her chest. She was once again walking away from people whose tongue she shared, people who were kind and whose ways she knew.

Bindra stopped still.

A welling dread was causing her steps and breath to falter.

The sudden, unruly cawing of crows drew her eyes up to the narrow strip of sky above their heads.

"Yes, you are right to laugh at my self-pity," she whispered.

Bindra closed her eyes and placed her bound right palm to her heart. "Kali Ma, I now choose to dispel my fear," she announced with new vigour. "I choose to let go of the delusion of separation, that I may see all life as a reflection of myself . . ."

"*Ama*," Jyothi interrupted, "are you certain you know where we're going?"

"We are going to the mountains," Bindra assured him with conviction. "We are going to Jiwan."

Ψ

It was barely dawn as I huddled on the upper verandah of the hotel, engulfed in woollen blankets. The night had brought an extraordinarily vivid dream that had prevented me from falling back to sleep.

I had seemed to wake to find my bed softly illuminated and surrounded by Hill Indians. I had sat bolt upright, whereupon a smiling woman had stepped forwards to place both her hands on the crown of my head.

"We're grateful that you've come," she had said in a strong, yet tender voice.

Over her shoulder, the smiles of her companions had broadened and I had felt myself enveloped in a remarkable, tangible warmth. She had gently lifted one hand and they had all seemed to shuffle backwards.

The light around them had quickly faded.

Their faces had dimmed.

And they had gone.

As I had sat staring into the new darkness, I was aware of a distant drumming. All the town dogs had begun to howl.

I had not been asleep at all, but fully, wide awake.

I repeatedly ran the apparition through my head as I sipped at my ginger tea on the verandah. I tried to make some sense, attempted to find some logic. Perhaps for the first time, I felt truly blinded by my Western eyes, shackled by my Western thinking. I had touched upon something that remained far beyond the finite perception permitted by my culture.

I concluded that to accept was better than to explain. I directed my attention instead to the promise of daybreak that had just illuminated a leafy ridge across the town, from which arose the pale, square tower and belfry windows of the incompatible silhouette of the MacFarlane church.

As the light began to rise, the clarity of the early morning air suddenly revealed a brilliant band of bright white, motionless clouds.

I gasped and rose to my feet.

These were no clouds, but the angular peaks and clefts of the snow-swathed Himalaya. This was the Kanchenjunga, the world's third highest peak!

Standing in motionless amazement, I understood why the Lepcha, the forest-dwelling, indigenous people of these hills, considered this mountain to be the masculine expression of their ever-loving Mother Goddess, Itbu-moo. I understood why they believed it to mark the Mayel Lyang, a utopian land of peace and perfection, in which all the knowledge and wisdom of their ancestors lay. I understood why, at the close of their lives, the Lepcha still chose to be buried sitting in a basket, facing its ineffable majesty. It seemed only right that, in respect to them, many of even the most feat-focused foreigners still agreed not to desecrate its summit with their crampons.

The descent to breakfast quickly shattered my reveries. The hotel had been overrun by a tour group of Swiss Germans. They invaded my paradisiacal peace by storming about with co-ordinated travel bags and shouting strangulated vowels, like determined, thick-ankled Valkyrie.

I declined a second round of buttery toast and escaped back across the town to Uncle Oscar's old home, but nobody was in. I sat on the front steps to wait.

With alarming speed, clouds billowed over the mountains in ambush. Rain began to podded-pea-patter across the red tin roof. I took cover on the verandah as the orchids began to tremble, and the fronds of the high bamboo began to hot-coal-hiss. I watched the ants battle to build breakers. I listened to the parakeets giggle at the droplets trickling down their ribbed-stockinged legs, as far away querulous thunder grumbled, and inside the house an heirloom solemnly chimed the hour.

Cecilia soon arrived, busy with apologies. She immediately sent servants to summon family members from their homes. In minutes, I was being formally introduced to my new cousins with their complicated Nepali familial titles of *dajoo* and *didi*, *bhai* and *bahini*. *Maila-mama* and *Kancha-kaka*. *Jethi*, *Saili*, *Maili* and *Kaili*. It was breathtaking.

Cousin Samuel was my elder by just four days. However, due to our difference in height, he insisted upon referring to me as *dajoo*, "elder brother", to avert confusion amongst his friends upon their introduction. He cuddled up beside me and affectionately clasped my hand.

"Just yesterday morning, my nephew woke me very early," Samuel began, looking into my eyes without the least reserve. "He said, 'Who is my new uncle arriving today?' I told him he was dreaming, but he said, 'No, no, your new brother is coming here from far away.' So you see, we knew."

At that moment, a figure appeared at the inner door. The gathered crowd fell quiet and respectfully made way for the eldest member of the family. I stood to greet a small woman wrapped in a white silk shawl from which shone sagacious eyes and a clement smile. I was instructed to call her *Phupu*, a term of affectionate respect meaning "Aunt". I could not hide my surprise at the familiarity I felt with this woman, still beautiful at eighty-six years old. It was as though my Grandmother had walked into the room.

Cecilia invited me to bow before this mellow matriarch, with hands pressed together at my heart. *Phupu* in turn placed her palms on the crown of my head. I was astonished. The woman in my dream had done exactly this during the previous night.

"This is *ahashis*," Cecilia explained, "the blessing of an elder. You may now give *ahashis* to your 'younger brother' *bhais* and 'younger sister' *bahinis*," whereupon I was inundated with dark heads on which to place my own palms. I, in turn, then bowed to receive the benedictions of my "elder brother" *dajoos* and "elder sister" *didis*, my *jethi* "aunts" and *kancha* "uncles".

"Welcome home!" *Phupu* smiled from the chair in which she was now resting. "Come, sit with me," she beckoned.

As I settled at her feet, she drew onto her knees a crumbling photograph album. My heart was pounding. I was back with my Grandmother in her Sussex cottage. I was back on the fraying harlequin pouffe, with Cesspit snoring by the fire and Bird in the kitchen battling with the bread bin.

As *Phupu* opened the front cover, a photograph slipped out onto the floor. I bent to pick it up and stared in wonder. Looking back at me were the unmistakable features of Rabindranath Tagore. He was wearing a traditional, black Nepali *dhaka topi* cap, his name written in his own hand across the bottom of the fading portrait in angular, Bengali script.

"You know who that is?" *Phupu* asked.

"Oh yes!" I exclaimed. "Tagore was my childhood hero! My Grandmother taught me his poems. And when I was older, my tutors would have me translate into German and French the *Gitanjali* she gave me, to practise my languages."

The gathered crowd murmured their approval.

"But how do you have his picture?" I pressed.

"Ah, *Gurudev* Tagore was a good friend to our family during those last years of his life spent here in Kalimpong," *Phupu* explained. "We children used to climb up on his knees and stroke his long, white beard as he sang to us his songs."

She leaned to rest her cheek against the backs of her fingers, just as my Grandmother used to do.

"*Your joy is mine, my mischief in your eyes,*" *Phupu* recited, smiling with the recollection, "*Your delight the country where my freedom lies . . .*"

She gave the fading photograph that rested on her palm one last, affectionate caress, before slipping it back between the pages of the album. She turned the book on her knees to face me and opened its cover once more.

"Now this," she announced warmly, indicating the picture on the first page, "is my mother, Lily. Oscar's eldest daughter."

I gasped and my skin duned into goose-pimples.

The distinctive face looking back from the sepia photograph was the very woman who had placed her hands on my head last night, in the hotel room.

Chapter Eighteen

Bindra had hidden herself amongst the other passengers' luggage on the long journey north-westwards across the Plains. The over-crowded carriage was noisy, dirty and comfortless, but through the night she and Jyothi had wrapped themselves in their ragged shawls and cuddled close. They had never been in a train before.

Despite his excitement, Jyothi had quickly fallen asleep in the oppressive heat. Bindra had quietly repeated her Ganesha mantra, to focus mind and body on this new venture, to remind herself to be open to the many changes this new beginning would bring.

And when a difficult and restless sleep eventually came, she dreamt of mountains. Of the Shakti Tree, *gundruk* and *churpi*. Of Jayashri, Jamini and Jiwan.

Back at Varanasi City Station, Bindra had explained in slow, clear Nepali to the man at the window that she needed two tickets to the mountains. She had told him that she was going to find her son. His name was Jiwan. Perhaps he had seen him some weeks ago? Small boy, dressed like an *Aghori Baba*.

Jyothi had opened the folded newspaper for his mother and had shown the disinterested ticket-*wallah* the money given to them by the temple priest, to prove that they could pay. The unexpected sight of a bundle of rupee notes in the possession of such a vagabond hill-woman and unkempt child had naturally caught the clerk's attention. He had counted up the money, then passed over the counter two G-class tickets to Dinantapur Junction, northwards in Rohilkhand.

"No seat guaranteed!" he had shouted at Bindra twice, in English. She had not understood.

Eighteen long hours later, the train finally dragged itself into Dinantapur Junction. Bindra struggled to her feet in the mayhem of a station arrival. She peered out of the small, barred window above them. She could see no hills. She breathed in the scalding air. She could smell no forest.

Jyothi clung to his mother's ragged sari as they anxiously descended into the boisterous crowds on the platform. Bindra directed him towards the communal tap, where they filled their water canister and washed their faces. They peered across the platforms in both directions. No mountains.

Bindra waited and watched. She decided they had better follow the jostling tide, but quickly found themselves forced and pushed until they were outside, exposed to the full flare of searing sunlight. Bindra was panting for air beneath her shawl, but did not dare expose her hands or head to public view. She did not fear for herself. Only for Jyothi.

Bindra drew her son towards the shade of the station canopy and sat to gather her thoughts.

"Are we where we're meant to be?" Jyothi asked, offering his mother gritty, metallic-tasting water from the canister.

Bindra scanned the horizon. A shimmering mirage of wilting rickshaw-*wallahs*, brightly painted lorries, rusting buses and crumbling concrete desiccated in an infernal haze.

Suddenly, the roar of "*Jaldi jao! Jao! Jao!*"

A policeman was storming towards them with fierce intent, raising his baton with every savage order for them to "Get moving fast!".

Bindra stood tall and drew Jyothi close to her side.

"*Dajoo*," she began, smiling at the perspiring officer, "elder brother, please tell us where we go to find the mountains . . ."

"*Saali kutti!*" he spat at her.

"We have come very far to find my youngest son. His name is Jiwan. Could you direct us to the *Aghori Babas*?"

"*Yahan se nikal ja, kutiyaa!*"

She did not understand the words. She did not need to.

Bindra and Jyothi turned their faces from the angry, vicious man and scuttled out into the sunlight.

𝕌

"Did you know *Sah'b-baje* took a princess as a wife?" *Phupu* asked, resting a papery hand on my shoulder. The day had passed with inexplicable speed, as we had acquainted each other with our family histories, giving credence to an array of inherited tales.

"*Sah'b-baje*?" I asked.

"British-master-grandfather," she awkwardly translated, sending the rest of the room into hearty guffaws. "Your Uncle Oscar."

"Ah yes, my Grandmother spoke of her, my great-aunt who was a princess," I nodded enthusiastically. "She said people stepped off the path when she approached and bowed their heads."

"Her name was Isi Mutanchi," *Phupu* smiled fondly, "but in our Nepali way, she was known as *Kaili-boju*, 'fourth-daughter-grandmother'. She was a Lepcha, one of the local tribe from these hills, whose father was the *Raja* of Phuptshering and the *Mandal* Overlord of Pachin – you know, where Margaret's Hope tea estate now lies, near Darjeeling." I did not. "Well, *Sah'b-baje* had fallen very sick with dysentery in his own tea-garden at Turzum. Very sick indeed. He was not just an important man, but was much liked and respected. He did so many good things to help the people and improve their lives. Clean water, medicines, cinchona, and all. So the *Raj-kumari*, the Princess Isi, nursed him. She saved his life, they fell in love . . . the rest you must know."

Phupu was brimming with history and proud of her past. Proud of her improbable mix of English, Swedish, Nepali and Lepcha blood.

"And do you understand her name, Mutanchi?" she asked.

I shook my head, longing for her to continue.

"Mutanchi is the name the Lepcha give themselves," she explained. "It means 'Beloved of the Mother', of the goddess Itbu-moo – Mother Nature, if you like. They're a remarkably friendly people, peace-loving and uncomplicated. They live in the forest, with names in their *Rongring* language for every bird, plant and butterfly to be found in these mountains, which delighted *Sah'b-baje*. He was a passionate naturalist and won awards in London for his lepidopteran studies – you see how he taught me that impossible word! But the Britishers just couldn't train the Lepchas to work the tea-gardens. They would throw off all the clothes that the planters and missionaries had made them wear in an instant – and run back into the trees, laughing and singing! Perhaps you already know of their reputation? It still enthrals anthropologists – and shocks priests of all persuasions!" she chuckled. "So the *sah'bs* shipped in the Nepalis instead."

I was fascinated.

"But, of course, *Sah'b-baje* lived in very different times. The Britishers did not approve of such mixed-race unions. Their Christian god-*wallahs* refused to marry them. He had to keep *Kaili-boju* secret, even here, and hide the children when Europeans passed through, to avoid a scandal. Even when Mallory and Irvine called in on their fateful route to Everest, we all had to stay down below without a whisper, until the coast was clear! And yet, you know, *Sah'b-baje* – your Uncle Oscar – loved and cared for all his family, unlike many of those Britishers in India who disowned and discarded their *chi-chi* children to the street, or abandoned them to orphanages."

Phupu rested back into her sagging chair and sighed with her memories. Again, I was back in Sussex, back with my Grandmother.

"It was in the same basement room where we used to hide," she continued, drawing me closer, "that, after *Sah'b-baje*'s passing, we found hidden bundles upon bundles of English pound notes. Perhaps it was the upheavals of Independence and Partition, but in those days rumours were running wild. My parents were assured that, with the demise of the Raj, the Bank of England had also collapsed, and because of the fall of the Bank of Simla some twenty years before, we all believed it. For months on end, these big bundles of *Sah'b-baje*'s money, his secret savings for our security, were played with by us children in our silly games, then used as kindling on the kitchen fire – yes, I know, I know! – until all were reduced to ashes . . ."

The appearance of a silent servant girl in the doorway brought the recounting of family tales to a disappointing end. She bowed her head and indicated to *Phupu* that dinner was served. I was led through unlit corridors and down a staircase to a feast illuminated by candle and oil lamp. Steaming pots of sticky rice, vegetable curries of ginger and garlic. Spicy raw salads, eggs baked in a creamy coriander sauce, served with a variety of fresh *rotis*.

As at distant Dalba, the family did not eat with me. Only Samuel kept me company at the table. The others stood to watch with manifest delight at my every mouthful, taking it in turns to plunge forwards with spoons piled high and refill my plate, despite my remonstrations.

As a band of "cousin-brothers" prepared once again to escort me through the darkness and back to the hotel, my indulgent "aunties" asked me to stay, to live with them in Kalimpong.

"Don't leave, cousin!" they begged. "Learn Nepali here with us. And we'll find you a good and beautiful wife!"

They all laughed out loud and slapped their palms.

So I laughed too, even as I fought to restrain the searing memory of slim, dark fingers that had once entwined and loved my own.

ψ

Bindra and Jyothi were tired. They had walked slowly, from stretch of shade to length of shadow. The heat was unbearable.

As they wilted behind the trunk of a dead tree, Bindra threw off her shawl and gasped for air, hair limp with perspiration, damaged scalp throbbing with new infection. She longed for a mountain stream in which to plunge. Even the thought brought a sighing smile.

"*Ama*," Jyothi mumbled through dry lips, "have you taken your foreigners' medicine today?"

She had not.

"We have to take care with our water and there isn't enough for me to swallow them," she admitted, trying to dip a narrow edge of her shawl into the canister to wipe his face and eyes. "Now drink," she insisted, awkwardly lifting the metal container to his mouth between her wrists.

"But *Ama*, you must!" Jyothi implored, his lips soft again and glistening as his thin, pink tongue explored their wetness. "I only needed a sip, so there's plenty left for your *paraiharuko dabai*."

Bindra was unconvinced she needed to continue taking the Doctor-Madam's pills. The kindly woman had already told her that the disease had been stopped in its destructive course. Surely it was better, then, to save the remaining medicine in case it ever returned. Surely it was better to keep it stored, in case she were ever to discover a new birthmark on any of her *chora-chori* children.

However, to appease the anxiety of her son, Bindra turned to her carrying cloth, cumbersome and heavy with the doctor's boxes. She pushed one towards him, and he drew out a single, silver strip, polka-dotted with three different-coloured tablets. Jyothi squinted as the aluminium flashed in the aestival blaze, then abruptly, instinctively flinched.

A thin man with high cheekbones and harshly coloured hair had silently appeared beside them. He was dressed in bright-bleached *kurta pajama* and exposed a bloody grin.

"*Namaste-ji*," he beamed, spitting a heavy globule of *supari*-stained saliva into the dust. "*Aap kaha aai ho?*" he enquired with a nasal whine through darkly discoloured teeth.

Jyothi moved closer to his mother and wrapped his fingers around her forearm. He did not like this man. He did not want him near her.

The intense heat had slowed Bindra's responses, and she suddenly realised the hairless scarring across her head was still openly exposed. She self-consciously drew up her shawl.

Having induced no response, the man turned to Jyothi and asked, "*Thik hai?*"

This Bindra understood. She rocked her head in courtesy, even as she turned away, to indicate that all was well.

Bindra drew Jyothi to sit on her other side and together they quickly wrapped the medicine back into the cloth.

"*Behenji, kya baat hai?*" the man asked, moving to sit beside Bindra.

She shook her head to show she did not understand his Hindi and hurriedly instructed Jyothi to tightly tie the knot.

"*Kya aapko chot lagee hai*?" he pressed, pointing to her head, then indicating with his smooth, raised chin towards her fingerless hands and heavily bound feet.

"*Aapka ghar kaha hai*?" he tried.

This Bindra thought she understood. He wanted to know where they lived.

"*Paharma*," she replied quietly, eager to move away from the unsettling, intrusive stranger. "In the mountains."

Despite her caution not to engage with his eyes, the man became animated with her concession to respond.

"*Dinantapurme*?" he continued. "And in Dinantapur?"

Bindra shook her head and struggled to her feet. She looked from side to side, but did not know in which direction to start walking. It was impossible for her to move in this heat. Impossible for her to think.

The man rose to stand in front of them. He grinned his scarlet gash at Jyothi and stretched out long, thin fingers to take his hand. Jyothi recoiled and plunged his face into his mother's *pharia sari*.

The man sniggered.

"*Aaiye*," he said, beckoning them to follow him. "*Ghar! Ghar!*" he pointed with affected excitement.

The tall, thin man in the bright-bleached *kurta* seemed to be promising them a house.

ॐ

I awoke to discover that I had slept through a great storm.

Rain squalled across perse peaks, filtering dawn light into fickle, iridian hues. Ghoulish clouds hung low over a sodden landscape, trailing in vast wreaths about fantastic hills.

My new cousin Samuel had insisted upon keeping me company at the Himalayan View the previous night. I had felt him tremble as his arm slipped round to hold me as I prepared to sleep. He had said it was their custom, that his parents would be proud, and with some glee asserted that his cousin-brothers would now be jealous that he had been "the chosen one".

After breakfast porridge, we shared a soapy bucket-bath, then strolled out into clarty streets. Samuel first led me up to the old Scottish church, its stained glass lately broken when a schism in an already diminished congregation had resulted in the hurling of bricks to vent a doctrinal sulk. We tried the doors, but found them locked, so squelched through soggy cottage garden, muddy chicken yard and on to forest in which a hillside graveyard lay. Above us, punk-fuzzed monkeys grumbled in the wet, whilst far below, beneath a pall of mist, the Teesta scored between Bengal and Sikkim its circuitous incision.

Samuel clutched fast my arm as we braved a dangerous declivity to press on amongst dense scrub and scattered stones. Monsoon-mellowed epitaphs bore witness to the lives of lowland missionaries who had arrived with foreign burr and Bible, only to soon sicken in exotic climes and swiftly merge with mountain humus.

Beneath dark, dripping trees, Samuel slowed us to a halt.

"This is where they lie," he whispered, I thought to mark respect. "So now let's go," he hissed and tugged to draw me back.

I stood astonished to have reached this isolated patch of unmarked ground, precariously perched on a Himalayan foothill's fragile slope. And yet to now know the tranquil saturation of this place, that to another would bear no significance or worldly worth, was the culmination of an abundant life of familial inheritance and grandmotherly affection.

"*Dajoo*, please!" Samuel intruded with a beseeching scowl. "I've got the proper creeps!"

"Just one last thing," I insisted, bending to place a hand upon the earth. I touched my heart and spoke aloud the names of Uncle Oscar and Aunt Isi, then chose a stone to fit my pocket.

Samuel crouched to peer in puzzlement at my quirk.

"A final gift my Grandmother asked of me," I explained. "From Uncle Oscar's resting place to hers . . ."

I looked hard into the trunk-cut mist. I had now eaten a mango from its tree, as she had asked, and held a *Dalit*. I had sat with *sadhus* and collected a memento of a grave. I had fulfilled her every wish, and yet found no solace in their attainment. Only sorrow at one more conclusion. Sadness at another end.

"Well, good! You've done your duty," Samuel hurried his approval, glancing anxiously around as though *bhut* ghosts might be prepared to leave their foggy peace and hunt us home. "So now," he spluttered in my ear, pulling on my shoulders to heave me upright, "let's please be getting out of here!"

We dredged our way back into town where, despite the weather, the *haat* market bustled, barter babbling over vegetables and fruits, bloody meat and stinking fish. Drifts of embroidered shawls and woolly jumpers, kitchen utensils and handmade tools. Neat bluffs of *churpi* yak's cheese and *murcha* yeast-pats to ferment *chhang* millet-brew. Tumbles of milk lollipops, flip-flops, Durga-covered calendars and all the paraphernalia of *puja*.

Then, the spices!

Multi-hued hillocks of clove, cassia, coriander seed and pepper-corn, heaped high onto squares of saffron cloth. Turmeric for colouring, preserving and treating tender inflammation. Pink garlic, bay and curry leaves for flavour. Sweet cardamom to fragrance puddings, and knotty clumps of ginger root to make digestive teas. Tamarind, fenugreek and mustard. Cumin, aniseed and mace. Mountainous rainbow ranges of tongue-scalding chillies of every size and shape, piled into sparkling pans of beaten brass.

I closed my eyes to draw the piquant air deep into my chest.

I was instantly back in Priya's house. Her mother cooking *dhansak* and chopping *kachumber*. Her sisters grating jaggery and nutmeg. Her father sitting in his armchair watching Betamax Bollywood and crunching crisp, peppery *papads* that glistened with warm peanut oil. The sudden clarity of memory offered unexpected comfort and I found myself smiling, even as it stole my spice-laced breath.

Samuel clasped tight my hand in his and drew me on through boisterous crowds. Deep amongst the throng, beside a stinking culvert clogged with sewage-caked plastic and rat-gnawed cat, I caught sight of an elderly Nepali in tatty traditional dress. The old man bowed, beaming in delight as we crouched to scan the dusty offerings scattered across his damp blanket stall. I rummaged through mouse-dropping-peppered piles of *mani* prayer wheels and *japamala* prayer beads, insect-riddled manuscripts and moth-munched cloth. And all the while, the aged peddler looked backwards and forwards, from Samuel to me.

He spoke and Samuel chuckled, translating that the old man had asked if it were possible we were related.

"Why would he think that?" I asked, bemused.

"He says we feel like brothers!" Samuel laughed and proudly hugged my arm with both of his.

Beneath the clutter, I found a wormy wooden plaque inscribed with angular calligraphy. I asked its price. The Nepali shook his head and told Samuel that he could not let me walk away with anything so beetle-tooled and broken. He attempted to direct my attention instead to a cardboard box of shiny, new trinkets. I insisted on the ancient board.

The old man smiled.

"He says you have an unfettered mind," grinned Samuel. "He wishes you to take it as a gift, because you are my *dajoo*."

I was deeply touched, but insisted upon giving him money, as a "donation". I bent to pass him the rupees with my right hand supported by my left, in an effort to show what I had learnt to be a traditional form of respect, when he took hold of my wrists and pulled me close. The man looked hard into my eyes.

Samuel intervened and an intense conversation was exchanged between them.

"David-*dajoo*," Samuel said, his face rumpling in perplexity, "he tells me the words on this piece of wood are hidden knowledge, written in the 'twilight' language of the *Tantras*. You know, our mountain tradition. He says this inscription was concealed thirteen hundred years ago, for future generations to discover and interpret – but no one ever has . . ."

Samuel raised a hand to silence the excited questions on my tongue.

"But the strangest thing of all," he continued, "is that he wants me to take you to a place in the mountains even I have never heard of. He says a man is waiting for you there."

I was astonished.

"And what is this place?" I asked.

"He calls it Lapu *basti*," Samuel replied. "The village of Lapu."

It was a hovel. One of at least a hundred shacks built of dismantled packing cases, corrugated iron and plastic sheeting that skulked below the entire length of the railway embankment.

Bindra shook her head, but the thin man just kept grinning his hematic slit. He pointed to a water pump, at which children were washing. He pointed to a reeking, communal toilet shack and partially buried sewage pipe.

"*Aacha ghar hai*!" he exclaimed joyfully, impressing that this was a good place to make a home. He kicked away a crippled chicken and shouted out, "Kavindra!"

An old woman, bent double and wheezing, peered around a length of sacking that hung across her empty doorframe. The man roughly pulled the woman into the light and smirked, "*Dekhiye*!" inviting Bindra to "Please look!" with disquieting courtesy.

Bindra was embarrassed. She bowed to the woman and respectfully called her "grandmother". She apologised in polite Nepali for the intrusion and asked her forgiveness. The old woman understood her meaning. She smiled kindly to Bindra and struggled to lift her skeletal arms in *pranam*. She had only one eye and no fingers.

Jyothi was rummaging in the bag given to them by the Nepali novices at Varanasi. He offered two bananas to the old woman with both his hands, as a sign of deference to her.

The thin man watched with swelling satisfaction. He lengthened one long finger to stroke the back of Jyothi's neck.

Bindra grasped hold of her son with her forearms in instinctive alarm and drew him tightly to her side. The thin man wagged his stiff digit in playful reprimand. He leaned in close with eager, heavy breath, wafting a sickly infusion of sweet spice, armpits and dental decay into Bindra's face.

She looked directly into his dry, bloodshot eyes, but held her breath. Bindra would not breathe in this man. She would not let him in to fan the full ferocity of her despair.

One last bleedy grin and the bright-bleached *kurta* turned as though to leave.

Suddenly, a bony arm extended towards Jyothi.

Before Bindra could respond, callous fingertips twisted hard the boy's unwary cheek, as the tall, thin man released from his lips a long, scarlet stream of muculent phlegm.

♆

It was early morning when Samuel and I mounted a borrowed motorbike, to make a difficult and bumpy ascent up Deolo Hill.

We broke our journey to pay respects to many-armed goddesses, whose scarlet dresses drew us from the road and into the dappled shade of deep forest. We found tiger-riding Durgas enwrapped by tree roots. Purifying Parvatis standing in the shallows of woodland springs. Long-tongued Kalis marking the entrances to womb-like caves.

We stopped at an army base that lay tucked into dense pine trees, to ask Sikh and Gurkha guards for directions to Lapu village. They pointed onwards, down into yet another distant valley.

We eventually drew to a halt near a scattering of neatly painted, wooden *kuti* cottages. The air was sheer, the mountain peaks lucid. An elderly woman approached, followed closely by two nanny-goats and six uninterested chickens. She expressed no surprise at our sudden appearance, but bowed and confirmed that Lapu *basti* lay below us, on the lower hillside. She looked intently at me, then spoke quietly to Samuel. His forehead wrinkled.

"I don't know what you've started, *dajoo*, but this woman says the man who's waiting for you lives down there!" he exclaimed, pointing to a narrow track that disappeared into thick jungle.

The powdery path down the hillside was treacherous, but as we stepped out of the trees, the entire Kanchenjunga range was revealed before us.

I held my breath.

It was as though both heart and time were momentarily suspended.

Ahead of us lay two small, wooden buildings. One a single-roomed hut, the second a simple temple. Both were surrounded by carefully tended flowers. Both were topped by quiet crows. The birds fixed their attention on us as we commenced our approach, only to come to an abrupt halt.

The man had been so motionless, sitting in the shade of the temple canopy, that neither of us had seen him. He smiled and bowed.

"*Dayagari aunuhos. Ma asa gardaitye,*" he said in a cheerful voice. "Please come. I have been expecting you."

Samuel turned to me with alarm in his eyes.

"David-*dajoo*, I don't understand why we're here," he whispered. "This man is a *jhankri*!"

"A what?" I hissed.

"The people here say the Goddess first formed man from earth and fire, wind and stone, leaf and water. But then she suffered to see the effects of all his self-inflicted afflictions – you know, like jealousy and anger." Samuel dropped his voice yet further and leant towards me. "So she took a handful of purest snow from the mountain Pundim Chyu, and formed the first *jhankri*, to heal mankind and oversee his welfare." He glanced back towards the man. "Well ... this is a *jhankri*! One of those very same hill shamans!"

I was enthralled.

"Look at the *marensi mala* around his neck!" Samuel exclaimed in an animated mutter. "Little skulls carved from old men's bones as a necklace. And you see that flute pipe in his lap?" I did. "Do you know what that's made from?"

I peered at its long, brown, knobbly length partially bound in cloth. I shrugged and innocently suggested, "Bamboo?"

"No, *dajoo!*" Samuel grimaced. "It's also bone! Cut from a dead man's forearm!"

I looked back, into the face of the quiet figure on the temple steps. He smiled warmly and nodded for me to approach.

"Be careful, *dajoo*," Samuel hissed. "The *jhankri* have great power . . ."

I stepped forwards alone and bowed in *pranam*.

"*Namaskar hajur!* Ma David *huñ*," I announced in introduction, courageously experimenting with my new Nepali.

"*Namaskar bhai*," he replied warmly, addressing me as "little brother". "*Ma* Kushal Magar *huñ*."

Bindra blamed the heat.

She had been unable to think. She had been unable to make a decision. Nobody had understood her questions about the mountains or the *Aghori Babas*. Nobody had seen Jiwan.

Bindra had told the tall, thin man that she had no money to pay him for the temporary use of the shack, to which she seemed to have inadvertently agreed. He had grinned in understanding. He had shrugged nonchalantly. She had assumed that it had been in lieu of rent that he had taken four boxes of her medicine and the oil for her deeply creviced skin. In return, he had given Jyothi two brightly coloured boiled sweets.

The tall, thin man lingered outside the hut for much longer than Bindra felt comfortable. Only when he finally left did they break the candy into pieces with a stone and share them with Kavindra. The old woman talked endlessly to them in her sibilant Hindi, frequently shaking her head and tutting, shaking her head and tutting. Bindra understood a few of her spittle-wet words, but little more.

As dusk fell and the biting flies began to rise, the sky was soon fluttering with paper kites. Jyothi was excited and ran up the steep railway embankment to watch them spiral and soar in daring dogfight. He clapped his hands and cheered as a small, green kite with glass-impregnated string cut free a bright blue opponent.

"Stay close!" Bindra called, as she watched Jyothi run along the railway line, laughing, to see if he could catch it. "Stay close where I can see you!"

The liberation of the chase sustained Jyothi's legs in their flight far further than he had intended.

His eyes were so fixed on the twisting, tumbling paper that he did not see the bright-bleached *kurta* until his face hit hard against the tall, thin, perspiring body to which it clung.

☙

"He says this is your time," Samuel announced, "that you are ready."

"Ready for what?" I asked, in puzzlement. "I don't even know why we're here."

I had removed my shoes and was sitting on the cold stone, before the inner doors of the *jhankri*'s temple.

"Well, *dajoo*, he's saying you have come for *diksha* – initiation," he insisted. "And these *jhankri* fellows are rarely wrong."

"Initiation into what?" I asked with a bemused chuckle.

Kushal Magar smiled with me. "*Thuture Veda*," he replied.

"The Spoken Knowledge," translated Samuel. "The *Paramparaa* – the Tradition."

I could not pretend to understand. But sitting there, beneath the fulgent heights of the Kanchenjunga, I knew that I instinctively trusted this quiet, gentle man.

I did not need to think.

I smiled and nodded, unperturbed by the fact that I had no knowledge as to what I had agreed.

☙

Bindra had collected sufficient twigs and dry leaves to bring to a boil the sandy hydrant water in her blackening canister. She scooped a little rice and lentils from the bag given by the temple novices back in Kashi and added it to the rolling foam.

248

She called out for Jyothi to come for his food, then turned to invite Kavindra to share their evening meal of plain *daal-bhat*.

Bindra stood quite still.

Her arms fell limp to her sides.

Sitting along the edge of the old woman's hut was a single line of silent crows.

ψ

The kindly *jhankri* placed his hands on my head in *ahashis*, then turned to prepare himself.

I watched as he donned his white tunic before positioning a headdress stitched with feathers and shells. He reverently opened the red wooden doors of the little shrine, to the accompaniment of an unintelligible stream of rhythmical syllables.

Kushal Magar turned to sit before me.

He placed a palm-worn drum in his lap. He unwrapped from its cloth binding an elaborate dagger of ornate metalwork and carved rock-crystal. He drew a circle on the ground and repeated a distinctive, reverberating chant.

Kushal Magar placed grains of rice upon my tongue and turned to face the altar. He burned handfuls of carefully selected mountain herbs in metal bowls. He lit pungent cones of incense in scorched, clay cups.

"I'm sorry, *dajoo*," Samuel muttered, "but the *jhankri* is asking that you remove your clothes. Yes, everything."

I inhaled a swell of scented smoke and found myself unhesitating. During these many weeks in India, I had learned that Westerners so often asked the wrong question. We asked 'Why?' Here they asked 'Why not?'

So it was that, in a moment, I sat again before the temple doors, oblivious to the chill of mountain air against my naked skin.

As Kushal Magar's palms began to voice the drum's taut top, I felt the union of earth, sky, mountain, breath. As our eyes drifted closed, as the vibration of his mantras seemed to mingle with my marrow, both he and I began to tremble.

249

All sense of time was slipping. All sense of self.

Had I been sitting before the scarlet temple for hours, days or months? How many moons had waxed and waned? Had I arrived today or was this the place in which I had been born? Was I infant, adolescent or ancient? Was I man or woman? Tree or crow? Earth or sky?

It was already darkening into dusk when the *jhankri* indicated for Samuel to lie me flat upon my back. Kushal Magar knelt to pour a viscous liquid into the pit of my throat, chest, belly and the hollows of my groin. He ran vermilion-stained fingertips in long lines across my skin as he mumbled unceasing, vibratory syllables.

He doused in new chrism a sudden, inexplicable tumescence, then pressed into my forehead and pubis with his thumbs. He dripped into my nostrils a bracing, bitter oil that set alight my sinuses and swelled my tongue. It seemed to cause my face to melt, my head to bloat, my eyes to open wider than the beam of every star.

Kushal Magar withdrew both hands to touch his heart, then plunged into my abdomen with tightened fists. He threw back his head to pronounce a chant that resounded through my cells. A chant that caused my limbs to shake without restraint.

My chest began to freeze, as though to mountain ice. My navel to ignite, as though some hidden, residual dock of my infantine umbilicus were now fiercely on fire.

I stretched down to grasp his wrists.

I tried to cry out, to restrain him in his rite.

But my entire body and mind were violently, rhythmically convulsing.

Chapter Nineteen

It was Kavindra who called for the neighbours.

Word spread quickly. The newly arrived Nepali boy was lost.

It was already dark when some of the men agreed to search amongst the haphazard rabble of shacks that squatted between the railway embankment and the stinking irrigation gully.

They soon tired. They would wait until morning. No point now. He would find his way back when he was hungry.

The women gathered to chatter and stare at the quiet outsider in their midst. One woman gave Bindra an onion; another, a paper twist of turmeric. One woman spared a green chilli; another, a measure of mustard oil and a small, round lemon.

Bindra was grateful. Really she was.

But all that she could do was to look beyond the sympathetic shaking of their heads and stare out into the darkness.

⚕

It had been a full five days before I had stopped trembling.

My new aunts had scolded Samuel for taking me to a *jhankri*, "of all people!" These men had great knowledge, they had been unable to deny. However, they considered that any close contact with mountain shamans was always best avoided.

Samuel had said nothing in his defence. Neither of us spoke of what we had witnessed in the wooden temple at Lapu *basti*. There was no need. I had experienced something that defied my understanding. All I knew was that a profound and lasting change

251

had been wrought, for which I had no words. An inner freedom for which I would have to wait many years to begin to comprehend.

Then, suddenly, it was time to leave. My permitted fifteen days in the militarily sensitive district were already spent.

The family was fearful at my departure. Kalimpong was in monsoon six weeks early. Shutters were closed and market stalls tarpaulined. Every street was a river of sludge and refuse. Trees had fallen, hillsides had slid. The few jeeps and buses that managed to reach the town were hailed as heroes, having slipped and veered their ascent through the watery mists of mountain jungle.

We all stood outside Uncle Oscar's house and hugged in the pouring rain. We all gave and received blessings. We all cried and kissed.

"*The morning light aches with the pain of parting,*" *Phupu* smiled forlornly, as she placed her hands on my head in *ahashis*, again quoting her beloved Tagore. She asked me to bear her love to her relatives in England, the family she would never meet. She begged me not to forget my new cousin-brothers and cousin-sisters, my new cousin-aunts and cousin-uncles. She implored me to return quickly, back to their eager arms.

"We shall never forget you," *Phupu* promised. "Please, do not forget us. We shall be waiting."

Cecilia stepped forwards and pressed her lips to mine. Through her tears, she said they had all grown to know and love me. That they would not be able to bear my leaving.

"I will return," I vowed.

"I know," she smiled, looking deeply into my moistening eyes. "And one day, David-*bhai*, you will write a book that describes this moment. Remember my words. You'll see . . ."

Samuel held my hand tightly as we walked up to the road through the sodden bamboo grove. I looked down at the dark fingers he had slipped between mine and caught my breath.

For a moment, it was Priya.

I stopped still.

"It's too hard to say goodbye," I mumbled, my hand purposely letting his slip free. I turned away to calm the savage surge that threatened to tear apart my chest and stared hard into the immensity of cloud that plunged before us.

"There are no goodbyes, *dajoo*," Samuel said gently by my side, insistently taking hold of my hand again. "Only gaps between hellos."

"Get that from a greeting card?" I winced.

"Oh no!" he assured me, squeezing my fingers hard. "June page of the Shanti Press calendar!"

As the breadth of his grin reached my heart, I caught a sudden glimpse of livid mountain peaks. They bobbed by, borne on a swelling silver sea, only to souse straight back into the torrent.

And in that moment, I understood that life *is* change. Breath in, breath out. Ebb and flow. Joy and sorrow. And ever the promise of joy again.

I understood that although the facts remained immovable, the past was done. My future did not need to be forever a reaction to it. A new and different life was waiting to be lived. All I had to do was make a choice. All I had to do was choose it well.

We reached the road to find the jeep already waiting to return me to the Plains and to an aeroplane bound for that other, distant life beyond the setting sun. As my rucksack was strapped to the roof, we held each other one last time.

I climbed in as the engine struggled to life, when Samuel suddenly lunged through the glassless window to press a kiss against my cheek.

"David-*dajoo*," he choked. "Dear *dajoo* . . ."

A grating of worn brakes, a grinding of ragged gears and he was gone.

Sobbing.

Running into the rain.

✼

Bindra washed her mouth, her damaged hands and feet.

She sat facing north, in defiance of the orthodoxy of the Plains that declared such a direction "unclean", worthy only of defecation.

For those of the old tradition, of the mountain *Tantras* and the *jhankri*, it was northwards that the fecund goddess sat as she mounted the eternally erect *lingam* of Shiva. For Bindra, north was the direction of wisdom.

Bindra lit the single wick she had made from a tag of cotton torn from her hem and dipped in mustard oil. She did her best to draw a simple pattern of interlocked triangles in the dust before her, a pattern her *bojudeuta* grandmother had tattooed on Bindra's body when she had been a child. Bindra had been taught to see in these intersecting lines a representation of the underlying reality of union in the universe. She now methodically stained these contours with the vermilion *sidur* she still carried in her cloth.

Bindra chanted the mantra of Ganesha as the kindly and benevolent Vighneshvara, elephant-headed Remover of Obstacles. Bindra reminded herself to release all her self-imposed restrictions, her doubts and fears. To find the truth within herself, within all life.

Bindra breathed out *kalapran*, the image of "black air" helping her choose to disengage from all anger and ignorance, possessiveness and hatred, vengefulness and greed.

Bindra honoured her teachers: her mother and her grandmother, her children and her lineage, the *jhankris* and crows.

She placed eight grains of rice in the centre of the *yantra* she had drawn, one for each of the qualities for which she strove: tolerance and self-discipline, generosity and patience, contemplation and honesty, dedicated intention and knowledge.

Bindra honoured Kubera, eight-toothed mountain Lord of Abundance, by adding the small, round lemon she had been given: symbol of her desire to dispel all fear of death, and thus all fear of life.

Bindra formed her hands into a fingerless *mudra* and touched head, mouth, heart, belly, pubis, knees and feet, reminding herself to identify not with the limited and individual, but with the limitless and universal.

She closed her eyes to repeat the *mulamantra* of Kali one hundred and eight times, until her body and mind reverberated with the activating syllables of action, discernment, and transformation.

Then, Bindra sat in stillness.

She slowly moved to touch her feet, knees, pubis, belly, heart, mouth and head. She extinguished the single flame and brushed the interlocking triangles back to dust. She offered the eight grains of rice to the solitary crow that waited at her door.

Bindra was ready.

♆

As the rains eased, the smudged stamp in my passport was suspiciously scrutinised by the same man who had originally made it. I looked out of the office door to watch the locals venture into puddles and through the torrential gutters of Teesta Bazaar. The narrow street began to ring again with the laughter of children. The melody of Nepali, Lepcha and Tibetan. The loquacious descant of unseen mountain birds.

When the jeep's engine refused to restart, I sat at a dripping tea-stall and waited. I waited until the sun began to dip away to waken Europe and the first stars began to brave benighting skies. I waited until viscous mists crept in, clinging to the ant-hollowed heaps of the little market town, lingering on its sopping shopfronts, skulking on its slippery wooden stairs. Transforming its damp inhabitants into phantasmic ghosts and incorporeal shadows.

I could barely conceive that my journey across India was over.

I had come in search of a house in the Hills, and discovered my father. I had determined to prove Grandmother right, and learned an unimagined truth. I had hoped for a mountain grave, and found a family. I had come to fulfil a duty, and found a way to say goodbye.

Where I had feared alienation, I had been deemed a brother and a son. Where I had anticipated exclusion, I had been embraced, kissed and inordinately loved.

India had shown me life in all its terrible, glorious extremes. She had laid bare both the utter horror and inexpressible wonder of humanity. And through it all, she had revealed that the meaning of life is not found in affluence or poverty, health or sickness.

Neither in fame or obscurity, science or politics. Nor in a belief in one, many or no gods. The true meaning of life is found simply in our relationships with one another.

A sudden, violent spluttering and excited, oil-stained hands were waving at me in triumph. I climbed back into the front seat and listened to distant thunder and startled dogs defying each other across the valley. I listened to monkeys arguing with the stall-holders, and owlets pronouncing votive offerings to forest gods.

As mud-encased wheels slowly turned and smiling, unknown faces wished me well, I wept for this most extraordinary of lands and its people who had changed me. I knew then that, until the day I flee this world, mighty India would forever invade my dreams. I knew that she had bound me to her with the very magic in which, as a child, I had believed. That she had captivated me, as I could never have imagined, with the enchantment beyond fairytales in search of which I had dared to come.

🔱

Bindra had made no attempt to sleep. She had wandered in the night through an unfamiliar terrain.

She had slipped and fallen. She had cut her arm and twisted her knee.

Bindra had struggled to climb the embankment to the railway tracks, grimacing through her task at the stench of urine and faeces.

She had called his name. She had called for Jyothi.

Bindra had stopped many times to ease her swelling leg. She had sat and sung his song, his "*Resam Phiriri*". She had held her breath to listen for his reply.

She had listened long.

"Kali Ma," Bindra had whispered into unresponsive silence, "I know I do not own my children. I know that they are but expressions of this body and this mind, just as all life is an expression of the forces in the universe personified by you . . ."

She looked towards the promise of daybreak on the horizon, towards the distant east from which she had come. She thought of home. Of hills and forest. A little house on an old burial ground. The loyal love of a man named Kailash. The laughter of sons and daughters.

"But in my foolishness, I have mislaid them," she confided to the coming dawn, "when neither my senses nor my breath are more precious to me. When all I long for is to smell their hair, to kiss their cheeks. To cook them *daal-bhat*, to watch them sleep . . ."

Bindra slowly slumped to one side and laid her head in the dry dirt. She was panting and exhausted.

"I have lost my children," she gasped, mouth muddying with suspended dust. "I have lost my children . . ."

Bindra closed her eyes and listened for a distant voice, a single footfall.

She heard nothing but an incessant wheezing in her throat, a tremulous rhythm in her chest.

When next she opened her eyes, a distant glow had begun to illuminate the haze. Bindra struggled to ease herself up and peered into the gloom.

Again she called out to Jyothi. Again there was no reply.

A sudden fluttering. A solitary caw.

Bindra looked towards the tracks, to the silhouette of a single crow perched upon the points lever.

"Oh Kali Ma," she choked. "What wisdom now?"

Bindra pulled herself to her feet with difficulty and stood squinting at the bird.

It sat still and staring.

Bindra stepped over the first rail and paused. The new light touched the metallic lines that intersected at the junction. A tangle of parallel, silver streaks that led her eyes back to the solitary crow on the upright lever.

"What, *kaag*?" she cried aloud towards the bird. "What do you know?"

She stepped over the second rail and paused again to stare at the junction point. The sky was steadily reddening, illuminating a neat bundle of smooth cloth.

The pounding of her heart silenced the blowing of an approaching whistle as she crossed the second track.

Not cloth.

Skin. Soft, young skin.

As the crow began to rhythmically bob on the crest of the lever, Bindra began to scream.

To cry.

To run.

To the naked body of a lifeless boy.

Chapter Twenty

I had kept my word. For fourteen winters I had returned to India.

As the years had passed, my months spent in England had steadily decreased, until they had become little more than a simple preparation for the next departure, a chance to earn a salary that would enable me to extend my stay by an extra month or two. I had chosen a professional life of self-employment, despite its insecurities, for it enabled me to return whenever the need to be back amongst loving cousins, mountain peaks and *jhankris* became too pressing.

My mother and father had been astonished at the discoveries I had made in those distant Hills. In my enthusiasm for Himalayan adventure, and my teaching in both Europe and India of the arcane yogic tradition of the North Bengal mountains, they had bestowed on me the mantle of "Hindoo Uncle" in the family. There could have been no greater compliment to be paid.

Indeed, my parents had been so struck by the changes my contact with India had wrought on me, and so delighted by the new intimacy that had flourished in our relationship, that it had awoken in them both the desire and confidence to retrace their own ancestral paths.

So it was that my father had accompanied me, after half a century away. He had wept at the sight of dahlia beds planted by his mother in the garden of Ketunky. At the fire-scorched floors in the ruins of his servants' go-downs. At the mimicry of mynahs on the school path to Sanawar. At the moistness of the mist on Monkey Point.

My mother had accompanied me, to meet her secret family. She had wept at the site of the grave of Uncle Oscar and Aunt Isi, swept into the Teesta by another monsoon landslide. At the embraces of her cousin-sisters and *pranams* of her cousin-brothers. At "*Sundari-boju!*" in the mouths of the children as they bowed to their "Beautiful Grandmother".

My fifteenth winter, and once again I made my way north-eastwards, but not alone. Beside me was tall, strong, blue-eyed Ben, my constant companion.

Ben had visited India in his early twenties, some years before we had met. Horrified by the filth and unwelcoming aggression offered by the country's overcrowded capital, he had spent four days locked in his hotel room staring out at the dust-dense smog and the gaunt wraiths that scavenged drifts of refuse beyond its gates. As soon as tickets had been changed and his prompt escape from Delhi secured, Ben had slunk back to the airport in an air-conditioned car with darkened windows, vowing never again to set foot on the Subcontinent.

And yet, when he had pressed to introduce me to his family on a sunny shore of New South Wales, I had agreed on the condition that he in turn meet mine in the jungled foothills of the Eastern Himalaya. He had consented to the adventure, and had discovered not only an entrancing, alien world, but a tribe of new relations eager to adopt him as their own. When it had come time for us to leave the loving arms of aunts and uncles, to commence our journey home, it had been Ben who had silently wept the length of our long descent back to the Plains, and had known that they had changed him.

Through the years of annual returns, our Kalimpong family had observed us with affectionate knowing. They had seen our friendship deepen to a devotion that surpassed the boundaries of gender, that disregarded the limitations of social expectation. It was they who had encouraged Ben and me to become ritually bound to one another in the old mountain tradition of *miteri*. We were of one heart, they had said, of one mind. We shared our breath.

It had been on an auspicious day in the month of *Magh*, under their attentive direction, that we had tied threads and shared food, knocked heads together and marked each other's brows with vermilion *sidur*.

"*When my days are done, my leave-taking hushed in a final silence,*" I had recited, "*my voice will linger in the autumn light and rain-laden clouds with the message that we had met.*"

It had been *Phupu* who had suggested that we include Tagore.

Ben and I had then embraced and exchanged gifts, made vows of lifelong loyalty and deference to each other's family. As is the custom, we had promised that all support, generosity, kindness and affection would be reciprocated, even if it required the defiance of cultural convention. And finally, we had pledged that when one died the other would oversee the Ritual of Severance and mourn as though he had lost his own brother.

"Look at our lovely boys!" Cecilia had cheered, as they had all gathered in excitement to place *khada* silk scarves and *saipattri-mala* marigold-strings around our necks in celebration. "Forever-more, Ben is David's *mit-dajoo* and David is Ben's *mit-bhai*!" she announced. "Brothers by affection! Already more loving and devoted than a married couple – and now as close as underpants!"

My own smiles on the day had been broadened yet further by the relief that the family held to the Nepali rather than the Lepcha *miteri* tradition, which would have required the public binding together of our upstanding manhoods.

For some years, even before our *mit launu* ceremony, Ben and I had kept a house in Kalimpong, newly built amongst the old family bungalows on the hillside of Uncle Oscar's Kalimpong estate. Weatherboard-clad and tin roof-topped, our very own "chummery" had been given as a gift by a loving aunt and uncle, in gratitude for supporting Samuel through university in Sussex, mere miles from where my Grandmother had once scolded Bird for his delinquency and cast her "hoodoos". It had been the least I could have done. For fourteen years, I had been submerged in love and kindness.

As Ben and I now passed through Kakariguri, the dry heat of the Plains quickly gave way to the peculiarly soft, sweet coolness that promises mountains. As our jeep skirted potholes on the forest road, the verdant wall again loomed before us. As we crossed the Teesta

River, monkey-ravaged teashops began to advertise *momos*, *masala chiya* and *puri aloo dum*.

As faces and statures swiftly changed from Bengali and Bihari, to Nepali, Lepcha and Tibetan, so the hillsides of towering poinsettia and datura rose ever steeper. Itinerant *roti-wallah* pastrymen appeared on the roadside with heavy metal trunks of tasty treats balanced on their heads. *Khelaune-wallah* toy-sellers wandered with vast bamboo lattices of gaudy playthings fanning out from narrow backs.

And so my bones seemed to sigh with relief, for more than anywhere in all the world, it was here that felt like home.

The welcome at Kalimpong was as warm and emotional as ever. They never seemed to tire of our annual arrival, nor we of the joyful embraces from cousin-brothers and cousin-sisters, the affectionate *ahashis* from cousin-uncles and cousin-aunts. Even Jethi-Auntie and Shiva-Uncle had travelled to greet us from their distant home at Patan, in the Kathmandu Valley, and had survived an attack on their bus by Maoist guerrillas.

Only *Phupu* was no longer there.

The last time I had sat beside her bed, she had tenderly recited her beloved Tagore to me.

"*There is love in each speck of earth and joy in the spread of the sky,*" she had sighed. "*And now, I care not if I become dust . . . for whatever I am I am blessed and blessed is this earth of dear dust . . .*"

I had never heard her speak again.

Once our gift-stuffed luggage had ascended the stairs, artfully balanced on sturdy heads, we were brought up to date on all the household gossip. The trauma of Premlal-Uncle's exploding boils, Cousin Othniel's snakebite and Barli-Auntie's dentures-in-the-daal dilemma. The shame of naughty servant Ashok, who had secreted the dainty separates of an unknown ladyfriend beneath his pillow. The tireless giggling of the Tibetan *lama*'s mistress in his meditation hut behind the chicken coop. The dismissal of gardener Tshering, who had been imprisoned in the lavatory by the cook when caught with muddy digits in the money drawer. And the four-legged *pothi* hen that had enjoyed a brief life of celebrity before being stolen by a mongoose.

Whilst their greetings were augmented with the usual cries of "How do our two sons remain so evergreen?", Ben alone was deemed to look in perfect health. I, as usual, was judged "far too thinny". Aunts tutted and shook their heads. A concerted programme of fattening-up immediately commenced.

Thereafter, our days began with breakfasts of steaming *masala kolay* spiced porridge and well-buttered, twice-cooked toast. Slabs of boiled cake and every aunt's own style of rice flour *sel roti* or crumbly *phinni*. Bowls of fragrant rice-pudding *khir*, and chunks of gelatinous, chilli-hot *pumbi*. Papayas from the garden, eaten with lemon juice and ground pepper. *Ghui kera* butter bananas, skins pierced and soft, creamy flesh sucked straight out of the hole. And finally their finest ginger brew, boiled with fresh pepper and cardamom, or hill-style Ovaltine made with cream-thick milk direct from a local udder.

All this, of course, was just a preparation for the morning tea, lunch, tiffin and dinner that followed, each a full-blown feast in its own right, for food, affection and respect were indivisible in these mountains. To decline, or not to leave a plate quite clean, remained the cause of great dismay, if not offence.

Thus every morning my waistline was scrutinised. And, as the days passed, the auntly tuts were gradually replaced by the cooing of increasingly satisfied approval.

ψ

Bindra had grown accustomed to the frequent cramps of hunger. They had become as ordinary as the biting insects that tumbled in callous clouds from the forest canopy with cruel mouth-parts primed. As common as the kicks and curses when she ventured beyond the charitable compound. As frequent as the sling-shot stones when she scavenged discarded vegetables in back alleys of the old bazaar.

The sparse monthly ration of flour, lentils, mustard oil, diluted milk and stale spices rarely lasted far beyond two weeks. But she was grateful. Still after all these years, it was a miracle to her that she should be given food without money or labour.

For her part, all she had to do was to keep the pot of vermilion *sidur* hidden beneath her blanket. The benevolent Christians would take it if they knew she defied their rules and practised *puja* after dark.

And yet, to be here, in the charity-funded colony for those disfigured and segregated by leprosy, was better than the years that she had toiled in the tarring gangs, in searing sun, devoid of shade. Better than the endless, open roads that cut their linear incisions across the harsh invariability of the Plains.

To be here was better than the burning pitch on insensate hands and feet, for which her fellow "lepers" had been specifically employed. Better than the star-bright nights of stinking, savage men who had sealed her mouth and forced her open, in the indifferent darkness of their roadside camp.

ψ

Fourteen winters with the *jhankri* at Lapu *basti*.

Puja and *sadhana*, ritual and practice.

Fourteen winters of the *jhankri*'s teaching, exploring beyond the limitations of the mind. Beyond the limitations of the ego.

And then the last initiation.

Liberty to enter the *jhankri*'s consecrated space, to circumambulate the hidden *lingam*. The drawing of the secret *yantra*, to represent the Goddess whose name is never spoken. The concluding covering of the head and the whispering of truths.

And then: bestowal of the final mantra.

"My teaching is done," Kushal Magar had smiled, to my dismay. "Listen with open ears. Approach the world with an unfettered mind. I have imparted all my learning," he revealed. "So go now. Learn wisdom."

♆

Bindra's smoke-filled hut sparkled with the voices of children. She fed one more green twig to the struggling flame and breathed onto it in optimistic encouragement.

"Burn a little brighter," she begged the listless fire. "Just enough to bring bubbles to the water."

"*Mataji*," the eldest of the girls courteously addressed Bindra in Hindi, "Respected Mother, take Baby for your cooking. She'll burn nicely."

Bindra chuckled. "Not today, my sweet Aarti. You can keep her until tomorrow," she promised. "Now hold her carefully and don't let her pretty dress fall."

Aarti hugged the stick doll back to her chest. Both Dipika and Poojita tried to help their elder sister wrap the rag a little tighter around its narrow, bark body.

"Now, will Baby want to share our *daal-chawal* tonight?" Bindra asked, maintaining the game as she dropped a frugal fistful of lentils and rice into simmering scum.

"She can have mine," offered Poojita without concern. She had often seen Bindra give up her share of food to ensure that she and her sisters were assured nourishment before they slept.

"You're a good, kind girl," Bindra smiled, shuffling along the dirt floor to rest against the mud-sealed walls. "But I think there'll be enough for all of us today."

She winced as she leant back to watch the three girls play Mother to their single, shared, treasured length of twig. She shuffled and winced again, struggling to find any relief from the persistent discomfort in her spine and hips. Often, it kept her from hobbling further than the stinking riverbank. Often, it prevented her from knowing any depth of sleep.

Bindra drew up her knees to rest her head forwards on her forearms. She closed her eyes for a moment and smiled for the sound of children in her home. She smiled for the memory of a bamboo hut on an abandoned burial ground. For a Shakti Tree, a sociable goat and an arid vegetable patch of sharp stones and dark bones. She smiled for a family whose names still stole her breath in their recollection.

"*Mataji*," Aarti interrupted, "if Baby sleeps, then she won't be hungry for *daal-chawal*. So shall we sing for her?"

Bindra chuckled again. It was this playful make-believe that had illuminated an impenetrable darkness. It was these innocent smiles that had delivered her from a dim twilight of confused thought and action from which she had once thought she would never be able to return.

There had been so many long years before these new games and new laughter. There had been so many long years out on the scorched roadways and in the tarring camps, when only the gift of hand-rolled balls of cremation ash mixed with buffalo *ghiu*, given by the *jhankri* all those years before at Lapu *basti*, had saved her.

"Throw one ball into fire for every *bija*, every seed of sound, of the mantra," Kushal Magar had instructed long ago, in the shadow of the Kanchenjunga. "Throw one ball into fire when you believe you have no more choices," he had directed, in that other place, that other life.

Bindra had often clutched at the greasy little bag when despair had threatened to steal away her heart and mind. Yet still the bag remained tied closed, for even when reason had seemed to have been snatched from her, Bindra had found she always had choices. Choices even when Jyothi had returned to fire and earth, plant and water, air and sky.

The *jhankri*'s gift had taught her that however isolated, however lost within herself, she alone was responsible for the ways in which she chose to respond to the natural ebb and flow of her life. She alone was the source of either her dark introversion and distress, or her bright clarity and peace.

Of course the *jhankri* had known it when he had given her the little bag of hand-rolled balls. This had been the very wisdom he had intended her to learn.

"*So jao*. Go to sleep," Aarti cooed, rocking the stick doll tenderly in her arms.

Bindra closed her eyes again and leant a heavy head against the soft, mud wall. She smiled as the biting insects, the burning spine and even the aching memories began to sweeten, as Aarti, Poojita and Dipika sang to their communal Baby the one song that Bindra had taught them in her own, long-silenced, mountain tongue:

"*Resam phiriri, resam phiriri udera jauki darama bhanjyang, resam phiriri . . .*"

ॐ

Clad in thermals, enrobed in woven shawls and topped with woollen *topis* we may have been, yet still Ben and I shivered in the deep darkness of Kalimpong's persistent power cuts. Still we shuddered at the murdered-infant howling of approaching jackals, and tried to ignore the spreading numbness in our toes.

And yet, now that we had once again to say goodbye, I knew that I would miss the arrival of the milk every morning, carried warm in its churn by the *gharwalni* milk-woman, who glimmered with ear discs, coin necklace and nose-ring. The family *dhurzi* tailor, who, before lunch, could whip up a shirt with cut-away collar and double-cuff sleeves. The *misteri* carpenter, who sat on the lawn to craft a new bedstead with nothing more than handmade tools and a handsome apprentice. The *naw-malissgarney* barber-masseur, who would squat on the verandah to whisk off fresh whiskers with cut-throat blade, and unknot tired shoulders with talented thumbs. The Bengali *dhunia* who thrummed cotton on his *dhanu* bow to re-plump old mattresses and winter quilts, whilst covering the garden in a fine, sneeze-inducing snow.

I would miss the group treading of clothes on washing day, accompanied by song, as though the task were a joyful, communal dance. And then the subsequent watching of the ants as they swarmed over wet garments to eat the remaining soap, which left them so intoxicated that they would curl up to thrill at who knows what sud-induced dreams.

I would miss the blissful hours spent pottering in the garden and bamboo thickets, playing games with the children and teaching the

Tibetan guard dogs to fetch us sticks. I would miss my cousin-uncles' patient daily lessons in Nepali irregular verbs and Bengali basics, and my cousin-aunts' instructions in the infinite medicinal uses of local flora, soil and sap.

But perhaps most of all, I would miss the many hours of chat and tales at the kitchen table. The laughter and unspoken understandings in every interaction.

It was never easy to say goodbye.

However, this year, we were not returning to the blossoming of an English spring. Instead, Ben and I were travelling westwards, across the Plains, to a charitable compound in a distant slum, into which those affected by leprosy had been gathered from the district's streets. I had read of the place ten years before in a Delhi newspaper. Its name had caught my eye as it stood outside the town to which, many years before, Priya had been sent for schooling. Even before I had reached the end of the article, I had vowed that, one day, I would offer myself to these people who had been rejected, ostracised and abandoned for no other reason than the stigma of a disease. People whose desperate and unrelenting plight had affected me more than any other in all my contact with India. This new journey was the consummation of a decade of determination.

Uncles were horrified. Four months in slums? Four months so far away, with Plains-men? With Hindi-speakers? With leprosy?

Aunts despaired. Where would we sleep? Who would wash our clothes? Who would understand our Hill Nepali? And, most troubling of all, who would cook our food?

Fourteen winters spent in India, yet still they gave us lessons in survival. Do not drink the water. Do not take tea from roadside stalls. Beware *bagala-mara* pickpockets and *dakait* bandits. Avoid orthodox *Bahun* priests and *bicho* scorpions.

"And sons, wherever you are, whatever you do," they begged, "keep well away from policemen and politicians!"

Stillness in the colony. An apprehensive anticipation, a fearful quiet.

It was Friday. Doctor Dunduka was coming.

Bindra swept the swathes of biting bugs from her doorway with a loose brush of dried grass, held clasped between her wrists. She paused to tensely arch her tormented back and called out in Hindi, "Jasoda-*didi, aap thik ho aaj*? You alright today?"

A lethargic shuffle and a cloth-bound head peered out from the shadows of the opposite hut. Sunken eyes struggled briefly in the morning sunlight, then listlessly withdrew, back into the gloom.

"*Didi*," Bindra tried again, "you not well?"

There was no reply.

Bindra shuffled the few steps to Jasoda's door. She eased herself down with effort and cautiously leant against the splintered doorframe.

"I'm boiling *tulsi* leaves, sister," she offered gently, brushing the biting bugs away from her bare feet with the hem of her shawl. "Good for your fever."

Jasoda gave a painful, choking cough in reply. She drew close to Bindra's side, curving her twisted spine against the brightness of the day.

"Not well today, *bhabhi*," she wheezed in apology, mistakenly addressing Bindra as "sister-in-law" in her muddled mind. "My feet have brought such *bukhar* fever!"

Bindra guided Jasoda to turn towards her, to lengthen her thin flaking shins, to brave the sunlight. The few toes she had retained were little more than shrivelled, oozing stumps. The ulcers on her deeply creviced soles, foul. The bone beneath, infected.

"Oh sister!" Bindra grimaced, biting her extended tongue. "In the Hills, I could have done so much to help you. We have good plants there. We have *putkako maha*, treasured insect honey that cures all wounds."

She blew away the flies from Jasoda's feet. She swept away the new flurry of biting bugs that had drifted from the *saal* trees.

"We must protect your sores, sister," she insisted. "We must keep them covered. But first, *tulsi* tea for the fever."

As Bindra struggled to stand again, a strident voice drew their attention down the alleyway.

"Quick, sister!" Jasoda cried in whisper. "Doctor Dunduka has come! Do not let him see you help me! You know his temper! You know what he can do!"

Bindra returned to her doorway. By the time she had swept away the bugs and eased herself back to the newly infested ground, he was there. Standing at a carefully judged, safe distance. Unblinking eyes monstrously magnified by heavy-rimmed spectacles.

"*Namaste Daktar-ji!*" Jasoda muttered with required respect.

Bindra touched hands to heart, but said nothing.

"Your medicine!" he called out with contempt, tossing toward them two plastic bags heavy with a colourful mix of pills. Jasoda offered thanks, but wanted him to know that the fever was growing much worse, that the holes in her feet were growing ever deeper.

"Then take a double dose, ungrateful hag!" he spat defensively. "A good handful might even silence your miserable complaining for good!"

Bindra stayed silent. She took nothing given by Doctor Dunduka. She knew he despised them. She knew he improved on his government salary by dealing in black-market tablets. She had watched too many in the colony die quickly and violently after a measure of his illegal medicine.

Every bag disdainfully thrown at her each week Bindra kept hidden in her bedding. And after dark, when the children buried them for her in the forest, she always paused to ask forgiveness of the *Punyajana* in the trees.

Bindra was comforted that the Good People also knew Doctor Dunduka was distributing poison.

ψ

Dawn was dissipating dense fog.

I peered through the grimy carriage window at vast sugar-cane plantations and enticing jungle, wild with boar, shimmering with peacock. I peered at children bursting from thatched huts to dance at the boisterous rhythm of the passing clickety-clack.

I had never tired of rail travel in India, even though for eight hours I had lain wide awake as the men in the lower bunks had snored like congested trufflers. One had repeatedly shaken the entire carriage with his sudden, chilling screams, until I had given up all hope of slumber. Instead, I had counted the cockroaches scuttling through the empty rivet holes on the rusting ceiling, and wondered at the demons by which my companion's dreams were haunted.

The last station at which we were to change trains already heaved with life, even at four o'clock in the morning.

Amongst cows, dogs, rats and crows, vociferous *chai-* and *chat-wallahs* competed for custom with many busy book and fruit stalls balanced on buckled wheels. Scarlet-clad porters strained beneath battered trunks and over-stuffed portmanteaux, between heavy-hipped *matajis*, who force-fed their sleepy broods with *dum aloo* and buttery *paranthas* from burnished towers of tiffin tins. Dignified tribals, with arms encased in dowry gold, nervously eyed mighty Pashtuns swathed in mountain wool. Enrobed Punjabi *sadars*, each with *pagri* turban, elaborate whiskers and splendid nose, swilled teeth at taps with old-time Congress-*wallahs* bearing Gandhi topi caps, unbleached "homespun" and defiant chins.

And between them all, steely-eyed urchins with Struwwelpeter hair and scabby, *sidur*-reddened cheeks cartwheeled and back-flipped in hope of alms from the indifferent throngs.

For two days we had travelled from Kalimpong to reach our final destination, which lay embedded in an overbuilt valley beneath dry and rocky hills, hard up against the border with Nepal. The nearest town proved a filthy, dreary place with virtually all remnants of its history eradicated. A crumbling colonial bungalow in abandoned, squatter-ravaged gardens. An exuberant Mughal façade, now dis-integrating and defaced, in a back street of the bazaar. A refined and elegant past reduced to little more than mere hints of long-lost wonder.

I was astonished to think that Priya had once been here, walking through this dust in pleated grey and navy blue. Satchel full of Shakespeare, Sassoon and Sukanta Bhattacharya.

"*I threw away my heart in the world; you took it up,*" I smiled at her memory. "*I sought for joy and gathered sorrow, you gave me sorrow and I found joy,*" I recited in gratitude for the way of loving that she had taught me.

The charitable colony for leprosy sufferers in which we were to work lay far to the north of the town, hard up against the remaining forest's darkness. It had once been entirely isolated within dense *saal* trees, but over the years many hundreds affected by disfiguring disease had gathered outside the official boundary. All waited in hope of a place within, for a convenient demise.

Over the years, these invading squatters had systematically cleared the once fertile land. Where there had been thorny *dhaak*, *tesu* and *babool*, stealthy leopard and shy musk deer, a noisy rabble of squalid homes now engulfed the arid ground. Where a fish-filled mountain river had gushed, a choked and viscous public drain now stagnated.

The official colony was a cluster of decades-old block buildings and wooden huts, which lay wedged between slum and hillside trees. The quarters in which Ben and I were to spend four months stood at the perimeter of the community. The two rooms were mouldering, dirty and infested. Upon arrival, we spent our first hours scrubbing and cleaning.

"You're sure we won't catch anything too nasty?" Ben coughed through mite-dense dust that now billowed from the open door.

"Don't worry!" I assured him, as we coaxed dark, mucus-like growths from concrete floors, knowing exactly to what he referred. "Most of us are born with a resistance to the leprosy bacillus. And even if we did catch it – which would be highly unlikely as our immune systems are in such good nick – we could be easily cured before it did us any lasting damage."

Ben nodded and chuckled at his enduring disquiet. He seemed content with my reply, as we swept crab-pincered spiders from hidden lairs. Yet still I wondered whether I had done a selfish thing to ask of him this sacrifice of precious savings, time and all the comforts to which we were so casually accustomed.

Ben had spent his working life in the management of opera companies, mingling with the artistic aristocracy of Western classical music on two continents. He was more familiar with millionaire budgets, champagne receptions and Green Room gossip than the pestilence and privation into which he had followed me. I watched him now as he crawled on his knees with a dirty rag in one hand and a long stick in the other, hectoring cockroaches from dark dens into sunlight, and felt my heart swell.

His support of me, in what had become a particularly personal objective to offer something of myself to both a country and a people that had played an essential part in who I had become, filled me with respectful wonder. Ben possessed a strength, compassion and integrity that constantly inspired me. I had found in him kindness, confidence and companionship that I had once believed would never again be mine. I watched him as he chuckled his apologies to the biting beetles he now banished with his broom, and knew that Ben was a man whom Priya and Grandmother would have very easily loved.

It was dusk when we finally sat back to survey our labours, relieved with the results achieved in our new home. Relieved, until a large section of the festering bedroom wall, the surface of which our enthusiastic cleaning had made unstable, exploded, leaving the entire room and our few belongings covered in a thick layer of lung-infesting fungal spores.

Bindra was woken by a choking wail.

"*Jyothi, ma yaha huñ!*" she cried out. "Jyothi, I'm here!"

Bindra opened her eyes wide in the lightless hut. She fought to raise herself from the sagging jute-twine of the wooden *charpai* bed on which she lay. Her violent heart vibrated listless air, pounding restless waves through inscrutable shadows.

Bindra felt her way to the sacking across her doorway and stepped out into a moon-bright vault. She breathed a temperate breeze into the deepest reaches of her tight lungs, and looked up to the brilliance of stars above.

There was not a night that she did not still hear the calls of her lost children. There was not a night that an insistent guilt did not threaten to consume her.

And then again, a suffocating cry.

Jasoda.

Bindra stumbled forwards, lifting the door-cloth high for starlight to cast its gentle gleam. The room was acrid with the stench of vomit. Jasoda was on the floor, fitting.

"*E didi!*" Bindra gasped. "What's happened here?"

Jasoda could not reply. The whites of her eyes flickered in the darkness. Her emaciated body shook.

"Oh sister, no!" Bindra exclaimed. "You've been taking his medicines!"

But Jasoda had no defence to give.

Her worn and weary heart had fallen still.

Chapter Twenty-One

"You people!" the retired army Major growled with an undisguised sneer through his inadequate moustache. "You come over here with your good intentions and your sentimental philanthropy, as though a fleeting charitable gesture might appease your colonial guilt . . ."

He interrupted his caustic sermon to beckon a man into the room, who had been hesitating apprehensively at the door. The secretary kept his narrow shoulders hunched and his precise, well-greased fringe bowed low as he nervously offered the ex-officer a handful of poorly typed letters to be signed. He did not once raise his face to acknowledge us.

"Good morning, sir," I offered, cheerfully. Both of them ignored me. "Perhaps we should come back at a more convenient time?" I directed at the Major with explicit purpose.

He raised a manicured finger, inadvertently pointing our attention to the unnaturally matt-black hair with its stark white roots that lay scraped across his scalp. He wagged the poised digit from side to side in rhythmical condescension, whilst he continued to scrawl his mark with an antiquated fountain pen.

This, our first meeting with the charity's director, was unpromising. He had already left us waiting in the corridor for an hour, whilst he drank his morning tea and leisurely emptied an entire tray of Vanilla Puffs. He evidently felt he had a point to make.

As the secretary slunk away, the Major once again turned his face towards the unfailing generosity of our pink-lipped smiles.

"We have never accepted two male foreigners here before," he stated blankly, as though in anticipation of gratitude for his concession. "Your work is solely in our hostel for the subnormal,

275

the mentally deficient. You never go out of the compound on your own. You never set foot in the neighbouring slum. You never send or receive post without the Office's approval of its contents. You fraternise with neither teachers nor staff. No alcohol. No assignations. Staff prayers and director's sermon in the chapel at seven thirty every morning. Understood?"

I was astonished by his tone.

"Thank you for your guidance, sir," I smiled, with perfect patience, "but there seems to be a little confusion."

His eyes tightened as though he had been slighted.

"We are here to work with those affected by leprosy," I reminded him, "a disease I've been privately studying for many years, ever since I was first touched by the desperate plight of the people outcast by its stigma. If you refer back to the letters exchanged last year regarding our application and your own confirmation . . ."

"It is you who is confused," he retorted with a new intensity. "You people may *never* approach the leper colony. You have *nothing* to do with them. You are here to assist the retarded. That is all. Without question. Understood?"

Ben and I were astonished.

The Major dialled the heavy number-wheel of his Bakelite telephone and began speaking in rapid Hindi.

He paused to glare back up at us, the lonely bristles of his moustache taut with his evident disquiet.

"You may leave," he impatiently hissed.

ψ

Bindra had spent all night beside the naked body of Jasoda.

She had first marked a boundary between the worlds of the living and the dead by stepping over the low fire she had lit, passing her unbandaged hands through the flames, and touching her senseless skin against a twig of sharp thorns.

Bindra had then washed Jasoda's skin with diluted *tulsi* tea and smeared her with turmeric paste. She had marked her disfigured feet, her shrunken pubis, wrinkled belly, desiccated breasts, sunken throat, crumpled forehead and near-hairless crown with careful lines of the *sidur* she kept concealed in her own bedding. At the intersections of these scarlet strokes she had laid the red hibiscus flowers sacred to Kali Ma that flourished on the bushes Bindra carefully tended around her hut.

Bindra now took a good, straight stick from Jasoda's meagre pile of kindling. She found the old, twine-bound blade used for wood, food, and the removal of dead flesh from decayed feet and hands. Into the dry bark, Bindra struggled to mark the nine notches of *Dharti*: the eight directions, plus the middle point of human awareness. She turned the stick to mark a further seven notches into its length: the seven levels of consciousness into the inner world of *Patal*.

Bindra laid the stick along Jasoda's motionless breastbone, then circled her body three times. She visualised specific *mudras*, formed by fingers she no longer possessed, and scattered a few grains of rice across the corpse. Three times she cried aloud the secret *bijas* of separation, followed by three moments of mindful silence.

Bindra lit a piece of the camphor she had long kept hidden, and slipped it between Jasoda's empty gums. She watched the yawning mouth flare, then plume back to darkness.

Bindra covered the quiescent face with a length of Jasoda's own head cloth. She lifted its corners to whisper the Mantra of Severance, once imparted on distant mountains by her long-departed grandmother, the much-loved *bojudeuta*.

Bindra slowly bowed in *pranam* to the husk of a woman whom she had considered a friend.

"*Behenji*," she spoke softly in Jasoda's Hindi, "respected elder sister, it is finished. Release your hold on this body and this place. The knot must now unravel. The wisdom of your life's experience must now be shared. Tomorrow's *shraddha* cremation will speed your return to animal and plant, earth and sky."

Bindra carefully drew the soiled cotton blanket around Jasoda's body and tied it at her feet and head.

"There is no need to fear," she assured the silent features, before finally drawing the cloth across them. "Just as all colours are expressions of the same light, so god and man, birth and death are all aspects of the same endless tide of universal knowledge, universal wisdom, universal truth."

Bindra sat at Jasoda's feet and closed her eyes.

When next Bindra looked up, golden light streamed in brilliant, rotating spirals onto the silent bundle before her.

Dawn had come.

The crows were calling.

Ben and I were unsure what to do.

The Major's refusal to allow us access to the very people with whom we had come to work had left us at a loss. We discussed leaving immediately in order to find another charitable leprosy colony, but had no idea where, from this remote location, we might begin our search.

We came to the decision that, having travelled so far from Kalimpong, we would give ourselves a fortnight to become accustomed to the climate and colloquial Hindi, whilst exploring the possibility of establishing new and more accommodating contacts in other districts.

During our first week at the charity hostel, the candid stares of children and teachers refused to tire. Over eighty inquisitive pairs of eyes fixed upon the pale-faced men amongst them. Pale-faced men inanely smiling, who taught the time with cardboard clocks and Hindi names of wild animals with poster-paint *jungli janvar*. Pale-faced men who taught long multiplication and times tables, volleyball and cricket. Seed planting, dental care and safe cooking. Skittles, Snap! and lice control.

As we clumsily attempted to lead lessons, without experience or preparation, we quickly learned "*Muh saf karo!*" for "Wipe your mouth!", and "*Naak saf karo!*" for "Wipe your nose!" "*Milkar bajao!*" for "Share it!", and "*Sabse mel rakho*" for "Be friends to all."

I spent my afternoons teaching Hatha Yoga on prickly grass. Every day, more caretakers, orderlies and cooks slipped in behind the children to become *gaya* cows and *magarmach* crocodiles, *hathi* elephants and *kaak* crows. *Paramvajra*, the Supreme *Lingam*, and *Perki Devi*, Goddess of the Trees. Together they learned to chant like *sadhus* and to hum like *bhramari* bees.

We spent our evenings with the bedridden, in their filthy, dingy rooms. Urine-soaked, unwashed, emaciated and ignored. Yet still they laughed, and through their smiles taught us.

Handsome Debdan, Gift of the Gods, beamed one such smile. He smiled, even though he had fallen from a tree and splintered his spine when still a child, provoking his starving mother to abandon him to a life alone in refuse-filled streets. He smiled, even though he was now often left unfed and confined to long-unchanged sheets.

Ben and I were seeking ways to secretly enable the bed-bound to earn a little pocket money. As Debdan had been taken in by an elderly *dhurzi* tailor who had trained him in his craft, I offered him my badly torn jeans for mending and asked his price.

"I need nothing, *beta*," he replied with simple consideration, clasping my hands. "Nothing at all, my son, but your love."

I sat staring into the forest for a long time that evening. I watched in a fading, dappled light the dusk-time rituals of red-crested woodpeckers, silver owls and emerald parakeets. Barely airborne flying beetles, hummingbird moths and butterflies. Hosts of stripy squirrels, squadrons of bats and pukish mobs of monkeys. I sat so long that the bright crescent moon was resting flat on its back in the treetops when I stirred from my silent solitude of thought.

As I wandered back to our quarters, I looked up to the ramshackle town that spread across the hills around us. The ugly clutter of dirty concrete reflected the last rays of day as though it were a translucent Shangri-la of water and glass. An unseen pack of pye-dogs beckoned with incessant barking. Vibrant drums and vivacious voices strenuously proclaimed yet another slum wedding that would last until dawn.

My own evening would be less colourful. Much-needed recuperation and quiet preparation for the following day's classes, whilst

Ben and I cleaned ourselves with care. Other's dribble, fleas, nits and worse were now part of the daily routine. We boiled eggs, ate nuts and fruit, and relished our ration of a single spoon of local honey.

We attempted to enhance communication with our charges by reading to each other from *Improve your Hindi in a Term Time*, a densely printed book picked up from a station stall, with pages so brittle they tore if turned with less than antiquarian attention. However, by Lesson IV – "In the Hotel" – we had already begun to doubt that the conversation practice it offered would advance our social skills or endear us to the local population:

"Darling, have you ever seen a cabaret?"
"Such foreign pastimes give little pleasure."
"Ha, now see how she dances very nice."
"But very shameless she is."
"Because she is naked?"
"Yes."

We abandoned our book, laughed out the candles and lay on top of damp sheets in the suffocating stillness of night air pungent with mildew and smoky wicks.

I closed my eyes to the darkness and pondered the peculiar intensity of the life I had known in India. Every day a rip-roaring ride from despair to bliss, bliss to despair.

I considered the life I had shared with Ben on two continents, his faithful presence an unfaltering stability in the erratic eddies of the years. His unalterable generosity of heart and spirit a refuge in the squall.

I heard him turn noisily on his mattress.

"Can't sleep?" I whispered.

"Too hot and too much in my head," he muttered. "Can you give me some Tagore to see me off?"

If it could be said that we had set our own tradition, then this was it. Favourite recitations when lights were out and sleep evaded.

"Alright," I considered, searching for the lines of a verse that might voice the feeling of that moment. "*As I stare on and on into the past, in the end you emerge,*" I whispered towards him, "*clad in the light of a pole-star piercing the darkness of time . . .*"

"*The memories of all loves merging with this one love of ours
. . .*" he whispered in return.

"*And the songs of every poet past and forever,*" we concluded
together, stretching out hands in the darkness to find affirmation
in fingertips.

I closed my eyes smiling, and sought for sleep. In far too few
hours we would be woken by the first call to prayer, bellowed once
more across the valley through distorting speakers, like the tortured
lament of a grief-stricken father.

I found instead an enchanted memory of mountain and cave
temple. Of an auntie's *ahashis* and a *jhankri*'s smile.

ॐ

Bindra had been called a witch before, on a mountain, long ago.
There she had been *bokshi*. Here she was *daayan*.

"How dare you!" Doctor Dunduka was still shouting at her.
"You had no right to desecrate this corpse with your mountain
sorcery, you filthy *daayan*!"

There, that word again.

"Only the priest is permitted to deal with the dead here! The
Christian priest!" he bellowed in emphasis.

Bindra looked him directly in the eyes.

"But Jasoda was a devotee of Kali. Not the foreigners' Jesus,"
she stated in quiet response.

"Your rations come from foreign Christians, woman! Your
blanket! Your medicine! All from foreign Christians!" His voice had
ascended to a porcine squeal.

"Church, *mandir*, mosque, *gompa*. What does it matter?" Bindra
replied with gentle conviction. "All is sacred. All divine. It is man
alone who discriminates. Not god. For all is god. All is one . . ."

Doctor Dunduka lurched towards her, as though to bring down
his trembling right hand hard against her face. Through his fury,
he remembered that these foul creatures were cursed. Cursed by
God for their sins. Cursed for their pagan profanities. He backed
away, panting for air in a narrow alley tight with bodies that

281

exposed through ugly deformity the true depths of their spiritual decay.

"You'll be reported to the Office!" he spat, his straining eyes wild and bloodshot. "I'll see the Major cuts your rations! Withholds all medication!"

The doctor's perspiring head pivoted dangerously on his pulsating neck.

"Let this be a lesson to all you ungrateful wretches! Let's see which of your ugly gods steps down from its rusting plinth to tend you now!"

He turned one last time towards Bindra.

"Christ alone can save you, *daayan!*" he grimaced, one petulant, plump finger pointing. "Christ alone!"

ॐ

Lesson VIII – "Pleasing & Surprising":

"You are my pride, O son. Let us take an evening stroll along the road."

"Nonsense, most worthy father. Heavy traffics a-coming and a-going, dins and bustles all around, dusts and rubbles."

"Come on boy, what does this matter, my joy knows no bounds. Annie dear, arrange for us a pompous dinner with sumptuous puddings."

"Good husband and lord, see me already busy in my wifely duties. Go take a stroll with your most honourable son, and soon return to a table fully spread with tasty treats."

Whilst we continued to struggle through our unfathomable Hindi language course, local eyes were peering up at the hills. Heads were shaken. Already no snow left upon their peaks. This was devastating. The temperature was too soon approaching that of early summer and, as foliage charred, the mountainsides were darkening into an ominous, desiccated black.

"By July there'll be no water!" they told us in despair. "Then what will happen to the poor?"

When I thought of the slum below us and the septic ooze upon which they would become reliant, I started losing sleep.

The early heat had also encouraged the biting *saal*-tree bugs to swarm. Great, black drifts of the belligerent beasts clogged the corners of the rooms and covered the floors in a crunchy carpet. We emptied our sheets every night only to find whole tribes of new bedfellows by dawn. Their unintentionally squished comrades left vivid, tie-dye prints of their demise. Indelible, accusatory stains.

Heavy stones were now placed on all internal drain covers to keep out cobras from the rooms and shoes were shaken to avoid a nasty case of scorpion-betwixt-the-toes. My youthful years of practice with red Wellingtons on kitchen steps had finally proved fruitful.

The unseasonable weather was blamed for the outbreak of gastric infections in the hostel. The subsequent loss of abdominal control amongst the children had resulted in the panicked evacuation of classes. Repeated summoning of the depressed *dhobi*. Frantic beckoning towards the grumpy man with his Dettol-drenched rag-on-a-stick.

It was amidst this explosion of heat, bugs and bowels that Ben and I had called a meeting. We had threatened to pack our bags and leave.

It was not just the misappropriation of foreign-raised funds. The new furniture and satellite television for the Office, the five-star hotel catering ordered in for Office staff meals, the first class air travel for the Major's fund-raising tour of North America. Nor was it just the self-congratulatory Office party, which consumed a budget of more than three times a teacher's annual salary.

Rather, it was the relentless beatings, kickings and slappings of the most vulnerable. The dragging by the hair of the unintelligible. The cruel twists of cheeks and nipples of the blind and deaf. The ever-inventive "punishments" meted out as a matter of course, by teachers, orderlies and *ayah* nannies alike.

It had become unbearable.

The Office personnel refused to attend. Only the hostel staff gathered, intrigued by our inscrutable passion, the inexplicable intensity of our purpose.

We addressed them with quiet confidence. We chose our words with care. We remained commendably calm, clear, concise.

Thereafter, the pale-faced men to whom the children ran were ostracised. The pale-faced men against whose chests the pupils laid their heads were avoided and ignored. Not only did the staff refuse to speak to us, but they would not even deign to rest their steely eyes upon our newly broadened shoulders.

Never again was any child in the charity hostel beaten in our presence.

Yet still we found bruises when we treated their ringworm. Still we found teeth marks when we powdered their fleas.

ૐ

A sudden detonation of light woke Bindra.

A moment of blinding brilliance before firm hands clasped tightly around her throat.

She threw her mouth open to cry out, but all sound had been silenced. She twisted and kicked, but a crushing weight had rendered her still.

Bindra closed her eyes and drew deep within.

She visualised Durga Ma riding into battle astride Her roaring tiger, bare breasts daubed with gore, arms and weapons raised against the enemies of fear and despair, restoring stability to both individual and universe.

"*Aung hring dhung Durga devyai namah-aung,*" Bindra struggled to voice within herself.

Fingers grasped her jaw. Gripped so hard, so fiercely that Bindra's teeth were forced apart.

All reverence to Durga Ma who is Vidya, knowledge personified! The knowledge into which all differentiations disappear, all perceptions of opposites, all concepts of duality, all separation and division!

"*Aung hring dhung . . .*"

Splintering wood pressed hard between her teeth. Nose crushed closed. Throat forced open.

"*Aung hring dhung . . .*"

All homage to wild, untameable Durga Ma, Her smile placid with non-attachment, devoid of self-interest! The ascendancy of truth over falsehood, knowledge over ignorance, liberation over self-limitation!

Objects small and solid pushed deep into Bindra's mouth, deep into her throat. She choked. Pushed deep again. Her tongue flexed.

She swallowed.

"*Aung hring dhung . . .*"

All honour to triumphant Durga Ma, as bright as sun, moon and fire combined! Once more She dances upon the corpse of Mahishasura, the Buffalo Demon! Once more, She destroys the destabilising forces of *krodha* anger and *mada* pride that separate man from his own inherent truth!

Wood roughly ripped from Bindra's mouth, cutting tongue, splitting lips.

The hands released their grip, leaving flesh to bruise darkly.

The crushing weight lifted, leaving brittle bone broken.

"*Aung hring dhung . . .*"

Salutation always to Durga Ma, who shows compassion even to Her enemies! Salutation always to Durga Ma, who embodies fearlessness of life, of death, of fear itself!

Hushed voices in the room.

The light fading. Fading.

Durga Ma.

Gone.

Chapter Twenty-Two

Ben and I had been banished.

The hostel staff so resented our popularity with the children and our interference in their abusive regime that they had finally ordered us out of the building.

Ben had turned his administrative skills instead to the Office, where he had been placed at the far end of the corridor, in a shabby little room with a wobbly table, broken chair, pickle jar of chewed pencils and dangerous electrics. Back home, he was accustomed to co-ordinating the working life of over a hundred singers, musicians, dancers and staff from all around the world, organising their schedules as far as five years ahead. Here, he was assigned the daily task of tidying drawers and uncluttering cabinets, filing damp paperwork in perpetual binders, and copying lists of residents' names into loose-leaf ledgers for no discernable benefit to anyone.

However, this new proximity to the charity's bureaucratic nub had afforded Ben unrestricted and increasingly unsupervised access to its records and accounts. As he had toiled to unravel an archaic and eccentric system, he had discovered extensive financial details, drafts of correspondence and lists of international sponsors. Ben had inadvertently become our mole.

One evening he returned to our room in an uncharacteristic depression. He sat slumped on the edge of his bed.

"These bloody people!" he suddenly roared in angry frustration. "Thirty thousand pounds they've been given over the last three years by one English parish alone that has been raising funds on their behalf! That's over twenty-five *lakhs*! Two and a half million rupees!"

He was shaking with fury.

"They've been sending back reports that claim they've used it to build a new school, open an IT centre for the children and staff a hi-tech medical centre – but it's all a lie! None of it exists. Instead, they neglect and even harm their defenceless charges, with no accounting for where all the funding's gone!"

He thrust towards me six crumpled sheets of paper. I sat beside him, staring at dense lists of names and addresses. Britain and the North American Bible Belt. Chennai and Bangalore. Sponsors. Well-meaning, but duped.

"This place is rich!" he thundered. "So where's the money?!"

Our instinct was to write to them all, to reveal the truth. But to what end?

If this charitable compound, with all its abuses and cruelties, were gone, what would become of its residents? Back into the slum that festered beyond its boundary fence. Back to the pitiless streets from which they had struggled and fought to reach its gates.

As the drift of dusk undid our day, we made no move to kindle candles. We dimmed with the darkening forest into which we stared, fading into the stupefied silence of our own impotence.

The following morning, we had barely swallowed two spoonfuls of spiced porridge when the peevish paper-*wallah* came panting to our quarters, careful to avoid all eye contact, all possibility of interaction. He timidly held out a scrap of foolscap, smudged with a barely decipherable scrawl. The inevitable command had arrived.

We were summoned to the Major. Now.

The prerequisite wait for an hour outside his door to ensure we fully understood our status. And then again, "You people!"

"You people come over here with your good intentions and your sentimental philanthropy . . ."

We had heard this speech before.

Even as my eyes were hypnotically drawn to those airy, open spaces between his facial hairs, I wanted to understand this angry man, fearful in his efforts to disguise feelings of inadequacy with the fragile façade of a military bearing.

My years of learning with the *jhankri* had encouraged me to see all life as an expression of a single truth. To try to see this defensive, fretful man, who hid behind the protection of his obsessively ordered desk, as an aspect of myself.

"Before you revere the 'good' or condemn the 'bad' in others," Kushal Magar had instructed on his distant mountain, "acknowledge the same wisdom and ignorance, balance and imbalance in your own thoughts and actions. Only then will you learn to liberate yourself from the self-defeating forces of envy and anger, pride and vanity. Only then will you find freedom from the delusion of separation."

"You people!" the Major was still bellowing, the stab of his scowl scattering my memories of *jhankri*, crows and Kanchenjunga. "You people understand nothing of our culture, our religions, or our languages! You see an impoverished India on your television documentaries. You hear a nostalgic narrative and your credulous consciences are pricked for the crimes of Empire! So here you come, relishing your short-lived discomfiture as 'adventure', as yet more dinner-party 'travellers' tales'. And yet you are nothing more than a disruptive influence, like your meddling forebears before you!" he swiped in disdain, sitting in an old colonial building, in his bureaucratic box, beside a plate of Britannia Bourbons, sermonising in highly articulated English, in his faux-tweed jacket and his regimental tie.

The truth was that the fundamental hypocrisy of this charitable compound had been exposed by our presence, its lies laid bare. From the day of our arrival, our presence had intimidated the teachers and attendants, inhibited their habitual mistreatment of the children, restrained their violent sadism.

"Sir, in which regiment did you serve?" I boldly interjected.

His fury faltered.

"My Grandfather was an officer in the army here, like your good self. Proud of the fact until his end," I smiled warmly. "In fact, my father has written to inform me that he was stationed close to here, at a camp you may well have known in your own time of service – but no doubt you have already read this for yourself when editing our post."

The Major was disarmed. His guard was down. His paltry bristles parted in a weak and silent flicker that dared to suggest an attempted smile.

"I also have two uncles living in North Bengal, who were both serving officers in the Pakistan War. The Indo-Sino conflict. Kashmir, of course. Kargil in '99," I persisted with measured solemnity, speedily composing my next question in what I imagined to be a pseudo-military style. "But back to the matter in hand: sir, have we been summoned to be discharged from our duties?"

He scanned his desk, as though an elusive memo might give promise of an appropriate reply.

"No," he coughed. "We just needed to clear the air. There is human psychology to take into account in such matters," he began, gathering his thoughts, rebuilding his confidence, searching for a new category into which to set us down. "Some of us speak at the level of a mature adult, just as I am speaking to you . . ."

I was intrigued to know where this was intended to take us.

"Others speak on the level of an immature juvenile. If one is speaking as a child and the other as an adult, then communication fails. Only when we speak on an equal level is information adequately exchanged . . ."

Ben and I waited.

The Major's eyes returned to their furtive exploration of the desk. He aligned his fountain pen with the border of his blotter.

The dialling of the telephone, the hurried Hindi. I now found myself doubting that there had ever been anyone at the other end.

He paused to look back up at us with an uneasy glare.

"Yes, you may leave," he testily suggested.

ψ

A slow and aimless "*Resam phiriri . . .*" seemed to stray around the room.

Bindra prised open unwieldy eyelids. The singing stopped.

She fought to focus on the formless faces that gathered into view.

"Bindra-*behenji*!" gasped a familiar voice. "Sister, are you comfortable?"

Bindra let her eyes close shut again and swallowed hard to deaden the nausea that threatened to engulf her.

She tried to speak. Her tongue was swollen.

She tried to move. She grimaced in pain.

"No, *behenji*, stay still," the voice advised. A warm hand rested on her shoulder. "I think your ankle's broken. But we've bound it with a compress from the forest. You'll soon be well again. You'll see."

Bindra could feel a soft and anxious breath against her cheek. She looked again to find the face that drew so close.

Sushmita. She who Smiles.

"My girls are here," Sushmita quietly announced, gathering Aarti, Poojita and Dipika into Bindra's dazed sight. "For three days they've been singing for you!"

"Three days?" Bindra rasped in incomprehension.

"Yes, *behenji*," Sushmita confirmed. "For three whole days you've slept . . ."

"For three whole days we've watched for you, *Mataji*!" Aarti burst. "We've all been waiting!"

Bindra tried to smile. Her mouth was raw with pain. "Good girls," she whispered to them all. "My four good girls."

"Do you remember what happened, *Mataji*?" Poojita gently pressed.

Bindra slowly shook her head.

"They've done it before, you know, to others here," Sushmita affirmed with distress in her voice. "It's too, too dangerous to anger him . . . that man . . ."

Bindra gingerly nodded from side to side.

"But at least . . ." Sushmita faltered, "at least it was only sleep they forced on you."

"What would it matter?" Bindra replied with effort. "I'm ready. I have no *dharma*, no duty to fulfil in life. Long, long ago, I lost my children . . ."

Sushmita wiped Bindra's face with a wet cloth, scented with crushed *tulsi* leaves.

"Rest now, sister," she insisted. "We'll stay with you."

Bindra's eyes closed as mind and memories began to drift.

She found a crowded bus in heavy rain, a foreign book beneath a pillow.

A brightly spinning, spreading flame, and a child long lost in a distant city.

A little red man amongst dark trees, an *Aghori Baba* on a burning *ghat*.

A bright-bleached *kurta*, a paper kite.

And a single, bobbing crow.

ψ

The path into the *saal* forest was long and dusty. Every step produced a billowing effervescence in my wake that glimmered in the morning sun.

The industry of communal life amongst the rows of block houses and huts ahead soon fell silent. All conversation, cleaning, cooking, card games ceased. All eyes came to rest on the foreigner approaching.

They met me at the peepal tree that spread its sheltering shade across the entrance to the colony. I honoured the *sidur*-laden *lingam* projecting from tentacular roots, then turned to raise hands to heart in *pranam*. They lifted their arms and bowed their heads in amicable return.

I introduced myself in clumsy, elementary Hindi. They were intrigued. I asked permission to call at every house and hut, to meet them all, to better understand their lives.

A sudden swell of smiles. A warmth of welcome.

With book and pen in hand, I began my rounds in the nearest narrow alley. I sat on thresholds to note names and simple histories, amongst mange-ridden pye-dogs, near-naked chickens, hostile scorpions and fearless rats. I examined disintegrated hips and buckled limbs; ran fingers across serpentine spines and swollen joints. I peered into seeping, empty eye-sockets, collapsed sinuses and infected bone; inspected weeping, stinking sores on cadaverous remains that were seemingly once hands and feet.

I listened to the residents of the forest colony sob out their pain and weep for Yama, God of Death, to swiftly end their suffering. I reached out my hands to hold distorted, inflamed stumps in soft, plump digits. And in return, they smiled through tired tears and kissed my pink fingers. They bent to touch my full-toed feet and praised gods for my presence.

No sense of time had passed and yet I wandered slowly home through kite-filled dusk. I looked for early stars, first glimpse of moon, but only found my own ineptitude, inadequacy – and nothing left to offer but the darkness of an empty, hollow chasm where once my heart had sounded.

Chapter Twenty-Three

Bindra had lost track of the days.

"*Shanivaar, behenji*!" Sushmita emphasised to her. "It's Saturday, sister. Are you awake? Are you ready?"

Saturday had once been marked by early morning Shiva *puja* in the forest. The drawing of the *yantra* of his secret, fierce form of Khadgaravana. The invocation of the necessary strength within herself to protect and heal her children.

Another place. Another family.

Bindra moistened her mouth and indicated towards the old tiffin tin, tucked far back on the single shelf.

"You'll have to climb on the *charpai* to reach it," she chuckled, "so don't you go falling on top of me and break the other leg!"

Aarti, Poojita and Dipika clapped as their mother brought down Bindra's money box. They all joined in the struggle to prise open the lid and peer inside.

"But *behenji*, this is not enough!" Sushmita whispered. She looked over her shoulder, as though she expected someone to be listening at the door.

"What to do?" Bindra shrugged. "Poor old thing, like me! Can't get very far on a good day, let alone with an ankle broken by the good doctor's midnight *goondas*!"

"But *behenji*," Sushmita persisted, "they never take excuses. You know how it is!"

"What to do?" Bindra repeated, with a sigh of resignation.

Sushmita shook her head. She slipped the good fingers of her right hand into the waistband of her sari skirt and drew out a twisted

293

loop of cloth. She removed two coins, dropped them into the tin and raised a chiding palm before Bindra could say a word.

"You'd do the same for any one of us, *behenji*," Sushmita insisted. "You've cared for us all and fed my daughters as though they were your own. Sister, if these tokens protect you from those *badirchand*," she spat the word, "then they make only little amends."

"We must find compassion even for the *badirchand* of this world," Bindra smiled, looking towards the three little girls. "Even those 'idiots' are but aspects of ourselves."

Sushmita's brow furrowed deeply.

"It's very hard to find compassion for those filthy men, *behenji*, when they come with foul words and stealing fingers," she growled, drawing her daughters close, "with cruel fists and brutal kicks."

"Then silently call them *Mataji*!" Bindra recommended, as much for herself as Sushmita. "Call them 'Respected Mother' and just see if your anger can become compassion for their ignorance. The greater our compassion, the greater our freedom from our own selfishness and suffering."

Sushmita's brow expressed dismay.

"Try it, sister," Bindra persisted, "for your own sake, just as I must do for mine. We must choose not to allow their deep disquiet to be ours. Let's call them *Mataji* and just see how it draws us away from our anger and hatred, our jealousies and fears."

She smiled at the attentive girls, with a fading recollection of teaching this same lesson to her own children. Bindra raised her gaze back to Sushmita. The two women looked at one another for a moment in affectionate silence and unspoken understanding.

Suddenly, Sushmita dropped her head and covered her mouth to stifle a single, choking sob. Her daughters looked up in alarm. Bindra beckoned them to draw their mother to the bedside, where Sushmita knelt heavily to cry her raging tears.

"Not this, *behenji*!" she stuttered, grasping her children to her breast. "Not this for my girls!"

Aarti, Poojita and Dipika hugged their mother in return, as Bindra put out a tight, thin arm to rest her bandaged palm on Sushmita's cheek.

"Sister, my children are well!" Sushmita burst in overpowering frustration. "Not one of them infected! Yet still they must live out their lives like this?" she cried aloud. "Their father abandoned us when my sickness was discovered and now my misfortune is forever theirs! No school will take my daughters! No vendor in the bazaar will take their money or sell them food! No healthy *dulhi* bridegroom will want them, when their time comes. And all this because of me!"

She clung hard to her frightened girls, as though they were to be stolen away. She pressed her teeming face against the crowns of their dark, quiet heads. Sushmita yearned to breathe them in, to keep them safe.

"And now this!" she cried, throwing back her head in fury. "Thirty rupees the Office gives us every month. Barely enough to buy one bag of dried peas! And every other Saturday, the slum master's Collectors slip through the fence to demand fifty-five!"

She was shouting now, almost as though she hoped she might be heard.

"They force us to beg! Force us to endure endless abuse from passers-by! And why? To buy their permission to purchase the good, clean medicine that Doctor Dunduka is employed to supply, instead of that toxic filth he doles out every week!"

She was shaking with the turbulence that stormed within her, even as Aarti stretched out a tender hand to stroke her mother's hair.

"You saw what they did to Aadarsh!" she exclaimed to Bindra, who sat quietly listening. "Gentle, old Aadarsh! For three months he'd sent his pitiful allowance to his sick sister at Naugunj. And now his back is so damaged after their beating that he cannot stand! All day and all night he weeps for his blind wife! 'Who will care for you?' he sobs. I hear him, *behenji*! 'Who will cook your food and nurse you?' . . ."

Voices in the alleyway. An argument. A cry.

"Hush now, sister," Bindra hissed. "It's time!"

With practised speed, the three girls slipped beneath the sagging *charpai*, as Sushmita drew close to cover them.

"Kali Ma, Kali Ma," Bindra muttered to herself as she tipped up the old tin onto her blanket and quickly rechecked the coins. "Alright, my good, sweet girls?" she whispered to the eyes staring up through the fraying jute-twine below her. "Stay still now. Sing softly on the inside – but outside not a sound!"

Bindra and Sushmita simultaneously looked up towards a sudden movement of shadows at the door.

"Kali Ma, Kali Ma," Bindra whispered, "the slum Collectors are here!"

ॐ

My rounds had not progressed further than the fourth alley of the charity's forest colony when I determined to confront the Major with the misery over which he ruled.

"Sir, may I ask when you last visited the leprosy colony?" I enquired with a conciliatory smile, feeling compelled to sit as neatly as I could in the compulsive order of his office. I knew from the residents that he had never once sullied his lustrous leather uppers in their settlement.

"You people . . .!" he began in defensive repetition. "You people have no permission to step beyond the hostel grounds! No permission!"

"Sir, are you aware that the residents of your colony have no fruit or vegetables in their diet?" I persisted with unfaltering gentility in my voice.

"You people come over here with your Western arrogance, trying to expurgate your colonial guilt . . ."

Today, especially today, I was not interested.

"Sir," I interrupted calmly, "the paucity of their diet may well be exacerbating the extensive signs of anaemia and scurvy. The swollen, spongy, bleeding gums. The red, sore tongues. The eye infections and exhaustion. And then there's the appalling bruising, not to mention the atrociously poor healing of their wounds . . ."

"You people . . .!" he was still bellowing.

I refused to be defeated.

"Of course, their medical conditions are complex, but the addition of some source of vitamin C to their diet could only help."

"Imperialist meddling . . .!" he was still shouting to drown me out, even as my eyes were drawn to newly blackened roots and the runny bruise of herbal hair dye that rimmed his forehead.

I had to try another tack.

"Sir, what if Ben and I were to find a source of regular fruit and vegetable provision? At no cost to your charity?"

He stopped. "How much money are you proposing to give?" he asked with sudden, animated interest.

"We won't be giving money," I emphasised. His upper lip curled. "We'll have the produce delivered directly."

His attention waned just as abruptly as it had arisen. A bored hand extended towards the telephone.

"It would require no additional expense or work to you," I smiled, quickly adding with feigned nostalgia, "You know, sir, your fine regimental tie is reminiscent of my Grandfather's. He was so very proud of his years of army service here, in his beloved India."

The hand paused in indecision, wavering above the handset.

"Inform me of the quantities you are prepared to provide and we shall deduct it from their usual food rations," he offered munificently.

"I'm sorry, sir," I responded in undisguised disbelief, "the whole point is that the fruit and veg are a supplement to their present diet – not a replacement!"

But the meticulously manicured fingers were dialling. The double-speed retroflexion on an agile tongue.

Nothing more needed to be said.

I had been dismissed.

🔱

"Why are some people so unkind?" asked Aarti.

"What a question for such a little girl to have to ask!" Sushmita sighed, striking a match. She lit a cotton wick and watched it struggle to feed a guttering flame from the small amount of mustard oil at the bottom of the clay cup in which it lay. "Let's hear how our good *guruma* would answer," she chuckled, glancing towards the *charpai*.

Bindra beckoned the little girl to her. Aarti approached, nursing the communal stick-doll in her arms.

"People are not born unkind," Bindra assured her. "They may grow up to think unkind thoughts, to do unkind acts, but they are not unkind by nature."

Aarti climbed onto the *charpai* beside her. Bindra slipped an arm around the sleepy-eyed girl, so she could lie against her shoulder.

"Then why do people think and do such unkind things, *Mataji*?" Aarti pressed.

Bindra paused for a moment to sift through the wisdom of her life.

"They do unkind things because they don't know who they really are," she carefully replied.

"So who are they?" Aarti puzzled.

"Well, just imagine you're standing alone, staring at a little twig. And that little twig is all you see."

Aarti lifted her stick Baby to examine its crooked length.

"Now, you're so busy thinking that little twig is all there is, that you don't look up to see the towering tree you're standing beneath. You don't even see the great *saal* forest you're walking in, which spreads far beyond the horizon, when it's this forest of which your twig, like innumerable other twigs, is an indivisible part!"

Sushmita listened intently as she bent to stroke the heads of Poojita and Dipika, who were already sleeping on the floor. Sushmita treasured these moments of learning from Bindra.

"In the same way," Bindra continued, "people live their lives seeing only *their* little twig, which they think is separate and solitary, with no connection to any other. They don't look up to see that they are just one integral part of the very same trees as everybody else, in the very same, endless forest of existence."

Aarti cuddled her stick Baby to her chest and closed her eyes, to better imagine the never-ending forest to which she belonged.

"So, to create a sense of who and what they are, people impose a false hierarchy. They begin to judge everything and everybody as either better or worse than them, as either good or bad. They decide that this person is worthwhile and this person is worthless. That this thing is sacred and this thing profane. Some food they pronounce pure, some impure. Parts of their own bodies they pronounce clean, others unclean . . ."

"They say we're unclean, don't they *Mataji*?" Aarti murmured.

"Only in their staring at their little twig do they, my lovely girl," answered Bindra emphatically, "when, in fact, all existence is an equal expression of the very same universal forces. My people in the Hills called it Mahadeva – the perfect union of Shiva and Shakti. Paramshiva – the perfect union of consciousness and energy."

"So, am I not unclean?" Aarti asked.

"Is the sun clean or unclean?" Bindra exclaimed. "Or the Himalaya? Or the seasons? Is Ganesha? Lord Shiva? Or Kali Ma?"

Aarti raised her eyebrows high and vigorously shook her head.

"Well, you and I are not separate, not different, from them," Bindra insisted. "Nothing is inferior or superior to anything else. Only man's limited understanding imposes such judgements, when it is not the reality of existence. It is only when man believes himself to be an independent, solitary twig that he grows vain, greedy, proud, jealous, even cruel and unkind in his ignorance."

She paused.

"Have I answered your question?" Bindra asked.

"I think so," whispered Aarti.

"That's why we need wise teachers, to guide us to look up from our little twigs and see the vast forest, mountains and eternal sky in which we move, and from which we are indivisible," Bindra smiled, her eyes closing for a moment in blissful reverie of another home.

"Who's your teacher, *Mataji*?" Aarti asked, her quiet voice beginning to fade yet further.

"Oh, my teachers have been many," Bindra replied, her heart swelling in gratitude for grandmother and *jhankri*, sons and daughters, weather and crows.

"And what did they teach you, *behenji*?" Sushmita asked, softly sitting at her feet.

"To see both the good and the bad, or rather the wise and ignorant, in myself, before finding them in others," Bindra explained. "They taught me to choose in every thought, word and act to turn anger into compassion, and jealousy into generosity. To transform hatred into love, and conflict into peace. To change chaos into order and ignorance into knowledge."

Bindra stroked the thick, dark head of hair that rested against her breast. "They have all taught me to understand, my sweet child, that in truth you and I are limitless sky!"

But Aarti was already fast asleep.

ψ

"A call for me?" I was baffled.

Bad news from home? Sickness? A death?

Ben ran with me to the Office, where a greasy telephone ear-piece was awaiting my arrival, clasped in a nervous secretarial hand.

"Good morning," I anxiously began. "Yes, speaking ... I'm sorry, who? Are you certain? This afternoon? Well, of course ... thank you. And you'll send a car?"

I grinned at Ben with eyes wide.

Without a word, I strolled directly to the Major's open door. I rapped confidently against the chipped paint of its wooden frame, causing him to start from his weekly task of sharpening all the pencils to identical lengths.

"Excuse me, sir," I beamed, purposefully stepping into the room in advance of his invitation. "Just to let you know that we shall be out of the compound this afternoon ..."

"No leave of absence without prior permission!" he barked.

"A car will be collecting us at three," I stated blankly.

"Requests for social interaction beyond the boundary fence must be submitted for official consideration a minimum of forty-eight hours in advance!" he ordered, flaccid cheeks reddening. "Any fraternisation with any member of the local population must be presented for initial clearance with the Office!"

I stood beaming in silent confidence, awaiting the inevitable question.

"And to whose residence are you requesting permission to travel?" he snapped, shoulders heaving in escalating tension.

"Oh, didn't I say, sir?" I smiled in apology. "We are invited to take tea at the *Raj Bhawan* palace, at the personal invitation of a dear, personal friend of my aunts in Kalimpong: His Excellency the State Governor."

The heaving shoulders had fallen still.

ψ

Bindra had lain on her back for much of the morning. The broken ankle caused her entire leg to throb unceasingly. Sushmita and the girls had been out since dawn, wandering deep into the *saal* forest to find the necessary plants to replace her poultice. It always ached more fiercely after they had changed the splints.

Bindra had little appetite. She had insisted that her remaining month's ration be taken for the girls. Sushmita had brought kindling and a little wood from their excursion amongst the trees. She had cooked on the fire in Bindra's hut, to keep her company, and had insisted that she eat a full portion of their combined *daal-chawal*.

As dusk now approached, Bindra was again alone. Sushmita had carried the surplus kindling to the river bridge, in the hope that she might sell it for a rupee or two at the dusty roadside.

Bindra watched a solitary lizard scurry across the ceiling. It paused to confront her upside-down world with an unblinking stare, before darkling back to shadow.

She listened to the laughter and songs of children in the alleyway. She could distinguish Aarti and her sisters by the confident, clear melody of their voices.

Bindra smiled and closed her eyes. Almost a bamboo hut on a hillside. Almost sons and daughters in their hunt for *iskus* and tapioca roots. Almost a nearly forgotten home.

A sudden quiet beyond the door.

And then, the explosive caw of crows.

Bindra opened her eyes and looked towards the single oblong of fading light.

"What is coming, Kali Ma?" she whispered out loud.

"*Mataji!*" Aarti and Poojita burst back into the room. Dipika and her friend, Tamanna, quickly followed behind. All ran to Bindra's *charpai* and turned back to face the door.

"*Kya baat hai?*" Bindra asked, awkwardly pulling herself onto her elbows. "What's the matter?"

"*Mataji,*" gasped Aarti, protectively clasping the stick-doll in her arms. "There's a man at the end of the alleyway!"

"Talking to Karishma and Sachi!" hissed Poojita.

Bindra was puzzled by their excited fear. She drew herself up to sit, ignoring the pain that scorched through broken bone and damaged flesh.

"The slum Collectors can't be back already!" she exclaimed, darting her eyes up to the high shelf and the empty tiffin tin.

"*Nahiñ-ji!* Not those *badirchand!*" replied Poojita, pulling a face in imitation of her mother.

"At the end of the alleyway, *Mataji,*" Aarti breathlessly burst, "we've seen a foreigner!"

Chapter Twenty-Four

The rain was so dense, the wind so wild that trees buckled. Tea-stalls and wing-clipped chickens took flight. Children and their grandmothers were knocked off flip-flop feet.

Two *dhoti*-wearing *malis* squatted on the flooding lawn, clutching an empty fertiliser bag above their sodden heads. They peered at us with forlorn eyes as the topsoil of carefully tended borders whelmed naked toes, splashed darkly across soggy nappies that flapped in frenzy around their loins.

Liveried *khansamah*s raised black umbrellas above our heads and accompanied us in our dash from a pot-plant-piled verandah towards an emblazoned state Ambassador. Both *malis* released their hold on the sheet of plastic to bow in reverential *pranam*. As yet more blooms were torn from straining stems and consumed by the slick of mud, we watched through cascading glass as two men danced on pin-thin legs across manicured grass, in pursuit of a volatile rectangle of billowing blue.

Our afternoon tea with the State Governor had been deeply unsettling, despite his warmth of welcome, his interest in the aunties' health in Kalimpong and the well-being of their seasonal neighbour, the Dowager Queen of Bhutan.

It was the proximity of the lives of those with whom we lived, beyond the formal gardens and twenty-foot-high ornamental gates, that I had found so disorientating. It was the contrast of slum, disease and despair, with tree-lined promenades, mock-Mughal gazebos and rifle-bearing guards in splendid ceremonial dress. The contrast of poverty, pain, abuse and squalor, with gaudy gilt, colonial chintz, antimacassars and fine china.

Seated on cushioned armchairs, in a cavernous state reception room of pretentious splendour, attended by a swarm of servants bearing silver platters of tongue-peelingly spiced savouries and succulent sweetmeats, the world into which we had been swept seemed to be nothing more than the fleeting fancy of my own deranged mind. It mattered to me that I could sit here when those others could not. It mattered to me greatly.

And yet, as our State Ambassador plunged back into the swell beyond the gates, Ben and I found ourselves brimming with new optimism. Such was the genial governor's interest in our efforts that we felt assured that our determined pleas would now be heard by newly opened, ex-military ears.

Perhaps now those who lived in the colony would be permitted fruit and vegetables, their monstrously infected wounds treated. Perhaps now the bedridden would be washed and fed, their urine-soaked clothes no longer left unchanged for days.

Perhaps now there was a difference to be made.

ψ

Sushmita was wet and breathless.

"There *has* been a foreigner here, *behenji*," she panted, squeezing out the rain-drenched cotton that clung to her gaunt frame. "Yes, it's true, a tall man. Not old. White skin, pink nose. He's been going to every door, one row every day."

"He carries bottles of hot water," added Aarti, "a big red bowl, clean bandages, a whole box of foreigners' medicine . . ."

"And he speaks our Hindi!" grinned Poojita, who was helping Dipika feed the stick-doll with a moist porridge of carefully crumbled leaves.

"Well, a sort of Hindi!" Sushmita clarified with a giggle. "But he talks to everyone. He even *touches* everyone! Some are saying he's the foreigner's Jesus, come to heal us!"

Bindra was intrigued. "Was I sleeping when he came?" she asked in disappointment, gently shifting her inflamed ankle in its home-made splints.

"No, *behenji*, he left early today, just before the rains," Sushmita assured her. "He stopped at Karishma's door. Gave her medicine and a big, prickly fruit he says is called *ananas*. Pravit says he's seen one before and that they cost fifty rupees in the market, *behenji*! Can you imagine? Fifty rupees for one fruit! This is the food of maharajas!"

Aarti expressed her own amazement for Bindra's benefit, with eyes stretched wide and brows arched high.

"We've never seen such a thing before!" Sushmita continued in excitement. "But the foreigner says it may help the swellings in Karishma's hands and elbows. She has no idea what to do with it – and nor do I! But she was too embarrassed to ask him, poor old thing. Does she eat the prickles? Does she cook it and rub it in her skin? He didn't say. Just handed it to her!"

"So what's she done with her maharaja's medicine-fruit?" Bindra asked.

"What could she do," Sushmita chuckled, "but hide it in her bed?" causing both women and all three girls to join in a chorus of unrestrained laughter.

ψ

The town into which our chauffeur cautiously drove was violently awash. Black, refuse-filled water tore down streets and stairways, driving their inhabitants into neckless huddles beneath straining trees, shop canopies and rickshaw hoods.

As we approached the river bridge, the car came to a choking halt. The waters had finally submerged hubcaps, extinguished sparkplugs, reached our feet. The chauffeur was more concerned about the condition of his shiny shoes than that of the state vehicle in which we had begun to wallow. He raised his legs to the safety of the dashboard and lit an asphyxiating cigarette.

Ben and I steeled ourselves as we stepped out into the swell with feet freshly bared and trousers rolled. The driver protested, briefly. Whilst he feared dismissal for the loss of his master's passengers to the storm beyond the windscreen, he had no wish to pursue his errant charges in their madness.

The filthy, flooding stream, where there had once been a potholed road, spliced into swirling rapids as it hit the solidity of our pale calves. We began to wade forwards, but paused in confusion. Ahead there was no bridge, only a single, raging torrent on which rolled corrugated iron, splintered wood, sewage froth and dead pig.

We had no option but to slop inland and follow higher ground to the only other river crossing: an unsteady wooden span that still maintained its passage above the intemperate surge. A single, narrow footbridge that led directly into the putrid heart of the forbidden slum.

ψ

Doctor Dunduka was angry.

He cast a long shadow as he peered across the small room towards Bindra.

"Where is it, *daayan*?" he snarled. "Give me the medicine, you old witch!"

Bindra pulled herself upright on the *charpai* and looked directly at the silhouette that filled her doorway.

"Good afternoon, brother!" she smiled cheekily. "How are you today?"

He had no patience with these people. No patience with their filthy morals or vile gods, their stinking rotting bodies.

"Give me the foreigners' medicine!" he spat. "They have no right! And *you* have no right! No right at all!" He was shouting through his perpetual grimace for all to hear.

Bindra's mouth lifted into a gentle smile of non-attachment, a smile devoid of self-interest. The smile of Durga Ma.

"No foreigner has come to see me," she declared in honesty. "You have nothing to fear," she assured the agitated black outline that now blocked out the light. "Nothing to fear from any foreigners, or their medicine. Or from me."

Doctor Dunduka swiftly stamped a shiny-shoed foot to crush out the life of another black scorpion that had sought escape from a flooded lair.

"Fear, desire, attachment, and all the conflict they bring, are just tangles of our own making in the threads of life," she continued calmly. "The tangles of a spiderwebbed fly that keep us from the innate joy that underlies all life."

The dark figure at the door did not move.

Bindra eased herself to the edge of the *charpai* and leant towards him.

"And this because we believe ourselves to be separate from each other, from Nature, from the cosmos," she persisted. "Separate from the very knowledge, wisdom and truth we seek. Only as we understand our innate unity with all life do we come to see that – like sunshine, foreigners and scorpions – we are an equal expression of the same perfect union of all its energies and consciousness."

But Doctor Dunduka had gone.

Bindra's room had already filled with light.

ॐ

The storm had passed as abruptly as the violent devastation it had wrought. It had come and gone as suddenly as the bursting of new froth-topped streams of raw sewage, the engorging of new foul pools in which children now splashed at every turn.

The slum was already busy with its own emergency reconstruction as we waded a route through its inundated alleyways. All industry fell silent as we approached. Hands dropped sopping bamboo poles to wave in astonished welcome. Straw-laden heads relieved their soggy loads to bob in *pranam*. Mouths of bent and rusting nails grinned in dismayed greeting, as we squeezed between spewing sewer pipe, pregnant cow, pack of balding pye-dogs, collapsed walls and elderly Pashtun with a tangerine beard.

It was in the rot and rabble of the slum that we came across a cluster of miserable shacks around which all others carefully skirted.

Shacks where there were no children hoisted on shoulders to re-patch shattered roofs, no men filling rain-blown walls with dung and straw, no women driving out black water from their rooms with beaten sheets of corroded tin.

Ben and I paused to watch a slow spiral of storm-dishevelled crows descend into the segregated compound ahead of us.

"*Nahiñ-ji, sah'b!*" a voice cried out behind us in warning. "*Nahiñ-ji!*"

We stepped into the yard, around which some twenty huts sagged, and found ourselves observed by filthy, dripping figures.

Our instincts had been accurate. Leprosy.

Men, women and children stared out from decrepit doorways at the two waterlogged aliens blown in on wind and rain. Only when we bowed in *pranam*, did their drawn faces crease into astonished smiles.

Two of their number slowly approached to introduce them-selves in unexpected English: brothers Bhim and Ajit Vir. They enthusiastically beckoned their companions to waddle, crouch and crawl, to gather at our feet. Broken plastic chairs were wiped with blackened rags, and offered to us with insistence that we sat. We declined, preferring to squat with them as equals in the steaming mud, only to concede when Ajit Vir begged, "*Sah'b-ji*, please be doing us the honour of accepting the only hospitality we have to give."

We listened to their stories of village homes and land forcibly removed. Of families lost. Of beatings, stonings, burnings.

We listened to stories of medicine given by doctors to declare them "cured", and then the subsequent removal of their names from all governmental and charitable lists. Of official dismissal. Of total abandonment.

We listened, and burned with anger that anyone should be deserted to endure such conditions. Anger that it would have evidently required simple, inexpensive intervention to significantly relieve their suffering. Anger that nobody cared.

We listened, unable to conceive of contracting a monstrously disfiguring disease that would condemn us to a life of gangrene, disablement, likely blindness and complete social exclusion. A disease that would prevent any dentist from considering treating the agonising abscesses in our mouths, even if we were ever able to pay for his attention. A disease that would prevent even our healthy children from open access to any education in state schools.

We listened, unable to conceive of a disease that would leave us with no possibility of an income, in a society that provided no free social services, clean water, or effective sewage system. A society in which the "official", orthodox philosophy justified its heartless indifference with the notion of *Karma* – that these people "deserved" their lot, that they had "earned" their suffering.

I found myself longing for the all-embracing *tantrikas* of the Eastern Himalaya. For smiling Lepchas, Nepali *bojudeutas* and mountain *jhankris*, who actively rejected all spiritual and social hierarchy. Who knew the intimate connection between all people, all life. Who taught that we each have a responsibility to maintain a balanced society in which all mankind, even the most vulnerable in our midst, may flourish according to their own natures.

I looked at the inhabitants of the slum colony one by one. Ruined eyes, buckled faces and ravaged limbs. Grossly thickened, rope-like nerves protruding beneath fragile skin. And I wondered at their simple dignity, their warmth and generosity of heart. Their humour and unfailing, fearless smiles.

For all the education, opportunity and security with which I had been able to indulge myself over an excessively comfortable four decades, I felt I knew nothing when sitting amongst these people. We always liked to think that we were the lucky ones, with our easy comforts and pleasures, pandering to our self-imposed isolation and decadent neuroses. But here, I truly wondered.

"So how can we best help you?" Ben asked, his voice muffled by restrained emotion.

An animated discussion ensued and a democratic decision was reached.

Bhim Vir, who had been elected as colony spokesman, first emphasised that they did not want money. Word would spread and bring far too great a price. Instead, they had just three requests:

Firstly, antiseptic, clean bandages, cotton wadding, "fever medicine" and pain relief. This we calculated we could supply from the local dispensary at the monthly cost of just 1,000 rupees – the equivalent of about £13 – for twenty people.

Secondly, they needed help to draw water. With only weeping wounds and protruding gristle with which to work, the residents found it impossible to use the cumbersome pump handle of the communal well during the dry season, when the water table plummeted.

Thirdly, they revealed a collective dream for some level of self-sufficiency. However, with no boundary wall for their isolated community within the slum, their attempts to grow food had been constantly thwarted by wandering dogs, goats, chickens and cows.

It was time to pull on our biggest, newest, chintz-upholstered string.

One phone call to the *Raj Bhawan* and we had a personal introduction to a contractor who could provide an electric, deep-bore water-pump that would function with the push of a button in all weathers. This was followed by the assurance that a sturdy brick wall would be constructed at the state's expense, to enclose and protect the entire, desolate quarter.

A difference could indeed be made.

The change had now begun.

Thereafter, Ben and I defied the dominant culture and sat with the residents of the slum colony, purposely emphasising their worth as fellow men and women to the gawping locals. Every day, we sat amongst dense clouds of flies that rested on open, stinking sores as we washed and treated deep ulcerations, dressed wounds from which bone and empty knuckle joints thrust.

Witty, welcoming and ever smiling amidst this horror, our gentle hosts sat quietly as we gently massaged healing oils into shattered, painful skin. Sat quietly as tears trickled down their cheeks that they feared to wipe away in case senseless, ruined hands crushed out remaining sight.

"Not even our parents touched us like this," they would softly choke and, in the low light of daily dying suns, hug us unreservedly.

"Jayashri! *Mero* Jayashri!" Bindra cried out into the darkness.

She had not been asleep long when the clamour of angry shouts had woken her abruptly. She strained to listen beyond the beating of her heart, beyond the cries of lost children she heard nightly in the darkness.

She strained to hear beyond the forest colony, beyond the trees. Strained to make sense of the rising commotion in the slum beyond the boundary fence.

The cries of fury.

The screams for mercy.

I woke with a start.

It was not a sound, but a smell.

Dirt. Decay. Death.

I sat bolt upright to stare into the indiscernible features of a figure at the foot of my bed.

"*Sah'b-ji!*" a voice trembled.

I fumbled to switch on the light, but the electricity was off.

"Who's there?" I hissed, in anxious return.

"*Sah'b-ji!*" repeated in unenlightening reply.

My hasty fumble for the torch caused Ben to stir. I scuffled with its loose switch and a cruel glare slammed into a startled, tear-stained grimace beyond my toes.

Both Ben and I cried out.

We fought with our bedclothes to reach the trembling intruder.

It was Bhim Vir.

He was bleeding.

Bindra was sitting in her doorway. It was the first day that she had felt able to shuffle from *charpai* into sunlight.

The broken ankle had been slow to mend and the fiery swelling in her lower leg had yet to subside. She winced as she sought the least painful position in which to rest against the wall. She now had new sores on her ankles, buttocks and back, mercilessly gouged by the slack jute-twine on which she had lain for far too long.

Bindra sighed and raised her face to smile at the caress of warm morning brightness against her skin.

"Kali Ma," she whispered towards the earth, the sky, the air she breathed. "Is it really today?"

"*Behenji*!" Sushmita suddenly interrupted. She was hurrying down the narrow lane towards her. Aarti, Poojita and Dipika followed close behind. "Have you heard?"

Bindra smiled broadly at the three girls, who scurried past their agitated mother and into the comfort of her waiting arms.

"Last night! Did you hear? Such a *burra danga* riot in the slum! They've beaten everyone in the colony down there. Even the women!"

"Who's been beating whom?" Bindra asked in distraction, as she stroked the three little heads with bandaged hands.

"Those *badirchand* Collectors paid residents – no doubt with our money! – to attack the colony last night. They smashed the water-pump. They cut off their electric powerline. They beat them with sticks and now two of them are dead! Of course, the police won't come near. They all benefit from the 'rents' with the rest of those *goondas*. The colony is already pulling down huts to try to build a *chitaa* pyre by the river."

Bindra hugged the quiet, nervous children to her breast.

"I will protect you with my life, my lovely girls," she whispered into their sweetly pungent, mustard-oiled hair. "With my life."

Bindra sealed her promise by touching each dark head in turn, then turned back to Sushmita. "Why would anyone do such a thing?" she asked.

Sushmita dropped her voice to a desperate whisper. "The slum colony said they wouldn't pay the Collectors any more!" she almost mouthed. "They said they no longer need their bad, expensive medicines or their 'protection'. Foreigners have come to give them all they need. The Collectors have lost their power. It seems the slum colony is free!"

Bindra pressed her cheek to the trio of warm heads that leant against her chest. A single caw rang out above them. She looked at the new shadow that stretched out on the ground before her. The shadow of a single crow that had alighted directly above her door.

She smiled.

"What is it, *behenji*?" Sushmita whispered. "You're not afraid?"

"Afraid?" Bindra chuckled. "Why would I be afraid? It is today that my son will find me."

Chapter Twenty-Five

I spent the morning in the charity hostel. The residents were delighted, the teachers tense and taciturn.

I taught volleyball in the dustbowl of the "sports ground" and yoga on the prickly grass, yet still my mind could not free itself from the violence of the previous night. Violence beyond the perimeter fence, cruelly perpetrated by the slum dwellers against the most vulnerable in their midst. Violence – and even deaths – because of us.

"Don't come, *sah'b-ji*," Bhim Vir had sobbed in the fading glow of last night's torchlight, as Ben and I had tended his bruised limbs, the cuts on his head and swollen eye. "Not safe for you. Not safe yet."

I had wanted to go straight down into the slum, to see for myself what we could do. But Bhim was adamant.

"Please be waiting, *sah'b-ji*. You come now and those damn *goondas* they'll be watching. They are saying they'll be cutting your throat. We leper-types are okay. All's too big danger now. *Sah'b-ji*, please be waiting."

As the morning bell was rung, I could not think of eating any lunch. Ben was already in the bazaar, buying up a long list of medical supplies, from both pharmacies and herbalist *pansaris*. I sipped at my boiled water with disinterest. I threw the remains of my banana to the waiting crows. They paid it no attention.

I knew that it was unproductive to indulge the fretful guilt that threatened to submerge me. If I could not yet enter the slum, then I would go back to the forest colony and continue my rounds until Bhim confirmed it was safe to return to his community.

I filtered and twice boiled water from the tap. I poured it, steaming, into thermos flasks. I bundled bandages, wadding, gauze, disinfectant, surgical gloves and jars of honey into my big red bowl.

I kicked at the dust and sun-crisped leaves beneath my feet as I began the long walk into the trees. I tried not to think of the slum beyond the boundary fence, from which I was temporarily forbidden for the sake of many more than me.

I thought instead of the cheery faces about to greet me at the *lingam* in the roots of the old peepal tree, at the entrance of the forest colony. Only then could I muster a smile for the promise of new friends, for the bright sky above, and for the flight of soundless crows that seemed to be deliberately following my route.

ψ

Bindra's fever had steadily, fiercely increased.

And yet she had spent the morning carefully brushing the floor of her hut with a loose bundle of dry grass. To disguise her shivering, she had struggled into a tatty jumper that had once belonged to Jasoda.

Bindra hobbled to the pump to wet her face and hair, to rinse her mouth, then hobbled back to rebind her head with cloth.

She was almost ready.

Between her bandaged feet, Bindra positioned the twine-bound blade. Between her bandaged hands, she took a stick to represent *Akash*: the world of gods, of all-encompassing consciousness. Into this, she cut nine notches for the levels of *Dharti*: man's limited, sense-bound experience of the external world. She turned the stick to cut into its soft bark seven more notches for the levels of *Patal*: the symbolic, inner world of water and crystal, the limitless, inner luminescence from which all else arises.

Bindra clasped the prepared wood between her palms and, with great effort, plunged its point into the ground at the centre of her hut. She closed her eyes to voice the secret *bija* of Shiva, the rarely spoken syllable of the Absolute. This, then, was now *Bindu*, symbol of man's limitless potential.

With steady sweeps across the smoothed earth, Bindra drew a *yantra* to represent her own, inseparable connection with the cosmos. She first scored three concentric circles around two interlocking triangles, and then the eight lotus petals of Kali Ma. These she enclosed with three firm squares to mark the four directions, the underlying structures of reality, surrounded by eight *trishul* tridents to denote the three qualities of Nature, the three primary streams of consciousness: time, space and that which surpasses both.

Finally, she marked out the sacrificial *khadga*, the Sword of Knowledge, to signify the battle against her own ignorance that prevented her from understanding the infinite reality of existence, and thereby her true nature.

Bindra scattered vermilion *sidur* and hibiscus flowers for Shakti. A little milk and *bilva patra* leaves for Shiva. She intoned the initiating mantra of Mahadeva's dynamic, hidden form, then sat back.

The *yantra* of Khadgaravana, for the welfare of her children, was now active.

Bindra had prepared the way for the son that was to come.

ψ

"*Namaste, sah'b-ji! Namaste!*" familiar voices called in welcome as I paused to mark my respects at the old stone *lingam*.

"*Namaste Pitaji! Mataji!*" I replied. "*Aap kaise haiñ?*"

"*Thik! Thik!*" they grinned, assuring me that all was well with them.

I wiped my brow and sat beneath the peepul tree, in which my companion crows had now alighted. Residents of the forest colony were quickly drawn into the shade to proudly show me that sores were healing. Deeply cracked skin had begun to soften and swellings had abated. Infected cysts had shrunk and putrid ulcers had lost their stench.

They cried aloud impassioned blessings, arms and faces cast skywards. Blessings upon my mother who had borne me safely. Blessings upon my father who had taught me well.

They wanted to bend and touch my feet. Indeed, since the heat had driven me out of shoes some weeks before, my intact toes had become the cause of great fascination. As I had sat amongst them, affectionate finger stumps had been regularly employed to transfer honorific kisses to every one of my pale, healthy digits in turn. I grasped their shoulders, insisting there was no need.

I made my way slowly through the colony to be greeted as "*Babu!*" by men squatting at their dice games, "Our dear son!" by women tending to their chores. Others, so damaged by disease and malnutrition that they could not lift themselves beyond their doors, stretched out thin arms to proclaim me"*Bhagavan!*" I laughed my protestations, insisting I was only as much "God" as any one of them. It was simply as their brother and their friend that their suffering was now mine and, in return, my heart forever theirs.

I called on old friends to gently clean sores on Drupada's distorted hands, wash self-inflicted slashes on Alka's shins, and smooth disinfecting lotion into Rekha's oozing scalp. I carefully massaged oil into the taut muscles of Kabir's contracted arms, lanced boils on Jaspal's back, and redressed Nanu's twisted, toeless feet.

Then on to a new, narrow lane of little huts. New skinny children, new smiles and blushes.

I laid my bowl with its weighty contents on the ground and crouched to face them. Only one small girl stepped forwards from amongst her shy playmates. She cocked her head and squinted to look me directly in the eyes. Her face was inquisitive and expectant, her hair wild and black. She wore a full-length dress that was torn and scarlet, the colour of the Goddess. A little Kali Ma.

"*Mataji!*" she called, without once allowing her unyielding gaze to lose its hold.

From the farthest hut behind the children, a thin, bent woman, her face shadowed by a heavy wrap of tattered cloth, shuffled out into the light.

"*Kya hua hai?*" she croaked. "What's up, Aarti?"

"*Namaste, Mataji,*" I greeted her in traditional respect, standing to touch hands to heart. I stepped towards her, momentarily distracted as the crow that had alighted above her doorway began to bob. "*Main* David *huñ*," I announced in simple introduction.

The woman suddenly drew herself upright and her smile broadened, as though in recognition. She bowed her head and touched her heart with bandaged hands, then opened her frail arms towards me, as though to offer an anticipated embrace.

"*Main* Bindra *huñ*," she replied.

Chapter Twenty-Six

The hut in which I squatted was dark and airless. The blaze of light beyond the door, beyond the breach of corrugated tin, blinding.

A *charpai* slumped to one side, its roughly carved legs long buckled, its jute-twine mesh sagging and torn. In the corner, a heat-charred mud hearth. Beside it, twigs and kindling grass neatly piled. Against the soot-blackened wall, a metal bucket of well water. On a high shelf, corroded tins of rice, lentils, flour and oil. Hanging from a rusty nail, a single, scorched *karai* cooking pot.

The little woman named Bindra agreed for me to remove the rough splints on her ankle and unwrap the black, stiff rags that bound both her feet. The silent audience of bright, wide eyes followed my every move. Three little girls and their mother, named Sushmita.

I tried to blow away the flies that fought to alight on soiled cloth and runny flesh. The child in the red dress shuffled forwards to assist me, waving her hands, flapping her wrists in every direction. The flies remained defiantly unperturbed.

As I moistened the last of the foul cloth bindings, as I eased them from the skin to which they had adhered, my companions leant forwards to catch a glimpse of the impending horror. They were not disappointed.

In the sweltering confines of the little room, I had to turn my head for a moment, to press mouth and nose into my shoulder. I breathed in the dusty sweetness of my own scent in an attempt to quell the straining in my belly.

"*Mujhe maaf karo*," I muttered into my sleeve. "Forgive me."

"It is I who should ask forgiveness," Bindra grimaced, biting her extended tongue as she peered at the putridity I had revealed.

I looked hard at her for a moment. I had only ever seen this idiosyncratic, lingual gesture in the Hills.

"These poor old feet are not only making *me* sick," she sighed in apology, "but now you too!"

It was no wonder this little woman endured a chronic fever. The ulceration of her feet, so common in those affected by leprosy, had evidently been unattended for years. With simple protection for extremities deficient in both sensation and blood supply, such secondary damage and infection could have been entirely avoided. The fire of anger began to tighten my already nauseated stomach.

"What has the charity doctor been doing?" I despaired.

Bindra indicated to the mother of the girls, who stood on tiptoes to run her hand along the length of the single shelf, bringing down a haze of dust and dead beetles.

"Here, *sah'b-ji*," Sushmita muttered as she passed me a weighty plastic bag filled with tablets of every shape, size and colour. "But please don't tell. Far too dangerous for you. For all of us." She was genuinely afraid.

"What are these?" I asked, studying the polychromatic contents in undisguised dismay.

"This week's medicine from Doctor Dunduka," she replied, dropping her voice to such a whisper that she merely mouthed his name.

"This cannot possibly be for one person, for one week!" I protested, rotating the bag in my hands. "How many do you take of each?"

"Oh, he never says, so we don't touch any of it," Sushmita continued, as her daughters joined us in what had now become a conspiratorial huddle. "It's poison, *sah'b-ji*!" she asserted. "Bad medicine that makes us sick, sick, sick, until we die!"

"But a doctor would never do that to you!" I declared, in disbelief.

"Not a good doctor, *sah'b-ji*. But ours is a bad doctor, who gives bad medicine!" she insisted.

"And what of your wounds?" I pressed. "Doesn't he see how infected they are? Doesn't he treat them?"

"Oh no!" she laughed crossly. "He would never touch us!" Sushmita's face suddenly became serious and still. "Doctor Dunduka despises us, *sah'b-ji*. He hates us!"

I looked to Bindra. She raised her eyebrows in affirmation and rocked her head from side to side. "We all have choices, we all have responsibility," she stated softly, "but not all of us have learned wisdom."

"Certainly not the doctor and his *goondas*!" Sushmita burst in anger, gathering all three children into a single, fearful sweep of her arms.

Aarti turned to look at Bindra.

"*Mataji*?" she asked, as though requesting comfort.

Bindra gave the little wild-haired child a smile of unqualified love.

"As hard as it can be, it's not for us to judge that the immature and foolish, the unwise and unkind have nothing good in them. However difficult it is to see, they all have something to teach us," she openly reminded herself. "It's only as we learn to see both the bound and the liberated, the ignorant and the wise in our own selves that we gain true wisdom."

I looked at the little crumpled woman, whose deep wounds I now packed with high-grade honey. I looked up at her and wondered at the gentility of her eyes, when her body had been so long damaged and neglected. I wondered at the way she seemed to illuminate the darkness of the dingy hovel to which she had been reduced.

I wondered just who this woman might be.

॥

"You people . . ." he bellowed. Bombastic, bellicose.

"Sir," I boldly interrupted in impatience, "I am not here to criticise, but to offer whatever help I can. You cannot need reminding that your charity was originally founded specifically to relieve the suffering of those reduced to living in this city's gutters?"

He evidently did not. The Major slammed his perspiring palm down hard onto his ink blotter, leaving the dark imprint of a comic-book crime scene.

"You have no right!" he squealed at such a pitch that the nervous secretary burst in through the curtained doorway, as though brusquely summoned by a dog-whistle.

"No right?" I exclaimed, no longer willing to temper my frustration. "It is my fundamental humanity that gives me a right to ask why simple wounds in the forest colony are being left unattended until they fester and rot? A right to ask why there are still no fruit or vegetables whatsoever in their diet, despite our repeated appeals? A right to ask why those without hands are left to carry water from the pump in buckets with metal handles that deeply lacerate their forearms? And a right to ask why those in your charge are being left to die in horrendous pain and needless suffering, simply due to inadequate – or rather incompetent – medical intervention?"

My carefully suppressed fury had finally begun to reveal itself by an intensifying quiver in my voice. The Major felt less inclination to quell his own.

"Get out!" he erupted, causing the timid secretary to tumble back through the very curtain he had just opened.

"It doesn't have to be like this, sir," I attempted in ineffective reconciliation. "I'm only offering the little I can, for the sake of . . ."

But he had grasped, not just the receiver, but the whole telephone in both his tremulous hands.

ॐ

The daily cleaning and rebinding of Bindra's feet and hands was a long, slow process. To ensure that all those who needed treatment in the forest colony received attention, I finished my day in her hut at the end of every afternoon.

Bindra preferred not to make conversation. I had quickly learned that she had no interest in social triviality. She preferred to sit and watch in delighted fascination at the disinfecting of my hands and the putting on of latex gloves. The laying out of tubes and tubs, spatulas and gauze. The pouring of boiling water from thermos flasks into my big, red bowl.

We were never without our well-mannered audience of three little girls. They had taken it upon themselves to be my official flitters-of-flies, brushers-of-bugs and scarers-of-scorpions. When all was cleaned, treated and rebound, our diminutive companions sang and danced at Bindra's request, to express gratitude and celebration.

The day I arrived with balloons, bottles of blowing-bubbles and stripy humbugs in deficient exchange for such tireless entertainments, neighbours gathered at the door. The cries of wonder at such exotic, previously unseen gifts had brightened the entire length of the alleyway. I attempted to encourage games with the *gubara* balloons, tossing the elongated, fluorescent pink, green and yellow sausages into the air. However, the children would have no such mindless foolery. They gently laid their emaciated stick-doll in a safe corner, in order to care for new, over-inflated infants.

Bindra sucked with surprise at the minty sweetness in her mouth and chuckled at the delight of the three girls as they tended to their tubby charges with motherly embraces. She then turned to look so long, so hard at me that I almost dared not breathe for fear of breaking an inexplicable spell.

Once Sushmita had returned from her wood-gathering and the neighbours had departed, I began my work. Bindra had admitted to intense pain in her spine and shoulders, so once the usual dressings were completed, I offered to massage her back. She called on Sushmita to assist in removing her tattered, dirty clothes until she sat before me naked. The years of suffering and sickness had eradicated all physical taboos, all embarrassment and shame. My own cultural politeness, however, caused me to avert my eyes.

"What shame is there in thought and action founded in integrity?" Bindra smiled, in return for the shawl I had offered as a covering. "What shame is there in sky or earth? In fire or air or water? What shame is there in the elements from which this old flesh and these old bones are made?" she chuckled, as she conceded to lay the cloth across her lap for my comfort, rather than her own.

I had heard such thoughts before.

As I moved to sit behind her, I noticed the intricate markings tattooed onto Bindra's mottled skin. The dark, interlocking triangles on her empty breasts, the concentric circles on her belly. The symbols inked onto her haggard limbs that, to my astonishment, I recognised.

"*Mataji*, where is your home?" I asked, as I began to trace the grooves of harshly protruding bones with my neem-oiled fingertips.

"*Parvatme*," she replied. "In the mountains."

"These mountains?" I pried.

"No, no," she answered. "Far from here."

I gently smoothed the thin, dry skin of her shoulders and tried to estimate her age beneath the mask of malnutrition, sun, exertion and disease. I doubted whether she would even know the answer. This was a culture that did not mark birthdays, nor count the years. Past, present and future were considered only subjective divisions imposed by man's limited viewpoint on the perpetual cycles of life.

I was about to press further for her place of birth when Aarti, who had been whispering to her big pink balloon, joyfully announced, "Baby wants Uncle to sing!"

I claimed to know few songs, but with the chorus of insistence that rose not only by proxy from the balloon baby, but also from Sushmita, all three of her daughters and my patient, I could but concede.

I cleared my throat.

The giggling settled into an expectant hush.

I began:

"*Resam phiriri, resam phiriri udera jauki darama bhanjyang, resam phiriri . . .*"

Bindra turned to stare at me and grasped my arm between her wrists.

"*Timi Nepali bolchau!*" she gasped.

It was my turn to stare and repeat her exclamation, "You speak Nepali!"

Our faces were suspended in shared astonishment.

"Then you are no longer *Mataji*, but *Ama*!" I declared in her mother tongue, instinctively bowing towards her for *ahashis*.

"And you are no longer *sah'b* . . ." she began.

But finding herself unable to speak another word, she drew me towards her to kiss my head, onto which she had begun to sob.

Chapter Twenty-Seven

As humid weeks sweltered into blistering months, the change in Bindra's feet and hands astonished us all. The daily round of careful cleaning and honey dressings in knuckle stumps, in deep ulcers and open holes where once toes sprouted, had steadily removed all sign of infection, banished all symptoms of fever. Where once there had been exposed bone and foul decay, there was now new flesh and skin – new life.

Nor was Bindra the only one to benefit from the unsophisticated attention I offered in the forest colony. Every day, communal cheers sounded as dressings were removed and seemingly miraculous changes revealed. Every day, tender arms tightened their embraces around my waist. Every day, lips pressed tireless kisses to my cheeks and hands.

Whilst Bhim Vir continued to insist that the slum colony remained too dangerous for us to visit, a new confidence in his isolated companions had become evident. They were now openly defying the slum Collectors, by applying directly to us for the provision of all their medical needs. The relief began to afford me a new peace in what had long been deeply troubled sleep.

In addition, Ben and I had been invited to speak at the town's only private boys' school. The old British institution was directed by a formidable maharani, who kept her privileged pupils in a blissful bubble of utterly-utter cricket-and-polo poshness. It was for this reason that the house master had requested we "broaden the social viewpoint" of his temporary sons, to whom he was devoted. Inspired by our well-attended lectures on the realities of leprosy in twenty-first-century India, he concocted the notion of mass tree-planting in the already leafy forest colony, as a school "social work" project. We redirected his well-meaning enthusiasm instead towards the provision of fresh food, vegetable seeds and gardening implements to the isolated leprosy colony in the slum.

When I warned the altruistic master about the "mafia" who had threatened to cut our throats due to our intervention, he shrugged.

"We know who's who and what's what," he assured me. "Those Collectors who work the slum are mostly teachers from that charity of yours."

I could barely breathe.

"But every hoodlum is the underdog of another," he continued nonchalantly. "And some of the high-ranking hoodlums are really quite important people. I know," he emphasised, "because I educate their sons."

ψ

It is impossible to say what caused the initial sickness.

Perhaps the water, despite its boiling, or the raw milk that curdled into yoghurt in our tea. Perhaps the rancid ghee that doused chapatis grilled on the hearth fire by Sushmita and fed to me at the end of every day to address my troubling loss of weight.

One afternoon, I sat on the ground and leant against Bindra's doorframe. I had just finished the daily cleaning and rebinding, when I found myself too exhausted to stand. Both Aarti and Poojita climbed into my lap. They laid their sweet-scented heads against my chest and sang a gentle tune "to make Nepali Uncle well."

I asked Bindra if I might rest on her *charpai* before attempting the long walk back through the trees to my room. I caught the fleeting look of concern she shared with Sushmita.

I fell onto the slack jute-twine, so loose that it hung like a lopsided hammock. My head was adrift in such a restless sea that I attempted to steady myself by staring into the wide eyes of the silver "ghost" lizard that kept an attentive watch from the ceiling.

I longed for the relentless heat to lessen. The crippling cramps in my belly to ease. The surging nausea to abate.

Bindra and Sushmita drew close to lay their damaged, shrunken hands on me, tenderly stroking my head, shoulders, arms.

"The least that we can offer, for all you do for us!" they declared, in defiance of my breathless protestations.

"Shall we sing for you, Uncle?" Aarti asked, but her mother had already guided all three girls from the room before I had found the words to answer.

Bindra sat beside me, perched on the bowing edge of the ant-hollowed bed.

"Close your eyes," she whispered in Nepali. "You've been working too hard for us. Every day, far too hard, *mero ramro, dayalu, shashi keto*," she gently smiled. "Now rest yourself, my good, kind, brave boy."

She tenderly stroked my fevered forehead, until my eyelids shut out inquisitive lizard, demented flies and luminous quills of dust that spiralled into the stifling shadows.

Until all I could hear was the soft mumble of her mantras.

Until all I could hear were the crows.

I woke shivering and wet.

Tongue swollen, stuck fast to my acrid mouth. Spine and joints so painful that I cried out as I tried to turn.

I was in my room, and yet had no memory of being carried by Ben and his companions along the forest path. No memory of day or night.

A solitary figure stealthily drew into partial focus. Thick-rimmed spectacles. The cloying tang of stale sweat.

"Ben?" I rasped. "Where's Ben?"

The blurred spectre approached my bedside, so close that I could smell his tobacco-tainted breath. So close that I could see the dark labyrinth of capillaries that webbed across the gelatinous yellowing of his unblinking, dilated eyes.

"Naughty Naughty," an unfamiliar voice hissed, "do what you're told and no trouble is coming. Be persisting in your naughtiness and all consequences are your own."

"Where's Ben?" I tried again, but my words submerged beneath another swell of bitter nausea.

"Time for your medicine, Naughty Naughty," Doctor Dunduka quietly replied.

$$\psi$$

Ben was frightened.

I thought it had only been a couple of days. He swore it had been well over a week.

"I can't get the doctor to come from town!" he choked. "I've tried everything! I've pleaded with him, bribed him. He just won't come out here! I've tried the Governor's office and even the house master and his maharani, but they're all 'out of station', gone to the Hills for the hot season. There's no one left . . ."

I had begged him to keep the charity doctor away from me and to destroy the five different sets of tablets I had been prescribed. Even in my fever, I recognised that Doctor Dunduka was treating me with the standard blend of illegal medication he forced on his unwitting patients amongst the *saal* trees. He was treating me as though I had leprosy.

"The colony," I tried. "Bindra . . ."

My breathing had become so shallow and erratic that I now struggled to form intelligible sounds. Ben poured a little water into my desiccated mouth.

"Don't worry about any of them," he pressed, wiping perspiration from my cheeks. "I'm there every day. I've tried to follow what you've done with the wound clinic, and they're doing their best to tell me. I'm managing the cleaning and bandaging, and I'll go back to do more this afternoon."

"Bindra?" I asked again.

"She's fine. You mustn't worry," he affirmed. "Look, she sent little Aarti with these."

He lifted into my eyeline a handful of scarlet hibiscus flowers.

My cracked lips flickered into a smile.

"Kali Ma," I whispered.

ψ

Tap. Tap. Tap.

The stench in the room was foul.

Tap. Tap. Tap.

I opened sticky eyes and struggled to focus on the metal mesh across the door, at which a solitary crow was rhythmically striking.

"What is it *kaag*?" I strained to whisper. "What wisdom . . .?"

Suddenly the mesh turned dark and two figures pushed through. One kicked at the bird to deter it from hopping into the room ahead of them. They paused to cover their noses for a moment.

"Oh, dirty Naughty!" a voice spat. "Dirty heart, dirty bedclothes!"

"Leave me alone!" I tried in defence, but the words made no sense as they struggled out into heavy, foetid air.

One of the figures moved quickly. He opened a tatty briefcase and placed a selection of plastic bags on the little table. My eyes flickered to his companion, who remained a silent silhouette against the door-mesh.

"Ben! Where's Ben?" I attempted, fearful that he might have already left the colony in search of some distant army cantonment he had mentioned, in the hope of procuring a military physician.

"Look how sweaty and skinny he's grown!" the shrill voice sneered, drawing nearer. "So, why are you shaking?" it barked in reprimand. "Why are you panting in that ridiculous fashion?" it scolded.

"I'm sick!" I tried in explosive exasperation.

"And no one to blame but you!" came the satisfied reply.

I looked back to the door in ripening alarm, to the vaguely familiar, military bearing of a motionless outline that impeded the light.

"All your doing, Naughty Naughty," the voice persisted, "coming over here uninvited. Not attending morning service. Thinking you can be doing this and that. Eating this and that . . ."

"Ben!" I tried to cry out.

"*Your* foolishness! *Your* wilfulness!" the figure shouted to silence my efforts. "*Your* fault!"

My determined attempt to sit up caused me to retch violently, partially into the bucket by my bedside.

"You see! No time for wasting, Naughty Naughty," the voice announced. "Only time for treating your chronic hypertension!"

I recoiled as he clumsily searched for a vein in my right arm. He pinched. He slapped. He dug his bloated fingers deep into my flesh.

"No line! No line!" the voice bellowed, as if I were being purposely awkward.

Moist hands threw off sodden, soiled sheets. They pointlessly pressed the cold pad of a stethoscope to my shoulders, my tender belly, my trembling thighs.

"No soundings!" the voice roared. "You're a *yogi*!" it angrily announced, as though in accusation. "You're damn well stopping your heart! Enough of your wicked sorceries, Naughty! Enough!"

A pause.

A muttered word.

A movement at the door.

Searing pain as a long, thick syringe needle twisted deeply into my wrist.

I attempted to struggle, but was too slow. I fought to resist, but all too late.

And the figures were gone.

I lay writhing on the damp foam mattress, my wrist swelling, swelling, ready to split.

I tried to cry for help.

I tried to stay awake.

Tried to focus on the return of the Tap. Tap. Tap.

The bright darkness of a full moon.

Another night so hot, so still, that my lungs seemed to remain empty even as I gasped for life.

I thought I called out, but the skin of Ben's naked shoulders in the bed beside me remained unmoved, glistening with his every breath.

I closed my eyes, defeated by delirium. My skull a scalding sea of seething foam. My bones a viscous slick of melting marrow.

I was dangerously dehydrated. My body was failing, I knew it. Every organ had grown so frail, so tired that I felt as though, if I were to allow my will to fade, I could slip into a quiet, easy death.

Again I fought for absent air.

And then, beneath the resonating tremor of heat-mad insects, a rhythmical voice. The murmur of mantra, the Words of Power.

"*Aung kring hung hring dakshine . . .*"

I opened my eyes.

It seemed as though Bindra was beside me, slowly moving unbound, umbral hands in full-fingered *mudras*.

"*Kalike kring hring hung svaha Aung . . .*"

I knew these *bijas*. The *jhankri* at Lapu *basti* had once taught their meaning, invoking the forces of dedicated action, purpose and awareness. The forces of change.

Bindra touched her pubis, navel, heart and head. She smiled into my eyes and bent to place her mouth on mine. To share my breath. To take my fever.

To initiate my healing.

I woke to the song of familiar birds. Bulbuls and drongos, bee-eaters and babblers.

I turned my head to the bolted door and opened my eyes wide in search of light.

I turned my head towards the shuttered window and took a deep breath in search of trees.

I sat up without pain, without fever.

The echoes of a febrile dream still resonated. The shadow of a woman in the room. Of Bindra.

"*Aung kring kalikaye namah-aung,*" I whispered to the dawn.

Chapter Twenty-Eight

I stepped off the forest path.

I moved slowly in the morning incalescence on legs that, since the fever had lifted, were not yet my own. I sought respite from daylight blaze in the dapple of dense trees. I sought reprieve from dust in the sweet humus of hot-season-deciduous.

The forest was not quiet. It bustled with the beat of butterflies, the hum of hornets, the mischief of monkeys. The listless canopy flared with golden woodpecker and emerald parakeet. The deeply furrowed bark glistened with fierce jewels of iridescent beetle.

A sudden, combustive caw of crows. An eruption of onyx feather, ebony claw.

I stopped.

No avian air. No simian chatter. No vespine bumble.

Between the tall, straight trunks of *saal*, I caught a flash of red. A flash of bright red running that prompted in me a sudden premonition.

"Nepali Uncle, *aaiye!*" a child's voice cried. It was Aarti, panting with effort. "Please come, Uncle! *Mataji* is calling your name. She says it's time!"

"Time for what, *choti behen*?" I asked my anxious "little sister". Even as I said the words, my heart quickened with inexplicable anticipation.

"You must come now, Uncle," she insisted, ignoring my question. "For *Mataji!*"

Such was her urgency that I tried to lift her into my arms, but found myself too weak. Instead, Aarti grasped my hand and together we hurried into the trees.

ψ

The hut was quiet.

Poojita and Dipika were standing still, stick-doll abandoned to the wood pile, their mother squatting beside the *charpai* on which Bindra lay.

"He's here," Sushmita whispered, as though in secret.

I bowed low to let Bindra place slow, bandaged hands upon my head in *ahashis*. She raised her face to smell my hair.

"What is it, *Ama*?" I asked, breathing heavily.

"So many days without you," she sighed, "without my good, brave boy."

"You know, I had a dream, *Ama*," I revealed with a chuckle. "A dream of you that made me well. And here I am! All better! Here to stay!"

She rocked her head and smiled, watery eyes held firm on me. She touched her heart and then my chest, and mouthed, "*Kalike kring hring hung svaha Aung.*"

My smile faltered.

"So many days without you," she repeated. "So many days without my good, brave boy."

Bindra stretched out a hand to stroke my face.

A sudden, threatening rasp and she was straining to draw in air. Her thin arms slumped to the *charpai*.

I looked to Sushmita, who shook her head.

"What has happened, *Ama*?" I asked. "Are you sick?"

"Not sick," she replied. "Just tired."

My heart began to pound, but before I could attempt a clumsy protestation, she simply stated:

"No medicine. No doctor. No tears."

Bindra looked up to Sushmita and the three girls who had joined us at the *charpai*.

"No one but my loving daughters. And my good, kind boy," she smiled far into my eyes.

"But what can I do?" I choked, struggling to contain a surge that threatened to break into the open.

"You know the *antyakarma* rites?" she asked. "The drawing of the *yantra*? The Mantra of Severance?"

"The *jhankri* taught me long ago," I confided, "but I've never used them."

Bindra sighed, as though in relief.

"Then trust his teaching," she advised me. "My good, brave boy, it is now time to trust yourself."

🔱

Bindra's eyes were closed.

Sushmita had lit the fire to boil *tulsi* tea for the washing and was already mixing the turmeric paste in careful preparation. Aarti had taken her sisters to search out hibiscus flowers. I had begun to cut the notches of *tintirilok*, the worlds of *Dharti* and *Patal*, into a length of wood that would symbolise *Akash*.

I looked up to linger on the serene smile of the woman who lay quietly beside me and recalled the *jhankri* teaching that as old age diminishes our senses, brings us frailty of body and mind, the quality of consciousness we have developed in our lives is ultimately exposed. "This is why some approach their end with peace," he had explained, "whilst others are consumed by 'demons' of their own making."

Bindra stirred.

"You are with me?" she asked, her voice weak, but calm.

"I'm here, *Ama*," I assured her, dropping the stick and knife to place my hands gently on her arm.

"You'll feed the crows?" she pressed.

"Of course," I promised, "before every meal for ten days. But they'll have to stay hungry for a long while yet . . ."

She looked into my eyes.

"You mustn't fear," she smiled. "This person, this Bindra, is but a fleeting knot that must unravel. The wisdom of my life's experience must now be shared with bird and tree, earth and sky . . ."

Her breath was growing increasingly slow and shallow.

"No need to talk," I tried to impress. But she was not yet ready.

"Everything in a constant state of ordered flux," she continued, "yet nothing lost from the whole. No star, no leaf. No bird, no child. No thought, no action. All is Shiva. All is Durga. All is Kali Ma . . ."

Her eyes flickered. Her voice faltered.

I lifted a clay bowl and moistened her lips with more warm water.

"Please, no grief for me," she entreated in a momentary return of strength. "For death, like life, is extraordinary!"

"Yes, *Ama*," I stuttered through struggling tears.

"This world of ours is not bleak, nor futile. It is not hopeless, my good, kind, loving boy," she smiled in broad, bright recollection. "For life – like love, like sky – is limitless."

"Quiet now, *Ama*," I wanted to say.

But Bindra was shining.

ψ

The hut was silent.

When the three girls returned, their hands were full of scarlet blooms. They laid them respectfully amongst the ready pots of *sidur*, *tulsi* tea and turmeric paste.

"Shall we sing you to sleep, *Mataji*?" asked Aarti brightly, as she joined me beside the *charpai*.

But Bindra was no longer able to reply. She had already gone too far away. To a snow-topped mountain and a friendly she-goat. To a Shakti Tree and an *iskus* vine. To a loving Kailash and laughing children.

Sushmita looked at me and nodded gently. It was time to offer a farewell that, many years before, I had been twice denied.

I bowed my head as Sushmita sprinkled me with *titepati*-steeped water.

She lit the hearth, over which I stepped before passing my hands through the flames. At a nod from her mother, Aarti lifted a spiny twig towards me and I pricked my fingers. As custom demanded, the line between the living and the dead had been defined with fire and thorn.

I turned to the *charpai* and placed my hands to my heart. I bowed and waited as though to receive one last *ahashis*.

I repeated quiet *bijas* of purification and dedication.

I laid along Bindra's breastbone the notched stick that marked the three worlds, as children's voices softly, slowly sang the song that always took her home.

"*Resam phiriri, resam phiriri udera jauki darama bhanjyang, resam phiriri ...*" – "Little bee who likes to fly, little bee who likes to fly, go and rest at the top of the hill, little bee who likes to fly ..."

I walked around the bed three times, moving my hands into dedicated *mudras*. I took the clean cloth on which I had drawn the *yantra* and laid it tenderly across Bindra's face. I lifted a corner and whispered into her left ear. Again, I circled the bed three times, then lifted the opposite corner to repeat the Mantra of Severance into her right.

I paused to raise the cloth one last time, to look into her face.

Peaceful. Smiling. Willing.

As I instinctively pressed my mouth to hers in gratitude and love, Bindra passed to me her final breath.

As the children sang.

As the *saal* bugs swarmed.

As the gathered crows ascended.

Postscript

Sushmita and her daughters are still living in the forest colony, where they have finally been delivered from the abusive attentions of Doctor Dunduka. The kindly State Governor fulfilled his promises, but no longer holds his influential position. The slum colony, of which brothers Bhim and Ajit Vir remain elected spokesmen, continues to benefit from clean water and medical supplies, and the long-wished-for protective wall. The latter has allowed for the planting of vegetable gardens, providing its residents with a previously unknown level of self-sufficiency, which has in turn inspired a new self-confidence. To date, its ostracised community remain entirely free from harassment by the slum "mafia" and its dreaded Collectors, who have lost all power over those isolated by leprosy in their midst.

As for Ben and me, we could not return to the indulgence of our lives and forget the courageous and cheerful people with whom we had had the honour to live and call our friends. Bindra's life and death, and the intimate interaction with those affected by leprosy with whom she shared the last years of her life, compelled us to found a registered charity named *Sarvashubhamkara*, a Sanskrit name meaning "he who does good to all".

It is thus in honour of Bindra's memory and of the family she lost that an ever-increasing number of girls and boys of leprosy parentage, who would have otherwise been excluded from normal interaction with their peers or the possibility of an independent future, are now benefiting from professional tuition, practical apprenticeships, and even nursing training in medical school. In the coming years, these children will include Aarti, Poojita and Dipika.

Donations

A percentage of the profit from this book is paid by Reportage Press directly to the charity *Sarvashubhamkara*. For ease of pronunciation in the UK, the abbreviated name of *Sarva* is employed.

With no religious or political affiliations, *Sarva* undertakes small-scale projects with "forgotten people" of the Indian subcontinent, to relieve poverty, sickness and distress of those in need. Central to its work is the development of a personal relationship with every recipient of the charity's support, in order that their needs may be fully understood and appropriately addressed. Its trustees are proud to be able to guarantee that not one penny donated is lost to administration, salaries or expenses.

In addition to the provision of medical attention, food, clean water and long-denied human contact, one of the principal projects of the charity is the maintenance of an education fund, which provides scholarships and bursaries for students excluded from state education due to their leprosy parentage, social status or extreme poverty. This offers an opportunity to those debarred from normal social integration not only to vastly improve their own futures, but also to finally break the desperate cycle of destitution and disease for both their impoverished families and communities.

If you would like to support the work of *Sarva*, please recommend this book to your friends, local book club, bookseller or school, and give it a good rating on your favourite Internet book site or on your Facebook profile. If you would like to know more about the charity's work, or would like to make a donation or set up a standing order, please visit the official website at www.sarva. org.uk, or write to *Sarva*, PO Box 3034, Eastbourne, East Sussex, BN21 9ED. We would be delighted to hear from you.

Author's Note

This book is inspired by real people and actual events, therefore personal names, places, times and details connected to some of the characters described have been altered to protect their true identities.

The account of Bindra's life has been constructed from her memories, those with whom she lived, and from personal knowledge of the people and culture from which she came. May its telling do justice to her memory.

Acknowledgements

I would never have found the confidence to tell this story had it not been for the untiring encouragement of friends and family.

My thanks must go to Chris, Kev and Briony who together sparked my first moment of determination. To Bulani, whose ardent interest in stories shared over Calcutta's finest fare shook me into action.

My thanks to Sarah and Emma for their invaluable enthusiasm, honesty and astute criticism. To Param, Ghanshyam, Michael, Ellie, Lynne, Flott, Gilly and Jo for their indulgence.

My thanks to my parents, whose belief in me has never faltered, in spite of the choices I have made that should have undermined it. To Shiva, Ananda and Shishir Uncles; Jethi and Kanchi Aunties; cousins Melita, Josiah, Yashashwi and Bal Krishna, who over the years have informed, enlightened, corrected and delighted me.

My thanks to Lizzie for a remarkable introduction. To my agent, Sheila Ableman, who dared to take the risk and in doing so became a friend. To Rosie Whitehouse, Henrietta Molinaro and Laura Keeling at Reportage Press, for their unfailing passion, attention and expertise.

My thanks to teachers who have asked for nothing in return, but that I seek out wisdom.

And to Bernard, whose breath I share.

REPORTAGE PRESS

REPORTAGE PRESS is a new publishing house specialising in books on foreign affairs or set in foreign countries; nonfiction, fiction, essays, travel books, or just books written from a stranger's viewpoint. Good books like this are now hard to come by – largely because British publishers have become frightened of publishing books that will not guarantee massive sales.

At REPORTAGE PRESS we are not averse to taking risks in order to bring to our readers the books they want to read. Visit our website: www.reportagepress.com. A percentage of the profits from each of our books go to a relevant charity chosen by the author.

The DESPATCHES series brings back into print classic pieces of journalism from the past.

You can buy further copies of *In the Shadow of Crows* directly from the website, where you can find out more about our authors and upcoming titles.

REPORTAGE PRESS